CRITICAL INTERVENTIONS IN CARIBBEAN POLITICS AND THEORY

Anton L. Allahar and Shona N. Jackson, Series Editors

Critical Interventions in Caribbean Politics and Theory

Brian Meeks

UNIVERSITY PRESS OF MISSISSIPPI   JACKSON

www.upress.state.ms.us

The University Press of Mississippi is a member
of the Association of American University Presses.

First printing 2014
∞

Library of Congress Cataloging-in-Publication Data

Meeks, Brian.
  Critical interventions in Caribbean politics and theory / Brian Meeks.
     pages cm. — (Caribbean studies series)
  Includes bibliographical references and index.
  ISBN 978-1-62846-121-3 (cloth : alkaline paper) — ISBN 978-1-62846-122-0 (ebook) 1. West
Indies—Politics and government. 2. Caribbean Area—Politics and government. 3. Political
science—West Indies. 4. Radicalism—West Indies. 5. Neoliberalism—West Indies. 6. Postcolo-
nialism—West Indies. 7. West Indies—Colonial influence. 8. Meeks, Brian. 9. University of the
West Indies. 10. Jamaica—Politics and government. I. Title.
  JL605.M44 2014
  320.9729—dc23   2014013903

British Library Cataloging-in-Publication Data available

CONTENTS

And so
if you see me
looking at your hands
listening when you speak
marching in your ranks
you must know
I do not sleep to dream, but dream to change
the world
    Martin Carter[1]

The essays in this collection are, in some respects, truly disparate, as they were written for many different purposes and delivered over an expansive span of some fourteen years. Yet, in the process of imagining them together as a single book, I discovered a surprising consistency underlying them all. They are all part of an extended conversation that I have been privileged to have with colleagues and friends,[2] and sometimes, hopefully, a wider audience, concerning the course of the radical movements of the 1970s as well as the possible paths for political and social change in the Caribbean since those momentous times. The last three decades have been a difficult and fallow interregnum for anyone convinced that the answers to the economic stasis, social inequality, and burgeoning problems of crime and violence in the Caribbean lay, in part, in some form of new, transformative political intervention. Earlier attempts in the immediate postcolonial period to forge a more radical direction in Caribbean politics had, of course, ended badly. Forbes Burnham's regime in Guyana, compromised from the very beginning by its status as the United States' favored alternative to Cheddi Jagan's Marxism, proved to be politically and spiritually corrupt. Michael Manley's Democratic Socialism, while advancing some basic foundations for a long-delayed social equality and a more activist international profile for Jamaica, was unable to withstand the combined offensive of the local elites, the international financial institutions, and the State Department. Most damaging of all, the People's Revolutionary Government (PRG) in Grenada, which had gone furthest in advancing a radical social agenda, imploded on itself with the tragic killing of its leader, Maurice Bishop, and some of his closest associates. The Grenadian events, culminating on October 25, 1983, with the U.S.-led invasion, confirmed the worst fears that radical initiatives were simply covers for an even more intrusive and undemocratic approach to politics than those practiced by the first post-independence generation of Caribbean leaders.

The invasion of Grenada occurred almost simultaneously with the consolidation of the Washington Consensus and its neo-liberal agenda, with the now familiar mantra that the expansion of the market was the one-stop solution to all economic problems. Together, these two phenomena contributed to a hermetic atmosphere in which many intellectuals abandoned the occupation of creative thinking for narrowly conceived consultancies and governments sought to abide by the letter of the international financial organizations, whether via the avenue of negotiated agreement or self-imposed edict.

Thirty years and many IMF agreements later, very little has changed. The entire region is still in the grip of the deepest economic crisis since the 1930s, generated in large measure by the U.S. housing and financial crash of 2008. There can be few sharper and more poignant lessons to be taught on the dangers of market fundamentalism and its inevitable outcome than the history of the events that led up to the crash of Lehmann Brothers and the financial denouement of 2008–9. Yet, these lessons seem not to have sufficiently percolated into the consciousness of regional political and business elites, many of whom continue to propose unmodified neo-liberal solutions for the intractable social and economic problems of the Caribbean. And even as elements within the IMF and World Bank, reflecting on the recent Greek meltdown, admit that structural adjustment policies may not be the best response in order to pull badly indebted countries out of recession,[3] such approaches continue unabated and unabashed as the official position of the Fund.

The time has certainly come, particularly in the fiftieth year of independence in the Commonwealth Caribbean, for new thinking around not only the political and economic policies related to growth, employment, and sustainability but more fundamental questions of the meaning and relevance of sovereignty, the continuing salience of nationalism as a motivating ideology, and even, as Norman Girvan[4] has suggested, the existential condition and survivability of the Caribbean and its people. The fourteen essays presented here anticipate such a debate, even as they are part of a lively conversation that has continued and grown in these difficult times.

The volume is divided into three sections, which correspond roughly with my main intellectual preoccupations over the past two decades. In Part One, "Theoretical Forays," the first three chapters—all written in the early 2000s—are part of a conscious attempt to engage with my contemporaries at a time when we were all looking for a relevant theoretical language and style to both explain the Caribbean's recent past and confront the difficult conditions in the first years of the new century. Energetic if occasionally rambunctious engagements are informed by an approach that, while deeply influenced by political economy, is searching for an idiom to explain the powerful intervention of culture, personality, place, and time in historical determination. Chapter 1, "The Frontline," sets the stage for the entire volume through an exploration of the reasons why the small Caribbean left of the seventies failed to gain greater political traction and eventually collapsed. The argument, developed via encounters with calypsonian Valentino, reggae singer Pablo Moses, and scholars Paget Henry and David Scott, is that the left in its philosophical approaches and praxis paid insufficient attention to the vibrant popular culture and organic philosophy of the times. Chapter 2 focuses more specifically on Paget Henry's influential book *Caliban's Reason: Introducing Afro-Caribbean Philosophy*.[5] Henry, I suggest, breaks new ground in the identification and mapping of Afro-Caribbean thought, yet there are notable flaws in the surprisingly scant attention paid to popular philosophical constructs and the failure to elaborate a relevant politics beyond his novel approach. Chapter 3, "Arguments within What's Left of the Left," takes the form of a sharp polemical engagement around theoretical questions—a somewhat rare occurrence in contemporary Caribbean social sciences. In the early nineties, I had reread C. L. R. James's classic history of the Haitian Revolution, *The Black Jacobins*, and argued that James had elaborated important insights on the role of agents in history, posing interesting questions for Marxist theory. Hilbourne Watson, in a broadside and published in a reader that I later co-edited,[6] criticized my approach, arguing inter alia that it was a break with Marxism and a celebration of neo-liberalism. The response, captured herein, was not only to counter his argument, but to suggest that there were lessons to be learned from Watson's method of criticism that reflected many of the flaws inherent in Caribbean radical political praxis of the late twentieth century. The fourth chapter on Michael Manley, though written purposefully for Anton Allahar's volume on *Caribbean Charisma*,[7] also seeks to grapple with the relationship between leaders and led in those rare openings when society is at boiling point and politics becomes more fluid than usual. The essay searches for the factors behind Michael Manley's mercurial rise to popularity in mid-late-twentieth-century Jamaica, while concluding that a theory of charismatic leadership is elusive and the era of Caribbean charisma may already have been eclipsed.

Part Two, "Caribbean Questions," is retrospective in nature as, from a consciously biographical stance, I try to reflect on my own engagement with, respectively, my intellectual home, the University of the West Indies (UWI), the short-lived but influential Caribbean Black Power movement, the work of seminal Trinidadian thinker and activist Lloyd Best, Cuba's relationship with

Jamaica, and the crisis and collapse of the Grenadian Revolution. Chapter 5, "Saving the Soul of the University," was written in 1998, in commemoration of the fiftieth anniversary of UWI. While appreciating that institution's remarkable ability to survive the economic and political vicissitudes of the previous half century, I suggest that unless the "soul" of the university as a place of free and critical engagement is rescued and nurtured, then the prospects for a democratic and meaningful Caribbean project are meager. Chapter 6, "Black Power Forty Years On," is a personal reflection on the Black Power movement that came to prominence after the expulsion of Guyanese historian Walter Rodney from Jamaica in 1968. The somewhat pessimistic conclusion is that while some of the underlying causes that led to the rise of the movement have changed, much of the intractable heritage of racial and color hierarchies still persists in twenty-first-century Caribbean society. Chapter 7, on Lloyd Best, recognizes the remarkable contribution of the late Trinidadian economist and thinker to the development of a critical Caribbean scholarship. However, it is suggested that while Best made real theoretical advances in the proposal of a more democratic and popular model of politics, his actual political interventions were, at the very least, enigmatic. Chapter 8 surveys perceptions of Cuba in post-independence Jamaica and argues that the genuine grassroots popularity of the Cuban Revolution derives not so much from actual Cuban politics and policy but from the powerful mythology of Cuba as a symbol of resistance. The final chapter in this section, on Grenada, revisits the tragic moments of October 1983 and calls for a careful, forensic reading of the evidence, as opposed to the common tendency to mythologize the events surrounding the crisis and collapse of the People's Revolutionary Government. The Grenadian Revolution's demise, I suggest, was not primarily the result—as typically portrayed—of a leadership struggle, but a chronic and shortsighted failure to deepen democracy in Grenada, which laid the foundation for the 1983 catastrophe.

Part Three, as evident in its title, "Jamaican Journeys," includes excerpts and extracts from my longer, rolling engagement with Jamaican politics and society. The overarching critique of the myriad scholarly and popular debates concerning the state of Jamaica has been their failure to look beyond the confines of immediate policy concerns and imagine, albeit with informed lenses, what the future might look like. Much of my argument is built around the notion that Jamaica is in a moment of "hegemonic dissolution" as developed in *Envisioning Caribbean Futures: Jamaican Perspectives.*[8] The essays presented here both precede those ideas and carry them beyond its conclusions. Chapters 10 and 11, "Reinventing the Jamaican Political System" and "Imagining the Future," reflect on the state of Jamaica at the turn of the century as they suggest a tentative agenda and pathways toward an alternative politics. Chapters 12 and 13 chronicle, respectively, Portia Simpson-Miller's first rise to national leadership and the tectonic events surrounding the arrest and extradition of Christopher "Dudus" Coke in 2010. Both attempt to track the changing socio-political impasse as they search for specific approaches and avenues out of the stasis of hegemonic dissolution. The final chapter[9] also explores the Dudus events, raising pertinent questions as to the diminished relevance of sovereignty in an age of globalization, while calling for a more democratic state alongside a new "guerrilla sovereignty" as a pertinent strategy for small states operating in the interstices of the increasingly "globalized" world system.

Much work still needs to be done in building a new, critical, and independent Caribbean approach to theory that is able both to inform policy and to provide a compass for navigating the difficult currents of the twenty-first century. While there is a growing body of local and regional scholarship critical of structural adjustment policies, there has been little frontal combat with the philosophical and, I suggest, vulnerable underbelly of neoliberalism, to the detriment of a more comprehensive critique. While Caribbean political scientists have, in recent times, been willing to tackle vital policy matters related to corruption, crime, and the environment, there is a noticeable retreat from the earlier enthusiasm to engage in more universal, theoretical interventions, related, for instance, to the flawed character of Caribbean democracies and their accompanying "Westminster export models." While in recent times, under the influence of the "linguistic turn," Caribbean scholars have focused more on the textual interrogation of foundational notions, there has been little effort to wed these explorations to a rigorous critique of governments, policies, and politics.[10] And, as mooted in the final chapter, while it is true that the notion of sovereignty, ephemeral from the outset, is even further eroded in these globalized times, politics nonetheless continues and there is an urgent need to propose and debate the political forms, strategies, and tactics that are necessary and effective both within and between small states in a more integrated and yet still deeply divided and unequal world. *Critical Interventions*, it is hoped, will be a small contribution to both the task of reflecting on the recent past and a stimulus to the new and unprecedented debates that will be necessary if we are to help in the dreaming, imagining, and making of a better future.

ACKNOWLEDGMENTS

I am grateful to my friends and collaborators Rupert Lewis and Anthony Bogues who provided moral support and intellectual companionship through the Centre for Caribbean Thought over a remarkable decade at the very beginning of the twenty-first century. Much of the work in this volume was written in that period and benefited from their critical interventions. Many others gave similar acts of intellectual solidarity, sometimes unknowingly, including Percy Hintzen, Norman Girvan, Paget Henry, Obika Gray, Cecilia Green, Pat Mohammed, Pedro Noguera, George Lamming, Stuart Hall, David Scott, Kari Levitt, Charles Mills, Bill Schwarz, Deborah Thomas, Aaron Kamugisha, Geri Augusto, Selwyn Ryan, Kate Quinn, Lewis Gordon, Hilbourne Watson, Anton Allahar, Anthony Harriott, Linden Lewis, Tennyson Joseph, Gina Ulysse, the late Barry Chevannes, the late Rex Nettleford, and the late Lloyd Best. I thank them all. I am particularly grateful to Carol Lawes, who stepped in late in the game and provided invaluable logistical assistance, and to the attentive and meticulous editorial team at the University Press of Mississippi, especially Vijay Shah, Anne Stascavage, Will Rigby, and Katie Keene. And none of this would have been possible without my wife and companion Patsy Lewis, whose own scholarship has assisted me greatly and whose unwavering care and attention is the bedrock on which all this has been built.

Brian Meeks
Kingston, January 2014

PART ONE

Theoretical Forays

1. The Frontline: Valentino, Pablo Moses, and Caribbean Organic Philosophy in the Seventies (2003)

Three Stories

Three anecdotal events from the early eighties serve as an introduction to the purposes of this chapter. The first relates to a close colleague and friend, the late Barrington Chevannes, former dean[1] of the faculty of social sciences at the University of the West Indies, Mona, then a member of the central committee of the Workers Party of Jamaica (WPJ). Barry had delivered a paper on revolutionary music in Jamaica at the Intellectual Workers Conference, held with much fanfare in revolutionary Grenada in 1982. To the great consternation and dissatisfaction of the audience, he spoke about the contribution of the small and relatively obscure musical trends that were emerging around the Jamaican Marxist left, including his own compositions, with very little if any reference to the broader field of reggae music which, even as he spoke, was blazing a trail across the world's stage. For this elision, he received the opprobrium of many in the gathering, who considered his approach as being contemptuous of those forms that were genuinely popular. The irony is that, among the leadership of the WPJ, Barry was one of the few who really had a handle on the nature and character of the consolidating popular music, which, had it been his intention, he could have elaborated in great detail.

The second and third events are related. The first was the impact of Bob Marley's funeral on Jamaican politics in 1981. At a time when Edward Seaga's pro-Reagan Jamaica Labour Party (JLP) had just triumphed, when "deliverance" from radicalism had yet to lose its gloss, when consumerism, America, and the greenback ruled supreme, when Michael Manley's People's National Party (PNP) and the broader organized left had been cowed, the massive turnout and enthusiasm for Marley's funeral reminded all that there was another and perhaps more profound social movement on which the politics of the seventies had built its foundation.

The third event was my own perceived response of some leaders of the WPJ after the funeral. I had written an article for *Struggle*, the WPJ newspaper, es-

3

sentially arguing that the size and enthusiasm of the crowd of mourners represented an important watershed, a symbolic reassertion of a popular ethos under the banner of Rastafari and an indication that the progressive forces had not simply dissipated after the recent electoral defeat. For this, a top member of the political bureau of the party roundly attacked me at the weekly study group meeting for overemphasizing the event. After all, I was told, we had to make a distinction between the struggle of the proletariat, led by the vanguard party, and petty bourgeois manifestations of populism, as this clearly was. Truly humbled by this display of superior ideological prowess, I never wrote for *Struggle* again.

What these three reflect in the Jamaican context was the half hidden, intermittent, yet barely recorded struggle for the hegemony of ideas in the radical Caribbean movement of the seventies. Crudely put, while the resilience of the Caribbean revolutionary movement was largely due to an alliance between middle strata intellectual tendencies and popular grassroots supporters, this alliance was fraught with contradictions. These surrounded questions of the appropriate philosophy that would guide these parties, the tactics to be applied to different phases of the popular struggle, and in some instances, which of these social tendencies should lead. Broadly generalizing, the intellectuals were Marxist, more often than not of the Marxist-Leninist variety, and adopted the strategies and tactics of a certain Marxism-Leninism of the seventies. Again, broadly generalizing, the popular grassroots supporters were not Marxist, even when on occasion they supported Leninist tactics, but had their own worldview of African-centered revolutionism.[2]

The failure to understand that such a worldview existed, much less to comprehend its critical components, contributed in no small measure to the demise of the once vibrant Caribbean left of the seventies. It is this failure that led Mervyn Alleyne, referring more specifically to the academic field, to write: ". . . studies of contemporary Jamaica have failed to come to grips with two fundamental aspects of Jamaican culture: its value system(s) (or ethos) and its worldview or cognitive orientations. But these are the aspects of culture that impinge most on political ideology and clash most with the culture and technology of modernization."[3]

This failure is also what Paget Henry, in his magisterial 2000 study *Caliban's Reason: Introducing Afro-Caribbean Philosophy*, is, in part, trying to correct, particularly when he asserts, "Afro-Caribbean philosophy needs to come to terms with the history of its own historicism."[4] The failure to theorize and come to terms with the popular perspective might help explain the early alienation of the NJM in Grenada from grassroots Muslim and Rastafarian elements that had given initial critical support to the revolution.[5] This sporadically documented event was, in turn, an early portent of the subsequent alienation of the entire party from the Grenadian people and the collapse of the revolution in 1983. Though there are obviously other causative factors, it can help explain the failure of the WPJ, despite (or, on closer scrutiny, because of) its almost hegemonic hold over a generation of young intellectuals, ever to seriously accumulate popular support in Jamaica. The December 1978 "Programme: Workers Party of Jamaica," for instance, calls for a cultural revolution, including the ending of illiteracy, modernization of the education system, and democratization of the media.[6] There is barely a nodding recognition of the specific strengths of the popular culture that precedes the revolution and its own potential as a fountainhead for popular organization and post-revolutionary reconstruction.

And, in an ironically contradictory fashion, it can help explain the failure of the revolutionary movement in Trinidad after 1970, where the intellectuals around the National Joint Action Committee (NJAC), unlike in Grenada and Jamaica, readily adopted Afro-Trinidadian cultural forms, but deprived them of revolutionary content. The end result, in a peculiarly convoluted Trinidadian way, was that NJAC lost its sting and evolved into a sort of cultural fraternity.[7] The reaction to this cultural turn was that grassroots revolutionaries grouped around the National United Freedom Fighters (NUFF) and sought to be Marxist, though with strong Africanist overtones and an uncompromising grassroots militancy, in order to distance themselves from the perceived elitist culturalism of the middle-class revolutionaries in NJAC.[8] The resulting guerrilla movement ended in a debacle in the mid-seventies, as Trinidad and Tobago segued into the early phases of its long oil boom.

Two Interventions

Radical Caribbean social and political theorizing, particularly around the upsurge and collapse of the popular movement of the seventies, has evolved in two distinct waves. The first, operating within the confines of Caribbean historicist traditions, sought to find essentially institutionalist, geopolitical, or narrowly ideological explanations. Thus, to take the best known instance, the extensive work surrounding the collapse of the Grenadian revolution, while necessarily varied in analysis and conclusion, is largely concerned with the role of parties, the CIA, the Cubans, or narrowly defined ideological issues.[9] Though it is not altogether absent,[10] there is very little on deeper questions of philosophy, of episteme—in other words, of worldview. A second wave, influenced by, or in opposition to, what Henry calls the "linguistic turn"[11] is far more sensitive to these matters.

Two recent and important contributions reflect this new thinking. Henry's

Caliban's Reason searches for an underlying ethos to Caribbean thinking. Critically scanning a variety of Caribbean theorists, from James to Fanon, Wilson Harris to Sylvia Wynter, and others including Jürgen Habermas, a number of Afro-American philosophers, and Caribbean Marxists, he concludes that this ethos is to be found in a veiled Afro-Caribbean philosophy. The fundamental weakness in Caribbean "historicist" thinking—the term Henry uses to refer broadly to historians, social scientists, and the like—is that it has failed to include in its focus matters of the self, of "ego-genesis" and ego-maintenance. The Afro-Caribbean self is differently constructed from the European self, he posits. It is deeply influenced by African "mythopoetic traditions" that advance the "immanent and transcendent" relationship between the spiritual and material worlds. This has profound implications for how man is perceived in relation to nature and, importantly, for notions of community, which trump the mythical, liberal construction of the unencumbered individual.

By placing psycho-existential matters on the agenda for legitimate Caribbean social theorizing, Henry has opened up an entire field. Future analyses of the Grenada crisis, for instance, can no longer ignore hypothesizing on the character of the Grenadian ego, its autonomous intervention, and its role as contributing element in the tragedy. Important, too, is that Henry maintains a space in his ideational framework for Marxist political economy and its respective categories, though the exact modalities of how, from the perspective of critical analysis, they operate within and around his notions of ego-genesis, are not sufficiently elaborated.

The most serious weakness, however, in an otherwise stimulating presentation is that Henry focuses too much on the ideas of the traditional intellectuals. Despite a promising start, in which he locates African philosophy as arising out of popular traditions, he then, in the Caribbean center of his study, largely elides discussion of popular philosophic forms. His only sustained discussion in this sphere—around Rastafari—ends up being less nuanced than his textured critiques of the "formal" intellectuals. Thus, for instance, while Henry considers Rastafarianism as being a "powerful and legitimating force for black identities,"[12] he argues unconvincingly that "Rastafarian historicism leaves the social and developmental problems of Jamaican society largely unaddressed."[13] This, as I have argued elsewhere,[14] fails to appreciate the extent to which Rastafarian notions of "livity" speak to an alternative relationship of individual to community, of community to environment and of humanity to commodity, countering, in significant respects, Western individualism and materialism. Henry's failure to seriously engage Rastafarian philosophy[15] reveals a critical weakness in an otherwise insightful study with broad theoretical implications.

The other perspective I wish to focus on is that of David Scott. In *Refashion-*

ing Futures: Criticism after Postcoloniality (1999), Scott engages in an equally, if not more ambitious attempt to redefine the parameters for radical thinking and (presumably) action in the contemporary world. Using his Sri Lankan and Jamaican roots and experiences as points of departure, Scott develops his perspective through a series of elegantly argued theses. First, the old narrative of revolution, associated with the myth of rapid social upheaval and cataclysmic change, if it ever had any real meaning, is now largely empty of content. This is a result both of geopolitical shifts that have transformed the terms of reference of that narrative and of new criticism that has undermined its philosophical assumptions. In his words, "Many of the epistemological assumptions that held (that narrative) together and guaranteed the salience of its emancipatory hopes—assumptions about history, about culture, politics, resistance, freedom, subjectivity—have been steadily eroded by the labour of antimetaphysical and antiteleological strategies of criticism."[16] Second, in the world that is emerging, the old dominant, hegemonic ruling alliances are collapsing and space is opening up for autonomous popular movements and strata to flourish and engage in their own self expression and "self fashioning."[17] Third, this New World requires new thinking. Scott codifies and encapsulates his approach in what he sees as a folding together of Fanon and Foucault.[18] By this, he means a borrowing and incorporation of Foucault's concern with power over the self and autonomy from overarching notions of domination, whether they are statal in origin or incorporated within the framework of societal norms.

Scott, however, is sensitive to the nihilistic dangers inherent in a certain interpretation of Foucault, in which there can be no emancipation, as all emancipatory projects ultimately end up reasserting dominance through power. The answer then, is to preserve a space for Fanon, who in *The Wretched of the Earth* epitomized the notion of anti-colonial revolution. It is a Fanon, however, from whom the state and the nation have been expunged. Instead, the notion of liberation is preserved toward the end of establishing vaguely defined communities of "self fashioned peoples," or as he describes it in his analysis of contemporary Jamaica:

> This will enable me to think of political society in Jamaica not as a domain centered on the state and the competition for its offices, but as a field of interdependent pluralities governed simultaneously by a desire for settled identities and by an unsettling genealogical ethic of pluralization. . . . On the one hand, I want to imagine spheres or constellations of discursive and performative activity which would be semi-autonomous and self governing in relation to each other, and in which embodied subjects—that is, not merely rights-bearing subjects, but subjects embodying lived traditions—would

be able so to speak, to stand forth and represent themselves in their own languages, stories, images and so on. On the other hand, I imagine that while these spheres would presuppose something held in common, they would not be presumed to be internally homogenous.[19]

Scott is not so much concerned with Henry's "self" and its construction as he is with the sort of epistemological and political framework that will allow a variety of selves to flourish. I am sympathetic with this central dimension of his argument, particularly out of the experience of the many national liberation movements that have disappointed by reimposing authoritarian structures on their presumably liberated citizenry. But, I suggest, Scott's analysis has important weaknesses that compromise its utility.

The first of these is his opening argument that the world of the immediate past, of Fanon's *Wretched*, is dead and buried. The Soviet Union is gone, U.S. hegemony has been asserted in international institutions in unprecedented ways, and the prestige of what he describes as "social-democratic energies"[20] has faded. Scott uses this fairly self-evident information to argue that the oppositional language of the old left is no longer effective and we therefore need to look beyond it, in the direction of his notion of refashioned futures. While it is certainly true that the old left is moribund, I disagree with the perspective that says that its projects and strategies must, therefore, be largely abandoned. The fundamental issues around which the older narratives of resistance were constructed are still very much present. The relentless transformation and domination of the world by capital has not changed. The ideological forms through which that domination is assured have certainly been modified to suit the new situation, but its central features—Euro-American centrism, racism, liberal individualism, and uncircumscribed materialism—are still remarkably intact. The recent moves by the United States government to penalize the Europeans for protecting Caribbean banana exports in favor of Chiquita is not some novel, postcolonial maneuver, but a classic, if prosaic instance of imperial domination in the interest of maximizing profits.[21]

Such a world requires not the abandonment of the old and tested forms of struggle but appropriate revisions and modifications to suit the complex new situation. By this, I suggest that in a world still composed of (albeit weakened) nation states, the struggle against capital and hegemony will, inevitably, have to take as one of its central forms a national struggle. This is the level on which governments battle with the International Monetary Fund (IMF) and World Trade Organization (WTO) to undermine their domination and push for a new international economic order. In his analysis, then, Scott seems to mistake unfavorable conditions for such a struggle for the absence of conditions altogether. The unprecedented local and international mobilization around the 1999 WTO conference in Seattle, including Internet mobilization and alliances between trade unions, environmental groups, and nation states, is but a first indicator of the new forms of struggle for old objectives.[22] Scott, by too quickly conceding defeat, theoretically excludes the possibility of a new frontal, more global, yet still very national confrontation with capital, a struggle that is emerging even as we write.

My second worry is with Scott's conclusions, his autonomous, self-fashioned communities. How do we get to this point where we have free-floating, critical, autonomous communities of free subjects? What is the process that takes us out of the contemporary state and into this new context? Who mediates between the communities when there are the inevitable disputes over resources, space, and conflicting rights to self-expression? Will any perspective be allowed to flourish in the new situation? Scott gives precedence in his analysis to communities of the poor, captured in his notion of the "ruud bwai,"[23] as epitome of autonomous, rebellious self-expression. But on what basis does he foreground the cultural assertiveness of the "ruud bwai" and the poor? What is it about the poor that makes them intrinsically interesting and worthy of theoretical precedence? Why not give equal weighting, for instance, to the increasing tendencies among the upper middle classes to refashion themselves with "Jamerican" identities? And what is the place, if any, of communities with embedded racial hierarchies, or gender biases? Will there be a body *über alles* to decide on which communities are allowed to flourish or not? Will this body be called "the state"?

I ask these decidedly leading questions to suggest that while I am sympathetic to Scott's search for modes of liberation beyond the Fanonian "national," there seems to be no shortcut through which to avoid a frontal political confrontation with the old state in order to transform it into a popular institution that will then facilitate popular, autonomous development. The question of mediation, of weighing between competing notions of the good, of even ruling certain collectively unacceptable forms of "the good" out of court, appears unavoidable, short of the Marxian notion of a post-socialist revolution in human consciousness. The real possibility then seems to lie in the democratizing of the state in such a way that it becomes a genuinely transparent tribune of the largest possible majority of the people and not the mechanism to ensconce the rule of a minority. This, clearly, is somewhat different from Scott's conclusions.

I want to suggest, further, that embedded in his foregrounding of the importance of ruud bwai is a continuing subterranean adherence to a narrative of resistance that invests the poor with a particular, intrinsic importance. This investiture of the poor as subject of historic transformation itself operates within multiple narratives. One version, of course, is Christian, and there are numerous contemporary instances before and beyond liberation theology to support this. The other is Marxist, and I suspect that Scott, even as he distances himself from Marx, is still beholden to him in this regard.

The sum of my argument is that, in searching for modes of autonomous self-fashioning beyond Fanonian "liberation," Marxist political economy and its central placement of the struggle against capital cannot be abandoned. What we certainly need to do, however, is rescue the baby from the bathwater. Much of what is Euro-centric in Marx's narrative needs to be jettisoned. A certain story needs to go, in which proletarians are forged in occidental factories, learn collectivity gradually, overcome "economism," and overthrow European capital "in the interests of" the poor, helpless, subjected masses in the rest of the world. Instead, we need to begin to write an alternative story, in which Jamaicans and Sri Lankans, African Americans and Peruvians, through developing their own modes of living, own cultures of resistance, form themselves and are simultaneously formed in the struggle to survive. These autonomous processes, with their own genealogies, give their own names to that struggle and in the course of this quite different notion of self-fashioning, in the battle against capital and for a better world, open up their own possibilities for a better future.

My own approach then, is closer to Henry's, with a strong appreciation of his incorporation of the self and of African culture, though it is also sympathetic to Scott's (and Foucault's) assertion that power extends and in turn must be curbed, beyond the barrel of the gun. It is closest, I would like to think, to Stuart Hall's approach in "The Problem of Ideology: Marxism Without Guarantees." Here, and elsewhere in his extensive (and still evolving) oeuvre, Hall makes the case for an approach to historical analysis that appreciates the importance of the economic, not in the sense of absolute "determinacy," but ". . . in terms of setting of limits, the establishment of parameters, the defining of the space of operations, the concrete conditions of existence, the 'givenness' of social practices, rather than in terms of the absolute predictability of particular outcomes. . . . The paradigm of perfectly closed, perfectly predictable systems of thought is religion or astrology, not science."[24]

Within these broad parameters, human subjects struggle to transform systems of domination with varying degrees of failure and success. The critical object of analysis then, is to understand how the complex, human construction of egos, of ideas, of cultural forms, and of leadership modalities operates within given, if constantly shifting constraints, to open or close the door to various possible futures. Or, as Hall more succinctly puts it:

This approach replaces the notion of fixed ideological meanings and class ascribed ideologies with the concept of ideological terrains of struggle and the task of ideological transformation. It is the general movement in this direction, away from an abstract general theory of ideology and towards the more concrete analysis of how, in particular historical situations, 'ideas organize human masses, and create the terrain on which men move, acquire consciousness of their position, struggle, etc.'[25]

Following from this, the tasks of critical Caribbean historical analysis would include, first, an attempt to understand the (contingent) boundaries to political and social action set by a particular socio-economic and geopolitical moment and from this to explore the ideological terrain, the contours of thinking that define it, and how these help to determine unique social and political outcomes.

Gramsci's notion of the organic philosopher is, in this regard, particularly useful. In "The Study of Philosophy,"[26] he makes the famous argument that all men are philosophers, but this "spontaneous philosophy," captured in language itself, "common sense," and popular religion, is limited, disjointed, and episodic. The thrust of Gramsci's argument is to understand the nature of "spontaneous philosophy," in order to push it in the direction of a "philosophy of praxis," i.e., one that would understand the world in its "true" nature and act upon it to change it for the better. His innovation here, certainly from a Marxist perspective, is that he conceptualizes his philosophy of praxis as building on spontaneous philosophy and not simply trumping it; thus, the thoughts and activities of "ordinary" people are to be taken seriously. Of a series of four notes, which he uses to elaborate the argument, I choose Note 3 to introduce my own addendum. In Note 3, Gramsci argues that language is not simply a means of communication, but is philosophic, in that the words themselves contain a conception of the world and of culture.[27] Gramsci then goes on to say: "Someone who only speaks dialect, or understands the standard language incompletely, necessarily has an intuition of the world which is more or less limited and provincial, which is fossilized and anachronistic in relation to the major currents of thought that dominate world history. His interests will be limited, more or less corporate or economistic, not universal."[28]

I both agree and disagree with this assertion. On the one hand, it is quite acceptable that there may be people who, through isolation, obscurity of language, and disconnection from the mainstream of modernity, simply do not have a full and proper grasp of the world around them. Parochialism of thought and philosophy is therefore conceivable. On the other hand, however, all is not necessarily as it appears to be. Thus, "dialect speakers," or persons apparently on the fringes of modernity, may in fact be in its engine room, at its very heart. In this respect, their insights and intuition as to its true nature may transcend that of persons with a formal, even rigorous understanding of its mechanics. Further, the very dialect(ic) through which they grasp and name this modernity gives to the struggle against it a particular quality and character. Finally, this quality and character is never transcended by a moment of truth, when philosophy of praxis merges with spontaneous philosophy; rather, the genealogical imprint of that dialect remains as a feature of that particular process of resistance, through defeat and victory and beyond any hypothetical transcendence of modernity.

If significantly greater weight is then to be placed on the speakers of dialect than Gramsci does, we need to take seriously the perspectives of the organic philosophers—those who most intimately represent the popular perspectives—and critically locate their ideas in a particular time and place. The concluding part of this chapter seeks to broach some of these issues in relation to two significant Afro-Caribbean organic philosophers of the seventies.

Two Singers

I use as illustration Valentino, the Trinidadian calypsonian, and Pablo Moses, the Jamaican reggae vocalist, two artistes who came to prominence in that era. Pablo Moses was born Pablita Henry, ca. 1953 in Plowden, Manchester, in rural Jamaica. Apart from a two-year stint in New York, he spent most of his youth in the countryside before traveling to Kingston. In school in Jamaica's capital, he formed a vocal group, the Canaries, which sought to record in the burgeoning music industry in the sixties, but they met with little success.[29] Moses gained some popularity in the mid-seventies with his single "Grasshopper," followed by his classic album *Revolutionary Dream*. This is how the liner notes for Pablo Moses's *Reggae Greats* album describes his appearance on the reggae stage:

> In a crowded East London record shack on a steamy August afternoon in 1975, Spy chalked up his current singles chart. High in the Top 20 appeared a parable-like single with the abstruse title of 'I Man a Grasshopper', the singer a mysterious Pablo Moses. The offbeat half-spoken, half-sung tale of a rum drinking ex-police officer who had informed on the herb-smoking singer, was delivered over a chugging rhythm, spliced with radical bursts of lead guitar. Produced for a mere hundred dollars, the mix bore all the hallmarks of Lee Perry's Black Ark Studio and the single was destined to elevate Pablo Moses to a near-myth status.[30]

Anthony Emrold Phillip began singing calypsos as the Lord Valentino in Port of Spain in the sixties.[31] His early compositions were in the traditional vein, with some social commentary, but largely in the celebratory mainstream. Under the influence of the Black Power Movement and the 1970 revolution, Valentino deleted the traditional "Lord" in his title for the popular "Brother." In the early part of the new decade, he was dubbed "the People's Calypsonian" and became closely associated with the many popular concerts initiated by the NJAC. As NJAC, however, became increasingly "culturalist," Valentino began to distance himself from the organization.[32] In the late seventies he took up the cause of the Grenadian revolution, though, like many other calypsonians, he was deeply disturbed by its fratricidal destruction. Valentino, now a Rastafarian, remains committed, in his most recent work, to a radical restructuring of Trinidad and the Caribbean.

I choose Moses and Valentino for a number of disparate reasons. The first is my own fascination with the quality of their music and lyrics and the fact (itself worth exploring) that neither of these artists ever truly broke into the mainstream.[33] Neither Moses nor Valentino were regular inhabitants of, in the first instance, the Top 100, or, in the second, the annual Calypso King finals. The second, as shall be further elaborated, is the evident and striking similarity in their form and content, even though they operated within distinct Afro-Caribbean genres. The third reason is that they fit neatly into the Trinidad/Jamaica dichotomy, providing rich comparative material from two of the most distinct cultures within the Caribbean continuum. The fourth and final is my own assessment that in the consistency of their messages is to be found the cutting edge of popular philosophical resistance to neocolonialism in the early phase after independence. I use two broad categories to organize a preliminary look at their work: style and content.

STYLE

Moses and Valentino, operating independently and a thousand miles apart, possessed a common, almost indefinable style. I was impressed when, as a young student at the University of the West Indies, I first saw Valentino perform in the tent in 1971, some months after the Black Power revolution—how different he was from all the other calypsonians. He stood, laconically, in a corner of the stage as though he was not really there, or certainly not the center of attention. He was dressed in a somber, full black outfit, hair combed in a neat, not massive Afro and "peepers"—the tiny, circular glasses then popular on the Port of Spain blocks. This contrasted dramatically with those who came before and those who followed him, who, for the most part, were clad in the traditionally gaudy, sequined garb and performed onstage in typical, physically ebullient manner.

A similar feeling was evoked when I first heard Pablo Moses sing "Blood Money" on a scratchy radio in 1975 and later when I saw him perform it. The cover of his first album, *Revolutionary Dream*, captures this mood, with Moses featured in mirrored dark glasses, obscuring all emotion, yet twice reflecting reality. If there is a common phrase to capture both, then, "cool and deadly" is as good as any. If as Hebdige suggests,[34] style is a critical space in which scripts of resistance are written, then Valentino and Pablo Moses occupied the same style corner. The key elements included a certain quiet dreadness,[35] exemplified in limited motion and an almost epic stillness of being, combined with the delivery of lyrics in a matter-of-fact way, yet possessing great profundity.

I make no attempt to understand the origins of this complex phenomenon. Certainly in the Jamaican case, there is a tradition of dreadness, of philosophical meditation, associated with ganja smoking and Rastafari, itself, perhaps, having a lineage into the African-derived authority of the griot. Undoubtedly, though, there are also other, newer elements. Thus, anyone who ever saw the Valentino of the early seventies perform would undoubtedly recognize the cool but deadly hero of the spaghetti western, arriving in town alone, but with a Gatling gun concealed in the ubiquitous box he drags around with him. He seems harmless, if a bit eccentric; but when confronted with vicious and seemingly overwhelming force, the Gatling gun appears and the hero (coolly) opens the box, cranks it up. and inevitably wins the day.[36] There is nothing novel in suggesting the western as a template for popular cultures of various kinds (including Jamaican Rude Boy of a decade earlier), but it is important to recognize it as a specific garb for a certain revolutionary discourse.

This question of style also segues into the matter of musical form. While it is true that the reggae music of the mid-seventies had slowed down into a walking beat,[37] Moses carries this to the extreme. It is very difficult to dance to "Blood Money," where the entire song appears to be at the wrong speed, like a 45-rpm being played at 33 and 1/3rd. A similar, though less extreme slowing down is to be found in pieces by Valentino like "Barking Dogs" (1973) and "Third World" (1972), though this might also be related to Valentino's tent style, where slowing down to listen to serious lyrics can trace its origins back to the early *Sans Humanite*[38] tradition. Thus, one simple explanation might be that both Moses and Valentino want their lyrics to be heard. There is also a certain "otherworldliness" in the style of both artistes. There is a casual off-stage quality, quite different from, say, the strident assertiveness of a Peter Tosh, or, in Trinidadian vein, the musical effervescence of a Black Stalin. This quality of being there and at the same time offstage, in the audience, is characteristic of both men.[39] It is as if to say "If you're ready to hear what I have to say, here it is, but if you aren't, here it is anyway. Store it up for the time when you are ready."

CONTENT

Moses and Valentino were on the frontline. They voice, perhaps more explicitly than any of their generation, an autonomous, African-centered[40] notion of revolution that operated around the parameters of the broader anti-imperialist and revolutionary movement of the Seventies, but never completely within it. Thus, Valentino, perhaps more than Superior, Stalin, or even Chalkdust, was the "People's Calypsonian" and Moses was the natural musical bridge between the more Rastafarian Marley and Burning Spear on the one hand and Mikey Smith, Joe Ruglass, and Barry Chevannes, who were clearly identified with left-wing politics. Among the critical elements in their oeuvres I mention:

1. The Assertion of Africa and Africans at the Center of Caribbean Life

Both artistes emphasize key themes surrounding the reclamation of an African identity and the struggle for African liberation. Both envisage a unity of the broader African diaspora. Moses carries this further by questioning whether it is feasible to effectively carry out a liberation process in the Caribbean alone, in what he derisively refers to as "this square of land." Similarly, Valentino's "Third World" proclaims and reclaims the biblical prophecy that "Ethiopia shall rise again":

> I no longer see the African
> Primitive man with a spear in his hand
> But I see a civilized intelligent man
> Walking that proud land
> And I see like Ethiopia go rise again
> And in the Third World the African shall reign.[41]

The glaring contradiction here is that, even as Valentino asserts pride in being African, he simultaneously falls into the primitive/civilized trap,[42] by characterizing traditional African society as something backward, to be turned away from. Thus, to be intelligent is coupled with being civilized, with its inevitable baggage of being like a European.

A further problem lies in assertion of an African predominance in a Third World of numerous ethnic and racial groups and, even more so, a Trinidad with a large Indian population and a history of ethnic contestation. It is appropriate to recall David Scott's expressed concern to avoid the essentializing of the native subject[43] and to allow differences to flourish freely and equally. Yet the reclamation of an African identity, denied most vehemently in the postcolonial period for a neutral nationalism, is a constant, irrepressible theme that is sustained far beyond these two, through the entire list of leading reggae artistes and calypsonians.

Moses, hailing from Jamaica—with an overwhelmingly African-descended population and a correspondingly strident official denial of Africanness—presents his assertion within the oppositionist Rastafarian tradition, though with his own revolutionary spin. Thus, in "Revolutionary Dream," he is a freedom fighter in Africa, but just when he is about to kill "the head man," he is awakened from his "wonderful vision."[44] In "We should be in Angola," he develops a theme not uncommon to other reggae compositions of the era, where unnecessary tribal warfare in tiny, marginalized Jamaica is counterposed to the need for a just war to free Africa from colonialism and racial hierarchies:

> Fighting here in Jamaica, it's a shame my brother
> Destroying our culture by killing one another . . .
> We should be in Angola, oh yes, my brothers
> We should be in Angola, oh yes, my sisters . . .[45]

And, in "Give I Fe I Name," Moses asserts the fairly well-trodden theme of reclaiming an African identity, but in a typically commonsense and humorous way:

> Take back you name and give I fe I name
> I and I don't want dis ya name . . .
> Because the name I have is for a European
> Not the name of a black, black African[46]

2. Revolution as a Turning of Things Upside Down

A consistent theme from both artistes is the well-developed notion of revolution. While there is little elaboration of what will happen post-insurrection, for both, the process of revolution is inevitable, necessary, and cleansing. Thus, to quote again from Valentino's "Third World," a calypso in the same vein as Moses's "Revolutionary Dream":

> Meditating in my house just the other day
> Is like I charge up myself and I trip away
> I travel whole day, I travel whole night,
> Where I went and what I saw

To tell you is my delight
Way over yonder I did behold
Because in front of my eyes
Was a brand new world
But like a wheel the world turn around
And all the people who was up they come right back down.[47]

This clarity on the possibility of a revolutionary outcome is equally demonstrated in Moses's classic "Blood Money." The youth have been held in thrall by the power of money, have taken up the gun, and are involved in fratricidal war. But with a supreme will and the guidance of God (Jah) they shall overcome. It should be underlined here that in both instances, revolution is simultaneously secular and associated with the spiritual. One gets to understand its possibility through higher meditation ("charge up myself"), and the act of upheaval itself is both carried out by man as it is fulfilled by spiritual cataclysm:

Oh there shall be lightning and thunder
For the heathens who take advantage of sufferer
To gain their vanity of power
They shall reach their final hour
They will be cut off forever[48]

And, in what is for me one of his most complete compositions, for its sense of timing, satirical lyrics, and plain good music, Valentino in "Dis Place Nice," chants that Trinidad is nice, but for the rich. The sting in the tail, left for the last line of the chorus, is that out of all of this hypocrisy, revolution is on the way:

They don't know their worth
Like they haven't a sense of value
They don't know their rights
Even that they cannot argue
Three quarters of a million people
Cannot get up and do something 'bout the struggle
But could plan for the next holiday
To fete their lives away
And forgetting that they own the soil
Of which their fore-parents toil
For the people who form the constitution laws
For the oppressors and foreign investors
Trinidad is nice, Trinidad is a paradise

Amoco and Shell business did went swell
On your oil them foreign parasites dwell
Trinidad is nice, Trinidad is a paradise
Yet the song I sing like if I hearing
The chorus singing "God save the King"
Trinidad is nice, Trinidad is a paradise
But the people getting ready for this revolution day
Change is on the way.[49]

In a feature common to both artistes, the nature of these earth-shattering changes is never really made clear.

3. The Naming of an Alternative Community of "Idrens"
The central feature in the work of both Valentino and Moses is the assertion of an alternative notion of community. It is not the Lockean commonwealth of self-seeking individuals, bound together by minimal contractual ties; nor is it the socialist unity of shared proletarian class interests, though this inhabits some of Valentino's work. There is, rather, a shared community of African survivors, who have, from bitter experience, forged their own notions of freedom, equality, and justice. This accords with Mervyn Alleyne's suggestion of an existent but besieged "collectivist ethos" that is at the heart of Jamaican culture. It is this collectivist approach that is at the fountainhead of the alternative community:

> Jamaicans, especially rural Jamaicans, tend toward a collectivist or communalist view of society—here too they follow Africa. For example, in Jamaica the whole community considers itself responsible for children. . . . Adherents of this European world view believe that the unbridled exploitation of nature is the inalienable right of individuals; that individuals can claim as their boundless property and boundlessly profit from however much forest or farmland, or natural wealth they conquer and stake out. . . . To put it at its most abstract, traditional Jamaican collectivism is being confronted by European individualism.[50]

The implicit purpose, present in the work of both artistes, is to excavate, rekindle, and, where necessary, reinvent this community for the purpose of a spiritually uplifted and better world.

This is most subtly illustrated in Moses's remarkable piece "Grasshopper." On one level it is a song written in favor of the legalization of ganja. Taken on this plane, it does a better job than, say, Peter Tosh's forthright "Legalize It" due to its subtle, indirect method of attack. Thus Moses presents his argument on the ground of equality of treatment, the cornerstone of Western jurisprudence. Yet, in the failure of the law to live up to its promise is revealed its hypocrisy. Beyond it, then, is the implicitly stated need for brotherly respect and the building of a world in which there is genuine freedom, and which demands a community with equality of treatment:

> That man saw I man eating I man Collie weed
> That man should never call Babylon to spoil I man irie feed
> I man don't want to cause any wrong
> I man only eating weed and thinking of love song
> To I man that man a fish da man deh love water
> I man I love collie weed I man a grasshopper
> That man love seed and fish bone
> I man love to keep high right in my soul[51]

This sense of brotherhood and community is even more explicit in Valentino's "Every Brother Is Not a Brother," where again, the question of hypocrisy is used to argue for a greater community of brothers and sisters that must find its true self and come together:

> Don't call me your brother
> If you know you come out to gesture
> This case is a serious matter
> But it's not so with your behavior
> The brotherhood to some doesn't mean a thing
> Daily this is what I'm experiencing
> If you don't check up on your foolish ways
> You will just dream about the better days
> You still backbiting, you not uniting
> And then you wishing one another the worst thing
> Your mental attitude towards each other
> Like you forget that we came from the same mother
> Vice-versa like a sister
> Every brother is not a brother[52]

And in "Blood Money," Moses calls for the "bredrens" to end their days of wrath and to unite for the greater cause of the joint community of blood and spirit:

So bredrens, bredrens, wrath no more
Let's inite in these troublous times
Vank the moneymen vank the oppressor
Let Jah spirit give guidance iternally
Let the moneymen be the sufferer
Then man I grow with like a brother
Will never shoot I for them nor them
Blood Money, Blood Donesa
I and I don't want them Blood money
Blood donesa[53]

This notion of community is a common, yet strangely underemphasized theme in analyses of mid-late-seventies reggae. Burning Spear's "Social Living," for example, cleverly counterpoises "Social Living" as a third option to capitalism and socialism, as he chants that it is the "best."[54] And, this sense of a collective task of survival is also present in the equally iconic "Row Fisherman Row" by the Congos. Myton, the lead, calls on the mythical fisherman (fishers of men?) to bring in his catch, for there are many hungry children to feed:

Row Fisherman row, keep on rowing your boat.
Row fisherman row
Lots of hungry belly pickney deh a shore.[55]

One Conclusion?

The preliminary conclusion here is, somewhat disingenuously, that this is still very much a work in progress. Beyond this, however, its most important innovation is, possibly, the attempt to place in the foreground this notion of community. David Scott, Tony Bogues, and others have sought to explore the concept of "dreadness" as metaphor for the recognition of alternative cultural forms and communities. In some respects, however, the concept of dreadness can be seen as one-sided. It is a stance of resistance to dominant narratives, not so much a construction of alternatives. The notion of community, of "social living" as "the best," provides a somewhat different space for exploration. Having asserted this, it should be noted that the section above is entitled a "community of Idrens" (brethrens), and purposively so. For while both Moses and Valentino reach for a revolutionary reconstruction of society, they operate within a certain paradigm of the revolutionary movement of the seventies in which women were largely relegated to the margins. Thus, there are numerous references to Idrens and bredrens, I-man and brothers, and while sisters and sistren are occasionally tacked on, it is more often as afterword, if not afterthought. The movement of the seventies, whether defined from the intellectual middle or from below, was led by men and reflected, in great measure, their interests. Any critical reappraisal of a popular philosophy from below must, therefore, also critique its glaring lacunae and weaknesses.

And it must be underlined that while Valentino, with his sense of African-Indian unity and inspired by the slogan of the 1970 Black Power revolution, was certainly not the most guilty, the assertion of Africanness in the peculiar topology of Trinidad was always fraught with the possibility of the exclusion or relegation to the margins of Indo-Trinidadians, and required a subtlety of exposition often missing in the popular discourse.

And finally, it should be restated that while organic philosophers sharply identified the need for substantial change, little was elaborated beyond the broadest parameters of community, providing only the barest blueprints for disenchanted multitudes to imagine their visions of utopia.

Much more needs to be done in this project of exploration. Thus, I have mentioned but not elaborated on the underlying commonality of the spiritual, as Chevannes, Henry, and others have argued, central to any understanding of worldview. Other differences need to be further considered. For instance, the differences between the more overtly political Valentino in his scathing attack against Reagan's Caribbean Basin Initiative (CBI), "The Basin Spring a Leak in the Caribbean," and the more metaphoric Moses of "Grasshopper" and "Where am I" suggest real distinctions in the way organic philosophers address matters of politics in Trinidad and Jamaica, requiring further thought and analysis.

Yet, as Valentino's and Moses's common construct of community suggests, the process of teasing out the peculiarities of the popular worldview is never an abstract act of excavation. For it is on the real foundation of lived histories and traditions of resistance, not a blank slate, that future projects of social and political transformation will have to be constructed.

2. Reasoning with Caliban: A Critical Reading of Paget Henry's *Caliban's Reason: Introducing Afro-Caribbean Philosophy* (2002)

Paget Henry has written an important book, breathtaking in its ambition, sweeping in its vision, and, certainly to someone trained in the narrow secularity of the social sciences, startling in its conclusions. Henry's purpose is nothing less than to explore and map a field that has not been previously charted: Afro-Caribbean philosophy.

His central thesis is to confirm that there does exist an Afro-Caribbean philosophy, but that it has been a minor tradition, operating in the interstices of the more dominant forms of Caribbean intellectual production. He suggests that it is divided into two sub-traditions, that of the historicists (Eric Williams, Arthur Lewis, and C. L. R. James, for instance) and that of the poeticists (Derek Walcott, Kamau Brathwaite, and Aime Cesaire, et al.). Though there are important individuals who span both traditions (including Frantz Fanon, James, and Sylvia Wynter), they have for the most part been separated; and this, as Wilson Harris has suggested,[1] has served to diminish the potential advances in social understanding that might have arisen from a closer affiliation.

More importantly, the absence of a self-conscious philosophical gaze has prevented Caribbean intellectuals from focusing on critical existential matters related to "ego genesis" and ontology. This weakness, argues Henry, has severely impaired Caribbean intellectual exploration, as it has affected Caribbean efforts toward social and economic liberation. In order for future social movements to have a better chance of succeeding, they will, as an indispensable part of their project, have to engage in the "setting afoot of a new man."[2] This will require a new focus on philosophical matters ignored by the social movements of the mid- to late twentieth century, including the nature of the innate creativity of the Caribbean people and, most of all, the formation and composition of the Caribbean self.[3]

In order to make this surprising psycho-existential turn, however, Henry embarks on a whirlwind tour of traditional African philosophy, through separate critiques of James, Fanon, Harris, Wynter, and Jürgen Habermas; further engagements with Pan Africanism, Afro-American philosophy, and contemporary Caribbean Marxism; and ending with a broad critique of the historicist position and suggestions as to how it might reposition itself.

Grappling with Caliban

At the heart of Henry's argument is the first chapter on African philosophy, which advances two proposals: that there is a coherent African philosophy, and that it has had a significant though subterranean impact on Caribbean thinking. African philosophy, apart from the most recent period, has not developed as a formal university discipline, but in the form of "mythopoetic traditions." This fact does not void it of its philosophical substance but, rather, informs us as to the particular character of the philosophy. Within the "mythopoetics"[4] of African philosophy, then, there exist origin narratives, which explain how the human ego is formed and sustained. These have as much validity as any, to the extent that all origin narratives affect and help to determine the behavior of living human beings. One of the tasks, then, is to grasp the nature of the mythologically constructed African ego and to understand its implications for social life.

Using examples primarily from West Africa, he posits that in the African conception there is a spiritual world that has both "immanent and transcendent relations to the material, social and individual worlds."[5] Generalizing from the Akan myth, he advances a view of the human being as the "ontic unity" of three component parts: the okra, or soul, the sunsum, or ego, and the honan, or body.[6] In order to achieve human fulfillment, the sunsum must develop within guidelines set by the okra, which is in turn set by god and is therefore predestined. To function effectively, the ego must cooperate with the soul, and though unity between the two counterpoised dimensions of the human self is never fully achieved, the process of attempting it is the purpose of human existence. Unlike either Western or Indian philosophy, which in different ways assert a radical separation of matter and spirit, Henry posits that there is an integration of the two in African philosophy.

Important addenda flow from this juxtaposition of ego and spirit. In the ethical sphere, the implication is that if the spirit dominates and there is a unity among all people at the spiritual level, then for the ego to be in harmony with the spirit, it must also seek, in everyday life, to be in harmony with that of other human beings. There is thus, arguably, a communitarian, as opposed to an individualist, ethic embedded in African philosophy. At the level of the relationship of man to the environment, it can also be argued that the ego/spirit binary is also an analogy for a more harmonious relationship between man and the broader spiritual world of nature, as opposed to the Western, Promethean ethic of man asserting his ego over and conquering nature.

In the concluding and, as I shall contend, insufficiently developed section of the chapter, Henry seeks to make the connection between traditional African philosophy and that of African descendants in the diaspora. Due to the erasures that took place under slavery and colonialism, African philosophy was eclipsed in the West as a conscious discipline, though it survives in Afro-Caribbean religion and in contemporary Afro-Caribbean literature. Two proposals follow: first, that we move beyond the prejudicial blinders that prevent us from appreciating the rich heritage, in order to recapture the elements of African philosophy that have survived; and second, that Afro-Caribbean philosophy be restored to its rightful place as a critical component in any new project toward Caribbean liberation.

The remainder of the book is dedicated to fleshing out these assertions, through a series of critical analyses of individuals and intellectual trends primarily, though not exclusively Caribbean. These take the form of negotiated exchanges, of givings and takings, in which Henry both seeks to identify the continuities that substantiate the existence of an Afro-Caribbean philosophy and simultaneously indicates his own preferred direction for it to develop in the near future. If one were, for the necessary sake of brevity, to focus on only the most critical of these exchanges, the following would be high on the list.

C. L. R. JAMES

Henry remains respectful of James's use of Marxian dialectics and political economy and of his brilliant attempts in his novel *Minty Alley* and through texts like *Beyond a Boundary, Mariners, Renegades and Castaways,* and elsewhere to organically link the historicist and poeticist traditions. Where James's approach is significantly flawed, however, is in its failure to see, and therefore explore an intellectual tradition before and beyond that of Europe. This restrictive blinder contributed to an insufficient exploration of the nature of the human ego as a cultural construct *sui generis* and not as an un-theorized given, or alternatively, a product of purely historical forces. Thus, for instance, even brilliant historical readings like *The Black Jacobins* failed to sufficiently grasp the extent to which leadership was molded and popular support was framed by African psycho-cultural imperatives and not simply by the class struggle within the France/St. Domingue sugar economy.

The Achilles' heel in James's work, Henry contends, is in his failure to transcend a certain modern/premodern dichotomy encoded in the intellectual practice of the West. And so, James, the quintessential Caribbean revolutionary thinker, is hobbled because he is confined to operating within the parameters and codes of the very system that he is struggling to overcome. It is not that James is Eurocentric, but in his struggle to overcome European domination he is restricted, has restricted himself, to the thought and weapons of the Europeans.

FRANTZ FANON

Henry's treatment of Fanon develops with themes similar to those employed with James, but he also recognizes and salutes Fanon's unique contribution. While engaging in perhaps the most original critique of anti-black racism, Fanon, like James, falls short in not recognizing the subterranean reality of and arguments within African philosophy. Where Fanon decisively goes beyond James, and almost everyone else in the historicist tradition, is in his psychoanalytic examination of the black self.

In his path-breaking study *Black Skin, White Masks*, Fanon explores the "zone of non-being" and the phenomenon of "ego-collapse" that, as a result of racism, have deeply scarred the personalities of black people. Thus, Fanon ventures into the territory of ontology, though only for a moment, as he then goes on to conclude that in the last instance, it is culture and history that determine the human self. Fanon, like James, fails to move beyond the confines of the European discourse in his search for a mode of analysis and the requisite weapons to dispense with European colonialism. In summarizing this chapter, Henry, in a statement relevant to his entire project, points to the general approach to intellectual engagement beyond both James and Fanon, that he sees as most appropriate: "Caribbean philosophy must creolize itself by breaking its misidentifications with European and African philosophies and allowing them to mix within the framework of more organic relations with local realities."[7] This is the place that neither James nor Fanon, despite their sterling contributions, was ultimately able to travel.

WILSON HARRIS

In the Guyanese novelist Wilson Harris, Henry recognizes and lauds one of the Caribbean's leading poeticists. Unlike critical assertions made respectively by C. L. R. James and Gregory Shaw,[8] Harris's work, in his complex novels and numerous essays, is neither Heideggerian nor Hegelian. Rather, it operates as a uniquely Caribbean discourse. First, in a feature common to Afro-Caribbean philosophy, it is a discourse of delegitimization against colonial rule and white

supremacy. Second, unlike the approach taken in the mainstream of the historicists, it consciously foregrounds and seeks to recover the pre- and postcolonial selves. Throughout his novels and critical discourses, the continual
invocation and questioning of the nature of the self, of consciousness, and of
spirituality brings Harris closer to the heart of the African tradition.

Henry borrows two critical concepts from Harris: he agrees with Harris's
repeated insistence that there be a greater convergence between "history" and
"the arts," with the latter often being a far more powerful source of understanding; and he agrees with Harris's continuing search for the inner self and his recognition that not everything can be understood through the methodological
techniques of the historian.

SYLVIA WYNTER

If, however, Henry borrows extensively from Wilson Harris, he owes an even
more profound debt to Sylvia Wynter, the Jamaican *femme de lettres*. Wynter,
like James, began her work in the poeticist tradition with her novel *The Hills of
Hebron*. Unlike James, however, who always maintained his loyalty to Marxism
with its insistence on the primacy in the last instance of material conditions,
Wynter develops her own bold interpretation of history.

Borrowing Foucault's notion of the episteme, she elaborates a theory of history driven not primarily by economic forces but by its inverse, culture and
consciousness. Epistemes, for Wynter, are the rough equivalents of the Marxian mode of production. They constitute knowledge systems that drive out
competition and dominate entire eras. They have elaborate rules, including
Manichean boundary markers that determine what ideas are good and bad and
what lies within or is excluded from the episteme. More specifically, they establish "liminal"[9] categories of radical otherness, which are, in effect, points of
"transgressive chaos"[10]—a no-man's-land of forbidden ideas. This, however, is
the fatal flaw in the episteme; for when, against all odds, the forbidden liminal
categories prove themselves to be true, the entire episteme collapses.

Henry suggests that Wynter's framework, when applied to the postcolonial
history of the Caribbean, possesses significant value. When Caribbean individuals and insurgent groups have sought to change neocolonial relationships
of power, they have largely failed. Wynter suggests that this is at least in part
due to their failure to break with the dominant episteme. Rather, what these
insurgent groups have done, operating within the confines of the old episteme,
is simply to refract the system of liminal categories onto new groups and individuals. The need, then, is for a radical break with the episteme, to "decenter
founding categories, recognize liminal opposites and control their social impact."[11]

Wynter, then, is suggesting that there should be a struggle to rise above systems of thought that automatically generate otherness and thus inevitably reproduce themselves in new clothing. In this, Henry asserts, she departs from the pessimism and nihilism present in much of the postmodernist/postcolonial tradition, in that she retains a central place for popular revolt and reconstruction beyond the master narrative.

But beyond this, Henry parts company with Wynter. He is unwilling in the end to abandon Marx's mode-of-production analysis for her tentatively constructed and imprecise ideational system. If the danger of the historicists has been an overrepresentation of institutional structures, then Wynter's lies in her relative underrepresentation. Yet, he concludes, in the detritus of failed attempts at institutional revolution, who can deny Wynter's demand that we take seriously the largely ignored field of consciousness?

SUMMARY

If one were to use this selective list of protagonists in order to summarize Henry's main arguments, they would go something like this:

First, there is a hidden dimension of the ego and its peculiar construction in Africa that is as critical to an understanding of the Caribbean past as it is necessary in the praxis of the Caribbean present.

Second, this subterranean philosophy has within it the feature of a binary struggle between the ego and the spirit that is diametrically opposed to the egocentric, Cartesian consciousness of the West.

Third, this has radical implications for who we Caribbean people are, what we do, and how we do it.

Fourth, this hidden dimension can only be appreciated by abandoning the restrictive, modern/premodern dichotomy inherited from the West, along with its inevitable racist baggage.

And fifth, this does not mean an abandonment of Marxist notions of political economy, but a thorough reworking of them, sensitive to the reality of the ego as social construct sui generis and not an effect of history.

Any new process of social emancipation, then, following arguments developed by Wynter, is probably doomed to failure if the focus is primarily institutional/material without a sufficient appreciation of matters related to the ego, consciousness, and the episteme.

DISCUSSION

I like Paget Henry's book not only, or primarily, because it is novel and lays the basis for an entirely new direction in Caribbean intellectual discourse but

because, for me, operating in the fields of political science and thought, it begins to address many unanswered questions in recent Caribbean politics and
praxis. There have been too many traumatic experiences of collapse, disappointment, betrayed promises, and defeat in the recent history of national and
social liberation in the Caribbean and beyond.

The well-known institutional explanations for these undoubtedly have
value, but leave many questions unanswered. My own practical and theoretical engagements with the Grenada revolution are as good a starting point as
any. Much of the analysis of its tragic collapse has operated at the geopolitical
level, with emphasis on the role of the United States, the Soviets, the Cubans,
and even the small (now defunct) Workers Party of Jamaica. Other approaches
have been ideological, focusing on the character of purportedly ultra-leftist
factions in the ruling New Jewel Movement, or, less popularly, on Prime Minister Maurice Bishop's (falsely) purported conversion to conservatism.[12]

To my knowledge, no analysis, including my own earlier work,[13] has sought
to probe beneath the surface and take seriously questions of the ego and Grenadian ego-genesis into consideration. None has sought to look at the nature
of consciousness and its formation beyond narrow ideological categories to
probe how deeply entrenched structures of "othering" might have contributed
to a damaging tendency toward demonization of opposition both during the
revolutionary years and at the time of the crisis in 1983. No one has, therefore,
drawn the conclusion that can be derived from Henry's approach (and is, of
course, explicit in Wynter's work) that in understanding the collapse of the
Grenadian revolution, the self and ego-genesis cannot be seen as unproblem-
atic, as simply determined by social being, but rather must be seen as matters
requiring serious intellectual focus and lie at the heart of any sensible explanation of the tragedy. *Caliban's Reason* has, therefore, put on the table in philosophical terms the matter of the Caribbean self, and for this alone it is historic.

There is, however, another reason why I find this book immensely attractive, in that Henry has sought, in the spirit of Wilson Harris's exhortation, to
bring the historicist and poeticist traditions closer together. I am in agreement
with Harris that, while neither of these streams is dispensable, if one wishes to
truly grasp the complexity of the Caribbean, then Caribbean literature and the
other arts, both plastic and performed, are often deeper and richer sources of
insight than the social sciences. Henry proposes that philosophy be the discipline that bridges the gap between the two, and his argument is compelling.

There are, however, important gaps in the study that weaken its otherwise
laudable conclusions. I suggest these in my concluding section as a series of
discussion points that may provide the basis for further debate and clarification.

1. An African Philosophy?

Henry scans, perhaps too rapidly, the field of African philosophy and samples certain features, which he chooses to emphasize. Akan notions of ego formation are, as noted, high on his list. He does not seem, however, to have made a watertight case for common features, sufficiently widespread and accepted as such, to speak of an African or even a West African philosophy. The identification and elaboration of an African philosophy is a major philosophical-anthropological exercise beyond the purposes of his book, yet Henry leaves us with very few sources and less discussion on what has been written, and moreso, what needs to be done to further this enterprise. Its assumed existence is at the very heart of his argument, which is weakened if the existence and coherence of an African philosophy is insufficiently developed. Yet precisely because Henry is, in his formal incarnation, a sociologist, one searches for a more rigorous confirmation of the character and definitive features of an African philosophy.

2. An Afro-Caribbean Philosophy?

It is never absolutely clear whether Henry is making a case for a retained Afro-Caribbean philosophical tradition with deep (if obviously modified) linkages to African traditions or whether, alternatively, he is recommending African philosophy as an important alternative approach for Caribbean thinkers. In his first chapter on the African philosophical heritage, he spends, for instance, some twenty-two pages outlining what African philosophy is and only three on the continuities in "Modern Africana Thought." There is insufficient elaboration for the reader to gain a purchase on what the retained traditions really are, how they have been modified and reproduced, and what their chances of survival are. In contrast to this, in Mervyn Alleyne's study on the African retentions in Jamaica,[14] there are rich insights on how notions such as community and time have survived in modified form from Africa and how postcolonial Jamaican society has further altered them. There is in Alleyne's book a sense of the concrete—of movement and of the way specific cultural constructs have evolved—that at best is only implied in Henry's work.

3. Where Are "the People"?

Reference to Alleyne's text also carries us to a third important gap, which is the relative paucity of "grass roots" philosophy in *Caliban's Reason*—a study that begins by attempting to legitimate African philosophy, despite its scarcity of formal texts, then proceeds to an almost exclusive reading of established Caribbean intellectuals and their texts. Henry is, of course, fully aware of and from time to time alludes to the rich tradition of popular religio-philosophical movements, but there is little serious critical discussion. Indeed, of the one movement which gains some significant space—the Rastafarians—his analysis and conclusions are found wanting. To take up Henry on this question, close to my own Jamaican tradition, I begin with his conclusions:

> First, like Blyden, Rastafarian historicism leaves the social and developmental problems of Jamaican society largely unaddressed. Second, it ignores the fact that the vast majority of Jamaicans do not want to repatriate. Third, the social and developmental problems that it wants to abandon in Jamaica and the larger Caribbean are just as, if not more, severe on the African continent today. Fourth and finally, its providential historicism conflates divine and human agency in a way that we saw as problematic in the case of Blyden. Thus, in spite of being a powerful subjective and legitimating force for black identities, we need to look beyond Rastafarianism as we examine the current crisis of Caribbean historicism.[15]

It is not that I disagree with his overall conclusion so much as with some of his earlier points. To address the first, it is unfair to say that Rastafarianism does not address critical Jamaican social and developmental problems. Rasta notions of "livity," incorporating community self-reliance, cooperation, natural organic living, and peaceful coexistence, provide critical alternative ethical and even economic approaches, in opposition to the unmitigated market, selfish individualism, and rampant materialism[16] of contemporary globalization. Henry's second and third points, on conditions on the African continent and repatriation, are surprisingly old and worn critiques of Rastafarianism that fail to appreciate the sophistication and diversity of contemporary Rastafarian arguments. Many Rastas fully appreciate the complexity of African politics and the difficulties African economies face and have developed far more sophisticated pan-African notions of diasporic struggle.[17] To advance these criticisms in the way he does suggests a lack of attention to nuance, not to be found in the well-crafted assessments of James, Wynter, and other, more formal intellectuals. Finally, his fourth point, the critique of the Rastafarian conflation of the "divine and human agency," is also too one-sided. While it is true that for Rastafari, the man Haile Selassie is God, it is equally true that god abides in all men.[18] With this simple conclusion, Fanon's negated African self not only is restored but is even given enhanced powers of creativity and self assurance, because in the conscious action of man is also to be found the hand of the divine. Henry's very central task of ego retrieval is, therefore, deeply embedded in the Rastafarian "I."

There is in this somewhat limited engagement a worrying indicator of a reassertion of the legitimate/illegitimate binary between the modern/premodern, between formal scholarship and grassroots reasoning, with all the implications of liminal categories, despite Henry's desire and stated intention to move beyond such an approach.

4. What Difference Do Healed Egos Make to Caribbean Politics?

Finally, I suggest that beyond the obvious societal benefit to be derived from more wholesome egos, Henry needs to suggest, if only tentatively, what difference the recovery of the self will make to Caribbean society and politics. It is true that *Caliban's Reason* is primarily an incursion into philosophy, but it is Henry himself who, quite appropriately in the tradition of radical Caribbean praxis, places the question of the political future on the agenda. When his tentative directions are examined (the continuation of the nation-state strategy with some version of federalism, more efficient management of the state, an improvement in its developmental capabilities, more local economic control),[19] the conclusions appear somewhat prosaic and time-worn. We hear the program of the Grenada revolution or even the PNP of the seventies, but little more.

Two criticisms seem relevant here. The first is the limited vision he proposes for the future. Surely there is room, if only in the concluding sentences, to engage in the discussion of the possible horizons of an invigorated democracy, new forms of community involvement and self-reliance, and new models and approaches to self-government and sovereignty that might be enhanced by a new, liberated Caribbean persona? The second is that there is no indicator as to a practical program to get to this new phase, beyond the scholarly task of unveiling and excavating the new approach. If Paget Henry's proposals are meant to have an effect on Caribbean politics, are intended as a move in praxis, then what he should be calling for, but does not actually do, is a cultural revolution, through scholarly discourse in universities, but also through schools, popular culture, and within the family, that would so transform the consciousness of the Caribbean people that the proverbial insurrectionary act would be a mere formality. But enigmatically, the question that would immediately have to be posed would be, can such a cultural revolution take place without a prior seizure of state power?

I make these critical comments to conclude where I began. This book is both ambitious and important. It certainly follows in the prophetic exhortation of Henry's mentor, C. L. R. James, that "To establish his own identity Caliban, after three centuries, must himself pioneer into regions that Caesar never knew."[20] And, importantly, it is an introduction. Henry has broken the bush and established the boundaries. Perhaps, he has even given the pitch its first roll with the heavy roller. Now it is time for the cricket match to begin.

3. Arguments within What's Left of the Left: James, Watson, and the Question of Method (2001)

> Not all the "Marxisms" have been of this wholly reactionary order. There
> have also been various Maoisms, Trotskyisms, and innumerable Marxist aca-
> demicisms. Most of these share, however, the same religious cast of thought,
> in which a Marxism is proposed as an ultimate system of truth; that is, a
> theology. All seek to put Marx back into the prison of Marxism.
> —E. P. Thompson

Genuine arguments in Caribbean social science scholarship are quite rare.[1]
Arguments within the left are even less frequent, as today the question might
realistically be asked, "What's left of the left?"[2] This is an eight-year-old argument, consisting of three parts. There is an initial statement, written by me in
1994. This was followed by a response, first delivered by my fellow Caribbean
social scientist Hilbourne Watson in 1997. And there is now this article, my
first defense, delivered at the auspicious C. L. R. James One Hundredth Anniversary Symposium in Trinidad in 2001 and elaborated in greater detail here.

Background

In September 1994 I edited a special issue of the UWI journal *Social and Economic Studies*, entitled "New Currents in Caribbean Thought."[3] The stated aim,
as developed in the preface, was to foster the development of critical thinking
from within the Caribbean, which, I suggested, had been on the retreat for
more than a decade. My own article in the volume was entitled "Re-Reading
the Black Jacobins: James, the Dialectic and the Revolutionary Conjuncture."[4]
The purpose of the article was, I thought, straightforward. As a young man, I
had been an active member of the Jamaican left as a cadre of the Workers Party
of Jamaica (WPJ) in the seventies and eighties. As an "internationalist worker"
in the two final years of the Grenada revolution, I had a firsthand appreciation
of its workings, as well as a keen sense of its tragic and bloody collapse. As a
postdoctoral fellow at Cambridge in the crucial year 1989–90, I had a close-up
view of the collapse of "really existing socialism" in Eastern Europe.

It was evident to me that the Marxism that had provided these movements
with a worldview, that had inscribed on their foreheads a certain explanation

of the course of modern history and that came with certain recommendations, indeed, prescriptions, as to how politics should be approached, was severely flawed. It was in this early post–Cold War period, shortly after the important James conference at Wellesley in 1991,[5] that I reread C. L. R. James's *The Black Jacobins: Toussaint L'Ouverture and the San Domingo Revolution*,[6] a favorite text of my undergraduate days, but gathering dust on my shelf for some two decades thereafter. It was a revelation. In James's profoundly creative endeavor I saw a concerted attempt to apply Marxist theory in a manner that would not only "explain" what happened in the course of the Haitian revolution, but also simultaneously, breathe life into its actors and explain their strengths and frailties, as not simply mechanistic effects of an economic system.

The purpose then, as it remains broadly my approach now, was not to abandon the powerful analytical tools elaborated by Marx, but to seek to use them better. The aim was to find a mode of analysis conscious of the formation and location of human beings within a given social moment, yet equally sensitive to the profound contributions these agents make in acting on and transforming the character and direction of that moment.[7] Put somewhat more succinctly, my underlying argument was that the theoretical failure of the Caribbean left of the seventies was to assume that history was on its way, already "overdetermined" by the course of accumulated events, by the "world balance of forces" and the strength of "really existing socialism." At the level of local politics, this implied that the need to convince people, in the broadest sense of that term, was subordinate to the imperative to take power. If the right insurrectionary situation developed, then the "proletarian party" should take power "in the interests of" the people, who, even though they might be politically "backward," would be guided and developed by the advanced party, as local representatives of the advanced class, in turn supported by the world socialist system. This led, at the level of the leadership as well as within many of these embryonic parties, to the most profound arrogance and sense of self-righteousness and ultimately contributed, I am certain, to the demise of the organized left, exemplified in the bitter collapse in 1983 of the Grenadian revolution.

The purpose of my rereading, then, was to open the door on an examination of human agency as neither simply a subset of economic forces nor necessarily a minor element in a complex and vaguely understood "overdetermination," but as a consideration, *sui generis*, in modern history, particularly at those rare moments of revolutionary boil.

Watson's Broadside

Hilbourne Watson took umbrage at my article and in "Themes in Liberalism, Modernity, Marxism, Postmodernism and Beyond: An Interpretation and Critique of Brian Meeks' Re-Reading the Black Jacobins" he took me to task.[8] He stridently asserted that I was not only rereading James's classic but announcing my break with Marxism[9] and that my ideas about historical determination were grounded in notions of the autonomous individual and autonomous self.[10] Having thus wedded me to a certain liberal and neo-liberal notion of the autonomous individual, he proceeded to make a breathtaking link with my ideas and the entire damaging course of American civilization: "There is a clear connection between ecological disaster, cultural strangulation, genocidal practices and the truculently free American civil society of Meeks's autonomous individuals."[11] And, he continued: "This allows Meeks's autonomous individuals to engage in debauchery, greed, destruction and other excesses of passion. Ecological destruction could be defined as the price of progress; capital accumulation as the progress of freedom's primary vocation."[12] Watson continued to assert: "Meeks finds relief in returning to ideological views put forward by Hayek and Nozick"[13] and further, though typically with no textual evidence to support his claim, that I have some ". . . new perspective on Fukuyama."[14] He suggested that I did not pay any attention to the dialectic between a politics of representation and a participatory politics, concluding, without any evidence, that I limit my notion of political democracy to narrow representational forms.[15] Most amazingly, he imputed in my analysis of Toussaint's overarching role in the Haitian revolution the very opposite of my statements. Thus, Watson, in an argument to which we shall return, claims that I speculate that had Toussaint been conciliatory to Leclerc—Napoleon's brother-in-law—history might have been quite different.

Indeed, this final example reflects Watson's failure both to read my article thoroughly and to understand the sequence of the Haitian revolution, as Toussaint was at first conciliatory to the French general, leading ultimately to his own arrest, exile, and death. My own query was to pose the counterfactual "What if Toussaint had not come to terms with Leclerc, but inspired by the early victories against the French had sought to resist?"[16] But we shall have more on this particularly egregious matter anon.

Not only does Watson play fast and furiously with the facts of my argument, purposefully avoiding painful encounters with the actual text, but he frequently makes gargantuan leaps of faith from the particulars of the intervention to the generalities of the entire history of the West; leaps that leave him with little intellectual tether to secure safe purchase, either to his original point of departure, or computed place of arrival.

It is not that Watson's entire effort is wasted. He does advance important, if well-rehearsed, assertions on the nature of Marxian dialectics and its flexibility as a methodological tool; of the rootedness of humanity in particular social relations; and of the fluidity and historicity of apparently solid social phenomena. There is much in what he has to say on these matters that I can, without hesitation, agree with, though embedded in his scholastic and didactic prose are central elements of a style of knowing and certainty that I find, to say the least, problematic.

In summary, his placement of my modest efforts in his sights; his completely unsympathetic and relentless trashing of the attempt to come to terms with a real historical and philosophical problem; his refusal to even acknowledge the legitimacy of the problematic—all with virtually no direct reference to the text—point to a philosophy of closure, of arrogance, and of exclusion that has deep and disturbing resonances in recent Caribbean and world history.

Re-Reading, Revisited

To appreciate the thrust of my original argument, it needs to be located within the context of "New Currents in Caribbean Thought" (*Social and Economic Studies* 43, no. 3). As my preface asserts, that volume was an attempt to accelerate theoretical discussion on matters of Caribbean politics and society. I suggested that theoretical debate on the Caribbean condition, certainly from the social scientists, contracted significantly in the eighties. "New Currents" was then identified as an attempt to "begin the process of redressing the imbalance against theory."[17] While for the Caribbean that decade was a fallow time, I suggested that in other parts of the world a series of events, most notably the collapse of Eastern European socialism,[18] had stimulated a broad deliberation around the usefulness of Marxism as an analytical tool, including varieties of feminism, cultural studies, postmodernism, postcolonialism, and beyond.

I mentioned these not as affirmation of any single perspective as necessarily providing superior insights, but as a recognition of what I saw as a potentially healthy loosening up of ossified theoretical positions after the collapse of "really existing socialism." I felt, and continue to feel, that a similar openness of debate and healthy contestation of contending views was needed in this region in order to kick-start and give momentum to a new round of critical thinking. I spend a moment on this because, in his introduction, Watson mentions my transition into "what seems like an unspecified postmodernism."[19] I can only conclude that this assertion derives from my reference to the emergence of a variety of "posts" in this period, though how this is then interpreted as my own perspective is another difficult-to-fathom leap of the imagination.

While the intention of the preface is to steer clear from a gratuitous location of my own position in these debates, it is, however, quite evidently located between the lines. I choose to mention, for instance, that missing from the volume is a needed critique of "a certain understanding of freedom and equality implicit in Hayekian-inspired structural adjustment policies (that) remains to be criticized from a purely philosophical perspective."[20] This comment is important, in the light of Watson's previous assertion that my views find convergence with those of Nozick and Hayek. That a mention of their significance as premier theoreticians of neo-liberalism and therefore requiring urgent and credible critique[21] can be interpreted as somehow succumbing to their ideological perspective, is, once again, hard to fathom. Yet a pattern is beginning to emerge.

Into the Text . . .

"Re-reading the Black Jacobins," as previously suggested, has one primary objective. It tries to bring into central focus a key methodological question that none other than James himself had placed on the agenda: the relationship between agency and structure in the making of history. James is clear that there is a problem that needs to be thought through. In his lucid assessment of Toussaint's personal role in the revolution, he argues that, on the one hand, he was a product of the revolution—its social forces had made him into the preeminent leader. Beyond this useful but limited explanation, however, there is the matter of his personality: "At a certain stage, the middle of 1794, the potentialities in the chaos began to be shaped and soldered by his powerful personality, and thenceforth it is impossible to say where the social forces end and the impress of personality begins. It is sufficient that, but for him, this history would be something entirely different."[22]

My approach begins by broadly concurring with James's analysis. He successfully paints a vivid picture of the international and national co-relationship of forces and of the economics and technology of the eighteenth century, and graphically suggests the limitations this placed on the revolting slaves and, implicitly, on Toussaint himself. My query begins at the line of thought generated by James's last sentence quoted above. If, but for Toussaint, the history might have been quite different, then, in order to understand the Haitian revolution in its totality, we must dig below the surface of the mode of production, of the rhythms of eighteenth century capitalism, of the technologies of wind and sail and of the individual's narrowly determined social location, in order to find out what really made Toussaint tick.

James himself actually starts to explore this line of enquiry. In what has been the grist for a highly charged debate,[23] he contrasts Toussaint's balance and level-headedness, indeed, his "civilization," with Dessalines's lack of diplomacy but relentless clarity of purpose. Toussaint's character served him well in the initial battles, in which alliances shifted and revolutionary France eventually emerged as an ally. But when it was time to strike the decisive blows against the local whites and the new France of Napoleon's army, Toussaint faltered and was lost. In his stead emerged Dessalines, without the veneer of Western "civilization" but with the full knowledge that freedom could only be won and held from the barrel of a gun. What shaped Toussaint and Dessalines to be the leaders they were? One of the central facts James focuses on is that Dessalines had been "warped" by the whip, whereas Toussaint, faithful house servant prior to the revolt, had never experienced this degradation.[24] Thus, James introduces the matter of the formation of the ego, of personality as not epiphenomenon but central problematic and legitimate object of inquiry.

My departure, to the extent that it can be considered as such, is to pose the next logical question: While it is true that men are shaped by social forces, if their intervention at critical moments in history can so transform the outcome as to create possibilities where none previously appeared to exist, what then is the implication for theory? The Haitian revolution, in a small, impoverished, destroyed, and embattled former French colony, could not, self-evidently, initiate a worldwide socialist revolution. This I think addresses the core Marxist assumption of what is possible and not within a given epoch. Yet, the Haitian revolution did not have to happen and, in happening, it transformed the world in smaller,[25] though very important ways. Haitian independence, for instance, critically doomed France to be a second-rate imperial power by cutting away her economic feet. Equally, it can be suggested, the decade of battles against the St. Domingue slaves, and particularly the independence war, so debilitated Napoleon's military prowess that his subsequent defeat at Waterloo was preordained. What if the black army had been defeated? What would the world have looked like with Napoleon consolidating his dominance there and on the continent? How much of world history at critical moments might then be placed at the door of the popular forces of St. Domingue and the chance intervention of their leaders, the Toussaints and the Dessalines, imbued with special personal qualities or lack thereof?

The purpose of this line of enquiry was never to abandon the undoubted strengths of Marx's historical method, but to consider its limitations, through a heightened awareness as to the peculiarity and serendipity of the agent, as captured in my concluding sentence in the article: "It is not that productive forces do not play their role in shaping events, but that people adamantly refuse to play the minor parts assigned to them."[26] This is an explicit appeal for theoreticians as well as future leaders of popular movements not to crush the popular perspective, nor the dissenting will, under the jackboot of justifications, such as "the wave of the future," "the direction of history," or "the will of the proletariat." It is a call for a greater appreciation as to how people are drawn into social movements and how they, as individuals and in the mass, transform in unprecedented ways these movements and broader social reality.

It is a concern of the utmost importance in the world we live in, as we contemplate the detritus of the past and begin to construct the new movements that will carry forward a popular struggle in the twenty-first century, a concern by no means limited to the radical movements of the recent past. For it is in the contemporary world, where there is one hyper power, that the danger of a new historical determinism is most rampant. For, how different is the world we live in from Orwell's *1984*, when cable television can offer one hundred different channels, but not one will carry a decent, truthful discussion on the history of the Palestinian conflict? How far are we from a totalitarian pole, when the president of the United States can threaten, with all of his tremendous military and economic might, that "if you are not with us, you are against us"?[27] The matter of determinism, raised here in relation to an intramural Marxist debate, cannot, in the world we live in, be limited to that terrain.

Once More, Watson

Watson carries us through three stages in his lengthy and somewhat arduous argument. In the first, he establishes by edict that I am fetishizing the individual. This is difficult to counterattack, as he fails to give instances. If by virtue of highlighting the pivotal role of Toussaint in the Haitian revolution I have made a declaration in favor of the liberal autonomous individual, then the sin is of course, shared with James. In the second stage he proceeds to give a somewhat didactic lesson on Marxian dialectics, sketching the outlines of Marx's general theory on the relationship between social being and embedded property relations, on the social and conjunctural nature of civil society and the emergence of the "individual" as a direct product of capitalism and liberalism. I have no objection to any of this as a textbook lesson on dialectics; however, my response at the end of it all is, so what? How does a restatement of classic Marxian theory carry us further than James's brilliant question? How does restating the theory of man's social locatedness,[28] that freedom is socially located,[29] that Toussaint himself was socially located and was interested in abolishing slavery only for the slavery of wage labor,[30] carry us any further along the way of understanding what was going on inside Toussaint's head and why? My response to this part of the critique then, is to offer thanks for the albeit gratuitous philosophical lesson, but it has not negated or trumped James's concern, nor my attempt to think through the implications of that concern.

Four Little Insights

In the course of this section of his paper, however, Watson raises a number of side issues that provide important insights into the character of what I consider his negatively scholastic bent. I mention four of the most significant. In reference to the history of Caribbean praxis in the seventies, Watson asserts: "The disappearance of the WPJ, the destruction of the former People's Revolutionary Government (PRG) in Grenada and the collapse of the 1970's social democratic strategies of the People's National party (PNP) in Jamaica simply will not serve to defend Meeks's claims against Marxism."[31] Aside from the now standard assertion that my article is anti-Marxist, this claim is particularly bothersome because I never mention the Grenada revolution, the WPJ, nor the PNP throughout the entire article. Perhaps it is that Watson suspects what I might say and is preempting my response. If so, then he may or may not be satisfied with this brief rejoinder. The Grenada revolution collapsed for many reasons, including the overwhelming pressure from the United States, but the central feature that contributed to the immediate collapse was a dogmatic Leninism that alienated the party from the people and contributed to the advancing of totally unrealistic organizational policies. These led to sharp divisions in the top leadership, which, in a militaristic climate, eventually led to a militaristic solution.[32] Such an analysis has little to do with Marx's thought, as it has to do with a certain Caribbean interpretation of Marxism Leninism. The Workers Party of Jamaica collapsed in part because of the overwhelming dominance of the two-party system in Jamaica as well as its own mechanistic assessment of the imminence of revolution, which prepared the party more for short-term insurrectional forms of struggle than for the long, positional haul.[33] Such a perspective, in turn, derives not so much from Marx but from the same Caribbean Marxism Leninism, which mechanically adopted forms of political organization wholesale from the Russian experience between 1905 and 1917. The crisis of the Caribbean left, therefore, certainly in these two instances, derived more from an interpretation of Leninism than it did specifically from Marx. Though I still stress that a certain ideologically monopolizing way of looking at the world is present and needs to be regularly exorcised in both Lenin and Marx.

My comments on the PNP, I reserve for the second instance. In a continuation of the above point, Watson asserts, "The PNP was consistently anti-Marxist and anticommunist."[34] This comment is particularly difficult to swallow and at the same time highly revealing of Watson's approach. If the PNP was consistently anti-Marxist and anticommunist, then what were the problems that plagued the U.S. State Department in relation to the party from at least 1974 until the mid-eighties? What accounted for Manley's deep and sincere friendship with Fidel Castro, which clearly went beyond personality to address matters of policy? What accounts for the fact that members of Manley's party studied Marxist classics in party study groups in the late seventies? What can account for the party's 1979 program "Principles and Objectives," which recognizes "class struggle as the necessary form of capitalist society"[35] and which concludes that "The struggle between social classes can only be resolved through the building of socialism"?[36] What explains Manley's own profound concerns with imperial dominance as captured in his testament on the seventies, *Struggle in the Periphery*?[37] Manley was never a committed Marxist; nor can it be said that his party ever dedicated itself to any variety of Marxism; yet, any approach that can simply dismiss the entire dialectical movement of the PNP from 1974 to 1980 under the phrase "consistently anti-Marxist and anticommunist," particularly in the wake of having delivered a long lesson on dialectics, is unbearably scholastic.

In the third stage, Watson responds to James's mention of the fact that Toussaint's father was an African chieftain and that this might have had some effect on his character. James fails to develop this point and in my footnote I take him up on this:

> Little more is made of this seminal fact. How did Toussaint's recent memory of an aristocratic African past influence his entire demeanour and character? Equally important, how did the African origin of the majority of revolutionary slaves—a point which James notes repeatedly—influence the militancy and obduracy of the movement? Were the slaves solely inspired by the revolutionary fervour of the times, or did they also bring with them a history of organization and rebellion from West Africa? More pointedly, was there a specific concentration of tribal groupings in the Haitian population that had arrived equipped with a propensity for the military arts? James, while tilling the soil of revolutionary spontaneity, is silent on the possible deeper rhythms of African continuity.[38]

Watson, as in his response to the PNP, is equally short and dismissive of any African influence:

> I see nothing in the social practices of Toussaint, Dessalines, Moise, Hedouville, or other leaders of the Haitian revolution to suggest that blackness defined their human nature or their way of thinking. Those men were not united in a common African origin for they did not come out of Africa; they came from different places on the continent of Africa, Africa having been a colonial construct. Nor did they share a common position in spite of their

broadly common experience with slavery and European oppression. Capitalist slavery, wage labour and their connection with modernity and imperial
domination influenced the development of their consciousness in Haiti.[39]

In his suspiciously rapid dismissal of the possibility of African continuity,
Watson misses the subtlety of the point raised, for my proposition is not of a
broad pan-African consciousness but the possibility of a solidarity determined
by tribal concentration and tribal hegemony.[40] Such a possibility existed elsewhere, as Alleyne[41] suggests, and a dominant tribe might so place its stamp
on the others present that its culture, however "creolized," comes to play an
inordinate role to its size in the overall population. While, undoubtedly, economic position influenced the development of their consciousness in Haiti, it
is precisely the search for the entire picture, the complexities beyond the narrow economic location that James wants us to explore and appreciate and that
Watson insists we turn away from.

The final instance is Watson's own assertion, in which he reminds us that
the freedom that Toussaint fought for was ". . . a contingent freedom, as those
men had a stake in the former slaves selling labour power on the plantation."[42]

For Watson, there is a place for everything and everything is neatly in its
place. The PNP of Manley was petit bourgeois and consistently anti-Marxist.
African culture had nothing to do with slave resistance, which was forged pristine on the economic foundations of the plantation and, in other words, is to be
pristinely located in the sphere of class struggle. Most disturbingly, Toussaint's
freedom is contingent freedom, the negative freedom, no doubt, of liberalism.
There is no sense here of the complexity of the social moment; of the spilling
over of categories; of the degree to which freedom taken by black slaves must
have brought with it different agendas from, say, that won by white American
merchants and yeomen. A quote from the Haitian Declaration of Independence brings home sharply the urgency of the moment, the extent to which
freedom was bound up in the human body and not externalized as "property
rights"; the extent to which freedom went beyond the polite terms of reference
expressed in its North American parallel:

> It is not enough to have thrown out of your country those barbarians who
> have soaked it in blood for two centuries; it is not sufficient to have curbed the
> factions that still play tricks on the spectre of liberty that France has revealed
> to you all; to guarantee the triumph of freedom in the country that you have
> seen born, you must make one last act of national authority. If the inhuman
> government that has held our spirits in the most humiliating torpor for so
> long is to give up all hope of subjugating us again, we must live free or we
> must die. Independence or death . . . these are the sacred words that unite us.[43]

This sense of the complex, of the indeterminate, of the possibilities created or denied by the intervention of specific social forces with their own strengths and weaknesses, is palpably missing in Watson's essay. What we are left with is the reassertion of vapid categories as the ultimate defense against an invasive apostasy.

Misreading the Speculation

In the final part of the essay, Watson goes completely overboard. Under the subhead "Speculation and the Counterfactual," he lambastes my argument for proposing a number of "what ifs" as alternative speculations on the possible course that the intertwined French and Haitian revolutions might have taken. The purpose of the exercise was simply to underline the tentativeness and uncertainty in history at a moment of severe crisis and to suggest how easily it might have gone a different way with unforeseeable consequences. This is not to deny that there were not necessarily finite options. Thus, as earlier stated, it is quite evident that the material conditions did not exist in the late eighteenth century for a socialist revolution in advanced France, much less economically dependent Haiti. It is important to quote from my intervention at length to appreciate the error in Watson's response:

> What if Toussaint had not come to terms with Leclerc, but inspired by the early victories against the French had sought to resist? Would he not have sooner, rather than later, come to Dessalines's conclusion that independence was necessary? Surely, if that were the case, then Toussaint's policies towards the whites would have been more conciliatory. Haiti would then have entered the new century not so much as an international pariah but as a legitimate part of the family of emergent Latin American states. That would not have prevented neo-colonialism, but what kind of example would a renascent, black Haiti, more of a success than a failure have set for the rest of the West Indies?[44]

Now, let us follow closely Watson's response. First, he misreads completely the thrust of my "what if":

> There is no validity to the counterfactual claim that Toussaint's lack of conciliation towards the French influenced or determined the future place of Haiti in the New World. Such an argument stretches history, facts and faith and it depoliticises history. Is it necessary to invent this myth to excuse such an unproblematic reading of European and American imperialism in their excesses against Haiti? Is it necessary to invent such reasoning to inform an

anti-Marxist reply to the Marxism of C. L. R. James and the failure of Marxism to liberate autonomous agency?[45]

He continues in this vein toward the end of the paper, elaborating on my supposed heresy in which he claims that I assert that the Haitian revolution should "not have beheaded Leclerc's army."[46] This, he concludes, is the ultimate indicator of my revisionism.

The simple fact, as evident in my prior quote, is that I make a case for the very inverse of what he asserts. I query how history might have gone had Toussaint resisted Leclerc from the start, on the beaches as he landed, instead of allowing him to gain a foothold and begin to undermine the black resistance. Watson's final thrust is thus directed at an imaginary, conciliatory invention.

My second "what if," to which with some generosity he may be confusedly referring, assumes that Toussaint had taken the aggressive stance, defeated Leclerc, and led Haiti to independence, instead of being captured and transported from the island to die in captivity. The argument then suggests that Toussaint, given his propensity for diplomacy, might have been conciliatory, in the sense of not massacring the surviving whites. It is James himself who argues that Dessalines's massacre of the surviving whites served to provide the excuse for the diplomatic isolation of Haiti, which crippled the country in its early years and from which, arguably, she has never recovered. James goes so far as to suggest in his play of the same title that the decision to massacre the surviving whites was a cynical, even treasonous move by Dessalines.[47] My argument, simply put, is, what would have been the future of Haiti if Toussaint had been at the helm? It may well have been that, in the face of renewed invasion from abroad and a determined and still powerful fifth column of former slave owners behind, there was little option but repression of the recalcitrant group. But was repression to be equated with elimination? Would Toussaint have had the wherewithal to restrain the whites, while not providing the excuse for the subsequent isolation of Haiti? Would he have been able to outmaneuver the concerted powers of Europe and America post-independence as he had so successfully done in the preceding years? The answer is moot, but it deserves to be asked even as it underlines the tentativeness in the entire process, a point James returns to again and again. Watson misses this nuance completely and wastes his concluding remarks on a falsely constructed opponent.

Conclusion

The picture is now relatively clear. Watson asserts my conversion to some sort of postmodernism when I allude to the existence of postmodern currents without indicating adherence to any one of them. He accuses me of "finding relief" in Hayek and Nozick when I am sharply critical of them both, though I also suspect that critical theory has failed to satisfactorily answer all the difficult questions they pose. He implies the same connection with Fukuyama, though this is even more spurious, as Fukuyama's name is never mentioned, although elsewhere I have expressed opposition to his end-of-history mantra. He asserts that in my critical "what ifs" I have invented a genuflecting Toussaint, when, on the contrary, I propose a more aggressive Toussaint, leading Haiti to victory and then outmaneuvering the West on the diplomatic field.

He undertakes this extensive exercise with no substantial quote from my article and absolutely no reference to my previous work in order to establish some overall trajectory or dynamic. The only logical conclusion is that Watson is not genuinely interested in what I have to say. He sees the word "individual" and downloads the category "liberal." He invents an entire intellectual profile of revisionism, compromise, and defeatism to fit the contours of this construct and then tears down his own scaffolding. In its place he constructs the pure model of Marx's theory in its pristine form. But the model is pure because it is unsullied, untouched by human hands. It has not been forced to come to terms with the harsh reality of practical politics, with, as in my instance, the lived Caribbean praxis of the seventies and eighties. For Watson such practical concerns are a bother: "Meeks assigns far too much credit to Maurice Bishop and the Grenada Revolution in relation to revolutionary Marxism."[48] For me, the Grenada revolution, with four and a half years of state power with a government whose intention was revolutionary social transformation, is a far richer model of practical experience than the brief interregnum of the Paris Commune, to which Marx returned repeatedly for intellectual nourishment as the one example, one possible outline, of what the future might look like.

In the end, Watson's is an academic and scholastic Marxism, jealously guarding the sacred truths from impostors, declaring certain lines of inquiry verboten, and sending out fatwahs against individuals who initiate uncomfortable lines of argument. It is a structured Marxism for a time when structures seem impenetrable and resistance futile. It is a Marxism in a time of stasis, not of movement.

It is not that Marxism is dead. Indeed, in the work of Paget Henry, Cecilia Green, Tony Bogues, Obika Gray, Percy Hintzen, Holger Henke, Tim Hector, Rhoda Reddock, Anton Allahar, David Scott, Pat Mohammed, Linden Lewis, and many others, there is a concerted attempt to use Marx creatively. There is a growing body of work that is searching, in the space of interaction between the economic formation and the grammars and identities through which social struggle is articulated,[49] for a better way to understand and act on Caribbean life. For despite its inevitable lacunae, how can one contemplate abandoning the single theory that has consistently sought to explain and, in so doing, transform the veil of tears that is modernity? It is not that Marxism is dead, but that Watson's article veers into a dead-end Marxism.

I leave the last word to E. P. Thompson, who in a somewhat intemperate frame of mind in *The Poverty of Theory*, engaged with Louis Althusser, an earlier keeper of the faith:

> If this is all that Althusserianism is, as ideology—if it is no more than one
> of the successive fashions by which the revolting Western Intelligentsia can
> do their thing without practical pain—then we have been wasting our time.
> But it is more serious than that. It is actively reinforcing and reproducing the
> effective passivity before "structure" which holds us all prisoners. It is enforc-
> ing the rupture between theory and practice. It is diverting good minds from
> active theoretical engagement. And, at a level of more vulgar theoretical
> discourse, it affords theoretical legitimations for all the stupidest and most
> dangerous half-truths, which, one had supposed, had at last gone away. That
> "morality equals the interests of the working class," that "philosophy equals
> class struggle," that "democratic rights and practices equals liberal ideology,"
> and so on. Such a theory, if ever afforded any power, so far from "liberating"
> the working class, would, in its insufferable arrogance and pretensions to
> "science," deliver them into the hands of a bureaucratic clerisy: the next rul-
> ing class, waiting on the line.[50]

Thompson continues to identify two traditions deriving from Marx: between Marxism as closure and tradition and, alternatively, Marxism as open investigation and critique. Thompson sided with the latter. Watson must decide whether he wishes to lay his bed in the camp of closure.

4. Michael Manley: Crossing the Contours of Charisma (2001)

"Let me catch a glimpse of m'boy," shouts Heather, a latter-day Juliet dreaming from her balcony, between snorts of her own laughter. "Michael—Young Boy, Kennedy gone! It's only you left now. The last hero!"
—Rachel Manley, *Slipstream*

Monday, March 17, 1997. It is the day after the funeral of Michael Manley. This is how the *Daily Gleaner* described the previous day's events in the western city of Montego Bay:

> They rented cars, chartered buses and car-pooled. Montego Bay was virtually empty yesterday as thousands of admirers made their way to Kingston to pay their last respects to the man tailor Ray Jarrett called "a great man who has left the world poorer at his departure, yet richer by his journey through." . . . Carol Spencer in Falmouth reported that the town was "very quiet," as most people were glued to their television sets while others were "gone to town" (Kingston). "Falmouth is silent today and you can understand why," she said. "I don't think there is another town in all of Jamaica where Michael Manley is loved as he is in Falmouth. The entire town seem to have gone there (the funeral). I know that most of them may have had to stay along the route and did not get to see much. But you think them care?"[1]

October 1917, Petrograd. The American journalist John Reed is describing the first appearance of the leader of the Russian Revolution, Lenin, before his triumphant supporters:

> . . . It was just 8.40 when a thundering wave of cheers announced the entrance of the presidium, with Lenin—great Lenin—among them. A short, stocky figure, with a big head set down in his shoulders, bald and bulging . . . Unimpressive to be the idol of a mob, loved and revered as perhaps few leaders in history have been. A strange popular leader—a leader purely by virtue of intellect; colorless, humourless, uncompromising and detached, without picturesque idiosyncrasies—but with the power of explaining profound ideas in simple terms, of analyzing a concrete situation. And combined with

shrewdness, the greatest intellectual audacity . . . His great mouth, seeming to smile, opened wide as he spoke; his voice was hoarse—not unpleasantly so, but as if it had hardened that way after years and years of speaking. . . . For emphasis, he bent forward slightly. No gestures. And before him, a thousand simple faces looking up in intent adoration.[2]

I use these two excerpts, exactly eight decades, though worlds apart, to focus for a moment on a peculiarity of the political world; that of the leader who is revered by his followers beyond the normal limits; for whom untold numbers are, on occasion, willing to die in battle; and whose aging but loyal supporters preserve his icons years beyond his death. Max Weber coined the notion of charismatic leadership to speak to this phenomenon. Weber's usage is, as shall be discussed, fraught; yet the dynamic of the hero and the crowd has been at the centre of modern politics, from Hitler to Mussolini, from Gandhi to Nkrumah, from Stalin to Sukarno, and from Lenin to Manley.

Is there a single identifiable set of criteria to be assigned to the charismatic leader? Is charisma a function of the leader's special qualities, of the crowd's perception of him, or both? Under what conditions does charisma develop and how does it wane? Can charisma abide within institutions, or does it reside solely in the personality? Are different instances of popular leadership common examples of charisma, or discrete instances of leader–follower interaction? Can a special case be made for Caribbean charisma as a sub-category of a general phenomenon? All of these questions cannot be answered here, but before an attempt is made to address some of them, we should return for a moment to two examples of Michael Manley at the height of his powers.

The first is what I refer to as the episode of "Double High Science." After winning the 1976 election with an overwhelming mandate, Manley, in an oft-discussed moment, was faced with an economic crisis of tremendous proportions. The coffers were empty and there was what seemed to be the almost unavoidable imperative of seeking IMF loans for survival. Faced with this option, which almost certainly would have meant an end to the social programs on which his popularity had been constructed, Manley set up a committee of left scholars to discuss the possibility of an alternative economic path.[3] When the proposed "Emergency Production Plan"—discussed in numerous forums across the length and breadth of the island—could not come up with satisfactory answers as to where the necessary funds would come from, Manley took the decision, in the face of sharp opposition from his new coterie of advisors and the influential left wing of the PNP, to travel the IMF route. In subsequent meetings with the party executive and members, he appeared to have convinced a working majority of his followers that, instead of retreating ignominiously, he had won a decisive battle with the IMF. At the subsequent September 1977 PNP conference, he called the purported victory, in true Ananse fashion, "double high science," implying—in touch with Jamaican popular culture—that he had managed to both gain the critical IMF approval *and* maintain the popular social programs. There was some truth in this, as the initial IMF agreement was mild, but then Jamaica failed the relatively moderate Christmas tests and shifted into full and (ultimately for the PNP) destructive structural adjustment[4] in 1978, contributing to his electoral defeat two years later.

The second instance surrounds the October 1980 electoral debacle. There had been anticipated, though in its scale unprecedented, violence leading up to the election, discussed in detail in his important, if little-read testament, *Struggle in the Periphery*.[5] Among the main features was the virtual insubordination of significant elements in the armed forces, the shooting to death by the police of the junior minister of national security,[6] the shooting up of a meeting in Spanish Town at which Manley was present, numerous incidents of terrorism by gunmen supportive of both major parties, and an atmosphere that led many to conclude that the country was bordering on a coup.

Jamaica Labour Party (JLP) opposition leader Edward Seaga, the record shows, won an overwhelming mandate. Many thought that if he had lost, the situation would have been uncontrollable and Manley would not have been able to govern. Immediately after the election there was sporadic violence, mainly from PNP areas in the city, and at least two communities—Arnett Gardens (Concrete Jungle) and Greenwich Town—opened direct hostilities against the armed forces. The youth of Greenwich Town—supportive of the Marxist Workers Party of Jamaica (WPJ)—in an unrecorded, though very real act of resistance, declared their community the People's Republic of Greenwich Town. And, in a critical moment after the results had become clear, the PNP general secretary, speaking from party headquarters, declared that the struggle had entered a new and revolutionary phase. Almost immediately, he was cut off the air.[7] Within two days things had calmed down and, aside from sporadic outbursts, what appeared to have been a localized, but definite insurrectional impetus ebbed. What was it that prevented the escalation of an insurrectionary wave among the militant and highly mobilized PNP supporters of downtown Kingston? It is my assessment, though the research is still incomplete, that Manley, against the wishes of some of his closest advisors and against the rising tide from downtown, gave the order to concede. That he was right is, in historical perspective, self-evident. Had there been a battle for state power, not only was it the case that the JLP irregulars, steeled in the internecine struggle of the past five years, were better armed, but the full force of the state and, if necessary, external support would have been brought to bear on what would then have been an insurrectionary and illegitimate party. More so, this would have been devastating from a political perspective, in a context where only a small part of its popular support base had been revolutionized by the previous months of urban guerrilla warfare.

I mention these cases to drive home the point that, in his generation in Jamaica, Manley was revered by the people and had popular influence and power like no other person, and further, that his intervention into the political process at critical junctures—which only he had the authority to implement—profoundly affected the future development of Jamaican politics and society. His longtime rival and competitor for power, Edward Seaga, pales in comparison. When Manley's support was up, as it was immediately after the then popular decision to call the state of emergency in 1976, he was considered the most outstanding leader by 60 per cent of Jamaicans. Seaga only gained 17 per cent of the poll. Even at the trough of his support in 1980, when there was no food on the shelves and machine guns were rattling every night, Seaga, on his most favorable terrain, when the question was posed as to "who is best able to run the country in times of crisis," garnered a narrow plurality of 39.8 to Manley's 36.3 per cent. Less than a year later, in what should still have been his honeymoon period in office, the old pattern had reasserted itself. When asked who was Jamaica's most outstanding leader, 33.4 per cent said Manley; 29.2 per cent supported Seaga.[8] It never changed again. When Manley died, a full 67.9 per cent supported the view that he should be made a national hero;[9] and three years after his death, national polls still considered him the prime minister who by far had done the most for the people.[10]

What was it that Manley had that his competitors did not? And can it be described in the formal sense as charisma? Let us for a moment return to Weber and two of his critics in order to begin formulating an answer.

Weber's Charisma

Charisma is one of Weber's three well-known categories through which leadership is legitimated, the others being the "traditional" and the "legal rational." He argues, inter alia, that in times of popular distress, a natural leader, rather than an appointed officer, emerges from the ranks. His supporters are won to him as they arrive at the conclusion that he possesses special gifts of body and mind, almost invariably considered supernatural.[11] Central to Weber's framework is the assertion that charismatic leaders become recognized as such by performing miraculous acts and, once they are recognized as having the gift of grace, need to continually prove themselves worthwhile in order to retain their charismatic appeal. Charisma is therefore essentially unstable; if miracles are not regularly performed, outwardly loyal followers will soon abandon their erstwhile champion.[12] However, for the time that he rules (and it is mostly, though not always "he") and the crowd continues to adore him, all autonomy is surrendered. No abstract laws restrain the charismatic ruler. To this extent, then, Weber saw charisma—with its absence of fealty to the past—as in direct opposition to traditional forms of power, indeed, as the "specifically creative revolutionary force of history."[13]

Further specifying, Weber suggests that charisma is essentially a localized, ethnically based, vocationally restricted phenomenon. It is therefore not only temporary in its scope, but also limited in its reach.[14] Finally, following his central theme of its instability, he notes that having emerged due to extraordinary circumstances, when those contextual conditions wane, charisma too subsides and becomes institutionalized. It is the fate of the charismatic leader to fade with the onset of permanent institutions.[15]

What is immediately striking about Weber's description is its specificity. Unlike subsequent theorists who have, on occasion, sought to apply the notion of charismatic leadership in mechanical fashion to diverse, modern social contexts, Weber is surprisingly cautious and tendentious. Indeed, for Weber, the emergence of modern bureaucratic society signals the death knell of charisma. It is interesting to note that, following this, many critics of the concept attack its theoretical usefulness, accusing it of being too generalized, an assertion of which Weber, perhaps, is least guilty.

Robert Tucker's Modification

In "The Theory of Charismatic Leadership,"[16] Robert Tucker argues for the essential Weber. An interpretation of Weber grounded in religion, which sees his propositions as absolute, is not useful in the contemporary world. However, if we take Weber's categories as a point of departure and look at tendencies, then we might come up with a useful framework. Thus, rather than the notion of followers giving automatic acquiescence to the leader, Tucker suggests that there is, rather, a tendency to acquiesce. He makes the important additional point that the charismatic leader is not just any leader, but the leader of a social movement. To this extent, he underlines Weber's argument that the issue is not simply one of personal qualities. The leader is not just charismatic, but is so to the extent that he develops a charismatic following and a charismatic movement.[17]

The essential feature to be maintained in any modern application of the notion, Tucker emphasizes, is that charismatic leaders arise in moments of distress and provide deliverance from that distress.[18] Equally, he adds the necessary caveat that charismatic leaders develop counter-charismatic hatreds. Yet, there is also the necessary search for specific qualities commonly possessed by the charismatic hero. Tucker stresses the sense of the rightness of mission and the personal sense of leadership. In summary:

> . . . charismatic movements for change arise and spread at times when painful forms of distress are prevalent in a society or in some particular stratum of a society. The unique personal authority of the leader and the rapturous response of many of the followers grow out of their feeling that he, by virtue of his special powers as a leader, embodies the movement's salvational promise, hence that which may be of supreme significance to them. Since he ministers to their most pressing need—the need to believe in the real possibility of escape from an oppressive life predicament—they not only follow him voluntarily and without thought of material recompense, but tend to revere him and surround him with that spontaneous cult of personality which appears to be one of the symptomatic marks of the charismatic leader-follower relationship.[19]

Danns's Intervention

In an important intervention, "Leadership, Legitimacy and the West Indian Experience," George Danns rigorously applies Weber's theory to the West Indies in the anti-colonial phase, with interesting results. Like Tucker, but with greater criticism of the core arguments, he suggests that Weber needs to be seriously modified if his theory is to be made applicable to the West Indies. He stresses the institutional and popular context of Caribbean leadership, arguing (though not in contradiction with Weber's theses) that support for leaders arises out of causes, not personally created principles.[20] The outwardly charismatic Caribbean leader gains his magnetism from the personification of the causes he fights for. Further, speaking of a generation of West Indian leaders, Danns concludes that the aim of the leader was never, pace Weber, to revolutionize the structures of society but to replace one leadership cadre with another.[21] Danns further suggests, in a rich but insufficiently explored diversion, that the ethnic diversity of the Caribbean constrains the charismatic leader's domination of his followers, by virtue of the necessity of having to compromise.[22]

The reality of the West Indian experience, then, is a lower-level "authoritarianism" and not "genuine" charisma as defined by Weber. Why, however, Danns chooses to see these two categories as mutually exclusive is difficult to fathom. It is precisely the fact of unlimited allegiance that makes the charismatic leader—no matter how well-meaning his intentions—potentially authoritarian. In summary, the charismatic leader today is different. He is oriented toward economic and utilitarian considerations and makes use of rational means toward this end. He gains support through a calculus of new ideas, rational endeavors, and personal magnetism.

But have Tucker and Danns, in their respective attempts to modernize and "West Indianize" Weber's notion, explained away the concept? Have they merged the charismatic leader with any leader, with the stuff of leadership in general? Let us for the moment go back to Manley and survey his origins and rise to power and influence in order to see if the signals point in one direction or the other.

Scanning Manley's Rise[23]

A rapid scan of Michael Manley's rise to prominence might suggest the following features as being critical:

THE PERSONAL

The most evident is that he was born with the proverbial "gift of grace." The son of prominent King's Council and later national leader Norman Manley and his English-born wife and leading artist Edna, he was blessed at birth by being the offspring of the emerging country's first family. This provided him with immense reserves of goodwill. And yet, the important parry here is to note that he was only the second son: his elder brother Douglas shared all these advantages and never strove for national leadership. We need, therefore, to conduct a wider search for what catapulted Michael to the fore.

The logical starting point is his personality. Unlike the phlegmatic, inwardly focused, and moody Douglas,[24] Michael from very early gave indications of the leadership qualities for which he would become famous. His oft-recounted resignation from Jamaica College is a necessary example. As a senior student at the prestigious grammar school, Michael had prospered under the "benign headmastership"[25] of Reginald Murray, who treated him like a "semi-adult."[26] But then Murray left and his replacement, J. W. S. Hardie, reverted to a more traditional authoritarian approach, committing the unspeakable crime of reproaching the monitor Manley in front of younger students. Manley wrote a protest letter, considered the height of impertinence by Hardie, and the tension between them worsened. What brought the situation to climax was Michael's perception that he was being victimized for his outspoken views. An English master gave him an extra essay and, when Michael asked why, was told abruptly that it was an order. The incensed Manley retorted "Do your damnedest!"

threw his books at the blackboard, and stormed out of the classroom. Hardie summoned him, offered the humiliating option of a caning or the alternative of expulsion. At eighteen years old, Michael responded: "You know something Mr Hardie, you'll never live to expel me. I resign!"[27] When he packed his bags to leave, his schoolmates bore him on their shoulders, chanting "We want Manley! Down with Hardie!"[28] It is an important coda to note that when his father Norman got wind of the incident, he told Hardie that if Michael were expelled he would be faced with a court case. The unprecedented resignation, then, as opposed to the more damaging expulsion was allowed to stand on the son's record.

Three features can perhaps be isolated from this incident. The first is the young Manley's courage and boldness, captured in the readiness to write the protest letter and then face the headmaster frontally, denying him the pleasure of either administering a caning or expulsion. The second is his rage in opposition to victimization. It was unfairness, both in the initial reprimand in front of younger students and the view that he had been singled out for unfair extra work, that precipitated his response. The third is the evident willingness of large numbers of students to support him. In the authoritarian atmosphere of Hardie's JC of the 1940s, it could not have been a simple decision for youngsters to break classes and bear Michael to the gate. Clearly his act of resistance had ridden a wave that was latent though widespread, but that no one else had been willing to ride. It is at the juncture of courage and the ability to recognize and voice the popular mood that the young Manley was borne to the gate, as the future Joshua would be borne to national leadership.

Following from the above coda, a further point should be underlined. Michael's courage in this instance is real, but it is bolstered about and carried aloft in the full knowledge that he is lawyer Manley's son and that, ultimately, resignation would not mean the squandering of his life chances and utter deprivation. Thus courage, and by implication leadership, is in this instance encouraged and supported by privilege.

An additional ascriptive feature of the young Manley needs to be brought into the picture, and this has to do with his physical appearance. Manley was fair, though not white. His father, though dark brown, was clearly of mixed African and European ancestry. His mother was for all outward appearances white, but she was the first cousin of Norman and the African roots were evident in her mother's family. This particular location distanced Michael from the vast majority of African Jamaicans, yet not enough to make him an outsider. Thus, in later years when the PNP bandwagon would play the popular rally song "My Father Born Ya," it directly counterpoised Manley's connectedness to the Afro-Jamaican continuum in contrast to Seaga's distance from it.[29]

Yet, Manley's "brownness" and privileged position gave him another advantage in color-stratified Jamaican society. In the 1938 labor uprising Norman's very light-skinned cousin and later political nemesis, Alexander Bustamante, had risen to national prominence when, in the face of imminent assault, he bared his chest and urged the police to shoot him but not his people. Both he and his supporters in the crowd survived. This relative immunity granted, to the elite of color in a highly stratified society, served Busta well and Michael certainly benefited from it. Simply put, it was safer to follow a brown leader than a black one, because not only was the leader's longevity more likely, but one's chances of survival were greater in the former's shadow. When one recalls the sharp confrontations between Manley and the police and military leading up to the 1980 elections,[30] it is moot as to whether he would have lived through them all had he been unambiguously black.

A related feature of this is what might be called the "gratefulness factor." In a society in which most well-off brown people prided themselves on their physical, social, economic, and cultural distance from the black majority and in which patronage with deep roots into slavery still flourished, for a brown man to take on the cause of the majority was in itself miraculous and ample cause to be grateful. The love for Manley deriving from this feature was evident at the time of his funeral, where many mourners perceived him, though in contradictory fashion, as the powerful, altruistic patron who had come down from his privileged heights to help the people. This slogan, neatly written on the side of a brown cardboard box and held proudly aloft by a poor, black middle-aged woman, is illustrative:

The Right Honorable Michael Manley
Government fonder of Jamaica
Both home and abroad
Intellect,
A great leader advocate and inspirator for the poor
One who was concerned about
The educational background for people
From all walks of life
He inteduce the jamal Foundation and free education
For all children at primary school to be awarded free places at tertiary institution.
This he did and many more for the betterment of the Jamaican people.

This is why he is hailed as gient.
May his soul res in peace.
Although you are sleeping
We closed with love comred.[31]

Yet there is one further, powerful, yet highly ephemeral dimension of the physical that needs to be mentioned, which is Manley's personal magnetism. He was a tall and undoubtedly handsome man. Yet, beyond these he possessed an indefinable quality of attractiveness. His mother certainly recognized it in him; in her insightful reminiscence *Slipstream*, Rachel Manley captures it in one of Michael's visits to his parents' mountain retreat Nomdmi:

> Mardi always looked at my father as though she were surprised to see him; as if he had recently grown taller. He did rather look as though he had suddenly sprouted from any spot where he was standing. That was how he emerged on any horizon—as if a sleeping giant had suddenly sat up. Things around him tended to get displaced. Like a bright light, he always attracted attention. . . . Mardi used to say that only mountains ignored my father. And maybe that was why he was always in awe of them.[32]

This larger-than-life presence, when combined with a quiet kindness, in which Manley would pay personal attention without fanfare to a child or sick friend,[33] made him an alluring leader of men, "always the band's drummer,"[34] long before he entered politics. It also made the young Manley, to his daughter Rachel's obvious chagrin,[35] irresistibly attractive and attracted to women. This, in the phallocentric universe of mid-twentieth-century Jamaica, was no millstone around his political neck.

THE MOMENT

Yet, being born to the first family and with a striking personality does not the leader of a nation make. Michael benefited from two further factors: his decision to enter the trade union movement when he did and the timing of his ascension to leadership of the People's National Party.

Since the birth of modern Jamaican politics out of the 1938 uprisings, trade unionism had been the acknowledged route to political power. Alexander Bustamante, who became a national leader through his powerful personalist trade union the Bustamante Industrial Trade Union (BITU), established this pattern. And it was only in the fifties, when the National Workers Union

(NWU) under Michael's leadership emerged as the affiliate of the PNP, that that party was able to triumph at the polls.

Organizing NWU workers, particularly in the strategic bauxite sector, gave Michael a requisite sense of the popular pulse as it simultaneously exposed tens of thousands of union members and their families to Norman Manley's son. It is very difficult to imagine the mature Joshua with his exquisite oratory without this apprenticeship. Michael, after all, grew up in the rarified world of Drumblair in an era before the Guyanese scholar Walter Rodney had demonstrated to the intellectuals that it was possible to "ground" with their brothers in the ghetto. And it can be argued in support of this point that Michael, even at his most populist, never spoke "broad" Jamaican in his formal speeches or elsewhere. Few, however, can question his sense of timing, brilliant rhetoric, or grasp of the popular mood that was honed, at least in part, on this formative experience.

Ironically, the trade union event that thrust Manley more than any other into national focus, involved middle-class workers at the state-owned Jamaica Broadcasting Corporation. In 1964, after two years in office, the JLP government had decided to fire two workers at the JBC. The NWU considered it political victimization and in Michael's reaction, as captured in *Slipstream*, we see again the enraged sixth former and his courageous response:

> Before going to work that first morning of the strike, my father had stormed
> up and down the hall, twisting knots into the length of the telephone cord as
> he talked. How dare they? Did they realize the course of history can change
> because of some small nettle of injustice? They had better reinstate these
> men or face one hell of a strike. He sucked up all the energy of the house and,
> dropping us off at school, roared on to battle.[36]

The chances of winning in a non-essential sector outside a broader national crisis were, of course, very slim. In the end, one worker was considered justifiably fired and the other given a tiny recompense. But Michael, like his cousin Bustamante before him, had now led workers defiantly into the streets. In a defining incident, while he lay, arms linked with other protesters on the ground, a police vehicle had raced up to him, stopping abruptly short of running over his head. Michael did not flinch. His mother called it a "legitimizing moment":[37]

> He was in the newspapers daily, photographed in moods of defiance, his jaw
> always leading the way. On the rival radio station, his name dominated the
> top story of every hour. His familiar voice came over in passionate clips. "He's

like the oboe," said Mardi sagely, as though she had expected all of this, "The whole orchestra will have to tune itself to him!" . . . At school I began to hear "Michael Manley" in a way that riveted people's attention. It was like hearing a name for the first time from the outside in, instead of from the inside out . . . "Michael Manley lie down in the road, and the traffic drive right up to his head and have to stop!" the girls said at school.[38]

Thus was the name of the new hero "Joshua" born, as Michael, rhetoric still immature, pointed at the radio station and said, "these are the walls of Jericho," and some unidentified person in the crowd retorted, "tear them down, Joshua."

But even with the creation of this myth, Michael might have ended up as the powerful but marginal leader of a trade union movement were it not for the national conjuncture. Norman Manley's long sojourn as leader of the PNP was drawing to an end. His final year in office coincided with the emergence of the Jamaican Black Power movement. In October 1968 the Hugh Shearer–led JLP government had declared University of the West Indies historian Walter Rodney persona non grata. Students had marched, the police attacked them, and the urban ghettoes of Kingston exploded in a day of rioting. The PNP's response, at first critical of the government, changed when "subversive" documents, purportedly coming from the students, surfaced in Parliament. It was evident that, in the new political climate, the old union/party anti-colonial alliance was insufficient to address the problems of the urban youth with their militancy and grassroots ideologies of black nationalism and Rastafarianism.[39]

Michael succeeded his father as president of the party some four months after these events. The rest is the proverbial history. In three years, due to force of personality, hard work, and political acumen, Michael rebuilt the party, sweeping to power with a decisive mandate in February 1972.[40] The new PNP, while formally committed to a multi-class alliance, had come to power with a clear mandate to change the social and economic lot of the poor. While the election slogan "power for the people" did not imply social revolution, it was interpreted as such by many among the urban and rural poor. The party's eight years in power can be interpreted as the attempt to resolve this tension between the expectations of its supporters and the party's weaknesses as a vehicle to address them.

In Power

The euphoria of victory was followed by a short honeymoon, during which innovative policies were tried, like the initiative of voluntary work on Labour Day, a National Youth Service, and an adult literacy program (JAMAL). Reflecting on the myriad initiatives undertaken by Manley's government from the distance of three decades, it is evident that the most enduring were those concerned with raising the dignity and personhood of the ordinary people.[41] Certainly, when one reads the numerous remembrances and reminiscences that were published in the popular media immediately after his death, the majority mentioned programs like the maternity leave with pay law, the status of children act (repealing the notion of bastardy), the literacy program, and the building of mass housing for the poor.

The fundamental issue of the unequal Jamaican social order, however, had barely been dented when, in 1974, the OPEC-inspired oil price increases sent the economy into a downward spiral. Manley's levy against the bauxite companies increased the country's earnings from the strategic mineral, and this marginally offset the worst effects of the oil crisis; but in retrospect, from at least 1974,[42] critical elements of the upper and middle classes had already bolted the alliance. And, in the face of increasing hardships on the poor, Manley and his party had to battle to retain their grassroots support. The PNP "rededicated" itself to democratic socialism in 1974 and this ideological hardening helped at first to rally the forces. Some further ground was secured as Manley's advocacy of a new international economic order, support for non-alignment, and opposition to apartheid in South Africa increased his international prestige and the small country's standing in world affairs.

In 1975 and 1976, in the face of a sustained and brutal tidal wave of violence that swept through the urban ghettoes and threatened to engulf the entire country, Manley and the party seemed at first to have no answer and there was fear among his closest advisors that they would lose even the core support among the urban poor. Then, at the peak of the violence in the middle of 1976, he threw down the gauntlet to his opposition by declaring a popularly received state of emergency. This appeared to hold the fort and served to rally his forces, contributing to his enlarged victory margin in the December 1976 election. At the height of his influence at the September 1976 PNP conference, Manley, on the basis of his social policies, symbolic representation on behalf of the poor, and now demonstrated willingness to fight back, had developed an organic, almost religious connection with the metaphorically appropriate PNP "massive." This excerpt from that speech captures, if only in pale shadow, the panache[43] and electricity generated between the hero and his believers at the peak of his powers:

PRIME MINISTER: Every worker who has ever had to go hungry on a picket line knows what it is to struggle. And when he has won his strike, then the suffering is over and he enters a new pasture of joy and principle. And they

are making us suffer but what they did not realize is that the masses would
show the capacity to struggle. (APPLAUSE) . . .
PRIME MINISTER: And we will remember then the Basic Schools that we
built, because we know where we are going. (APPLAUSE) We will remember
the Day Care Centres that we are building because we know where we are going. (APPLAUSE) The National Youth Service that we have started, because
we know where we are going. (APPLAUSE) JAMAL and literacy and into the
light for the masses because we know where we are going (APPLAUSE) . . .
And my comrades, there is now equal pay for work because we know where
we are going. We have a minimum wage law now because we know where we
are going. (APPLAUSE) We have a Family Court for mothers now because
we know where we are going. (ECHO FROM CROWD) There is status for
children now because . . .
VOICES: We know where we are going.
PRIME MINISTER: We are having worker participation in industry now
because . . .
VOICES: We know where we are going . . .
PRIME MINISTER: We know where we are going. We are creating a new
man. We have begun the building of socialist man. We are working towards
the day when there will be no more masters and no more servants but only
one together in the Lord. (LOUD APPLAUSE)
And we are learning now to go not upon our knees, but as true, sovereign,
human, dignified human beings, because we know where we are going . . .
In the name of every victim that ever lived, in the name of every martyr
that ever died, we will not fail. We shall overcome. (THUNDEROUS AP-
PLAUSE)[44]

This indefatigable bond between Joshua and his people was never severed after
this. He had gone beyond the grace of his birth and his early legitimation to enter the realm of myth and prophecy. Hereafter, no matter what he did, no matter the vicissitudes of the real economic and political situation, among the true
believers he had been forever canonized. For Joshua had come down from the
empyrean heights and delivered simple, mundane, but—from the experience
of Jamaica's post-slavery history—profound social justice. The narrative was
being related and, in turn, received in the rhetorical call-and-response style of
the popular wayside preacher and the prophets in Kingston's markets.
    Through the IMF travails and violence of the next four years, despite the un-
certainty and vacillation of the government's policies, through the long decade
of opposition in the eighties, through his reconciliation[45] with neo-liberalism

and reelection in 1989 and beyond his death, the image of the "true" Manley, at the moment of this stance in 1976, remained intact among the faithful.

By Way of Conclusion

How does this narrative fit with Weber's analysis or the subsequent above-mentioned modifications? The simple answer is that much in Manley's rise does not conform to the details of Weber's analysis, though it would be foolish to altogether abandon the notion. Michael Manley certainly did not emerge from the ranks but was, in the end, the scion of the PNP, some might argue the model, of the constitutionally based, procedurally driven postwar, anti-colonial party. Far from being limited and localized in his reach, Manley's influence extended across Jamaica and into the Jamaican and, debatably, the wider Caribbean diaspora. Finally and importantly, Manley, despite his fiery rhetoric, was personally and in private quite self-effacing and consciously sought to avoid the outward trappings of charisma.[46] The compromise would seem to be a "paper thin theory" of charisma that would, somewhat along the lines advocated by Tucker, preserve the essence of the powerful, deified leader who arises in a crisis, though retaining great sensitivity to the specific features of that leader's location in a particular sequential history connected into late modernity.

With this and the previous narrative, we might suggest that Manley in his time became a leader with inordinate authority and influence, though not to say that, as Danns suggests, he should be described as "authoritarian." Even then, there is need for further clarification. Manley's authority was strongest at the PNP grassroots level and among poor and working people generally. His influence among the middle classes, as evidenced in the seventies, gradually ebbed as his policies became less "national" and more "social." Any understanding of his charisma has then to be rooted in the social soil of a particular place, focusing especially on the relationship between the leader and the social forces that form the core of his alliance.

But a further issue is raised by the trajectory of Manley's career that, while mentioned by Tucker and Danns, is in opposition to Weber. This relates to the autonomy of the leader from his popular following. While, as suggested at the beginning of this chapter, Manley possessed sufficient autonomy to make decisions that were against the run of the popular mood, it is also true to say that his course, from moderate politician in 1972 to anti-imperialist rhetorician in 1976, suggests that he too was very much a creature of the increasingly militant positions of his support base. Indeed, as has been mooted, at a certain point the myth of Joshua takes flight quite independently of the man and serves as its own mythical symbol and organizing force. In the end, Weber's proposal, while not to be abandoned, is neither template nor model. This brief sketch of Manley's rise suggests the importance of the specific interplay of class and caste, birth and personality quirk, conjunctural moment and chance of fate that come together to determine the rise of the hero. Heroes there are, but the assertion of a general overarching theory should be approached with care.

Postnote: A Gramscian Alternative?

In *The Modern Prince*, Antonio Gramsci hints at an alternative to Weberian charisma:

> At a certain point in their historical life, social groups detach themselves from their traditional parties in that given organizational form, when the men who constitute, represent and lead them, are no longer recognized as the proper representation of their class or fraction of a class. When these crises occur the immediate situation becomes delicate and dangerous, since the field is open to solutions of force, to the activity of obscure powers represented by "men of destiny" or "divine men."[47]

Gramsci here, with potentially useful effect, nuances the debate, by placing the phenomenon on a field of social classes and at a rare moment of conjunctural crisis. The somewhat sweeping assumption is that, in the normal world of class struggle, classes are led by recognized parties, though occasionally there is a crisis point. When the old parties and old representatives are unable to provide leadership, a "dangerous" alternative emerges. This, far more explicitly than the Weberian template, raises issues of the social and historical foundations of crisis and suggests—though only if Gramsci's Marxist foundations are read into the statement—that there may well be quite different types of leaders depending on the particular character of the social formation and the nature of the conjunctural moment. But this is not elaborated.

Applying Gramsci's implicit assumption, the relevant question for the Caribbean is, what is the possible outcome in a context where there is no articulated history of leaders and (overtly) class-based parties? What, further, if the conjunctural crisis is persistent because of the inability of any social force to seriously take hold of and set the agenda for the future of the state? In other words, what if the ability of the postcolonial state to significantly improve the lives of its citizens, via patron-client means or otherwise, has been so undermined as to make it moribund? In such a context, the room is always more or less open for intervention from "dangerous men" or, in the absence of intervention, the likelihood of the collapse of the political project altogether.

Returning for a moment to Weber's notion of the charismatic hero as enchanted, though likely to lose this quality if he does not perform, we might also suggest that if the state fails to perform even minor miracles, then it too becomes subject to disenchantment. Thus, subsequent heroes who would step in to rescue distressed masses in such a context of widespread disillusionment find themselves in a no man's land in which the political itself is negated as a space for reconstruction. This, more than the danger of the quixotic hero, is the imminent risk in the current moment in Jamaica.

Or, there is a third imaginary, in which the inscribed image of the hero accompanied by his loyal following is subverted; in which worship and gratefulness are replaced by fraternity, sorority, and respect; in which democracy trumps hierarchy; and in which the single charismatic hero is replaced by the entire heroic people. This, while the less likely option, would seem also to be a necessary consideration for the yet to be determined future.

PART TWO

Caribbean Questions

5. Saving the Soul of the University (1998)

My conscious memory of the University of the West Indies (UWI) qua university dates back to the first week in fifth form at Jamaica College. Jimmy Carnegie, whose skill at throwing chalk at miscreants was even more finely tuned than his not insignificant grasp of West Indian history, had thrown his chalk (accurately) and, in response to an early "radical" comment from me, which itself has been forgotten in the mists of time, responded: "If you want to be radical at least do what Trevor Munroe[1] did."

At the time, I did not know who Trevor Munroe was or what he had done, and was vague at very best as what "to be radical" really meant. But Carnegie's comments did stir my inquisitiveness and attuned it to what turned out to be an immeasurably attractive place in which I developed the impression that very bright people engaged freely in debates about esoteric things and where the highest standards prevailed.

My second memory is in early 1970, when, like most of my fellow sixth formers, I was deciding what to do after A Levels. For me, it had come down to two choices: Columbia in New York City, with all the attendant glamor, or UWI, both of which had accepted my application. Then one morning in February—I was still only 16 years old—I opened the papers to read that UWI student-led demonstrations had blossomed to nationwide black power protests[2] against the government in Trinidad. Columbia was no longer in the contest. I decided then and there that I would have to go to St. Augustine in Trinidad to find my future, where the students and the people were redefining theirs. I give these two biographical anecdotes because they mirror important historical features of the University of the West Indies and what it meant to my generation. It is critical for us to remember them because in many respects they helped constitute the essence, the soul of the place, a soul that is in grave danger of being lost.

If my recollections are accurate and do, indeed, reflect real perceptions about the institution, then, for my generation, two notions dominated.

First, the UWI was seen as a place of intellectual inquiry and excellence. I do not recall ever conceiving UWI as a second-rate option, one taken only if the foreign applications failed or the overseas fees were too high. For me, it was as good a place to be as Columbia, nay, far better, because of its rootedness in the Caribbean soil and the deep concern of its intellectuals with the task of understanding and changing the Caribbean condition.

Second, the UWI was also perceived as a fount of activism. It was assumed that students and academics at Mona were intimately involved not only in the life of the campus but in that of the wider community, and that scholarship was ultimately to be put to the service of the Caribbean people, especially the poor and dispossessed. These notions, of course, like all perceptions, were in part myth. There has always been a large fraction of the student body that is apolitical and/or deeply conservative. But I suggest that despite the element of myth, they do reflect a time that has largely passed, even as, for the good of the region, aspects of it need urgently to be recovered.

I want to suggest three phases[3] in the evolution of the university as a place of excellence, intellectual inquiry, and activism. I shall use my own home base, the Faculty of Social Sciences, because it has always been at the heart of the regional debate on the character and fate of the university and, after more than half my life associated with it, I do have a cursory familiarity.

PHASE 1: WEST INDIAN NATIONALISM: 1950S–1968

This period was associated with the formation of the university and its consolidation. It was recognized that a tremendous amount of work needed to be done. The entire Anglo-Caribbean social order had to be mapped. There was the urgent requirement to categorize, theorize, measure, account, and to play a role in the establishment of new systems of independent government. The driving ideology of this period was undoubtedly a certain West Indian nationalism, undergirded by meta-theoretical notions of empiricism, behavioralism, and positivism. There prevailed a belief in the "science" in social sciences, accompanied by a tremendous energy and optimism, associated with the approach of what was thought to be regional autonomy and independence. On rereading the important journals and papers of the day, however, it seems that a major flaw was that these philosophical issues remained subterranean and were seldom if ever debated frontally. Despite these limiting ideological and meta-theoretical notions, which falsely assumed a certain natural, linear, and progressive future for Caribbean development, much of lasting import was accomplished. Examples of the important pioneering work would have to include M. G. Smith's plural society thesis and the debates with R. T. Smith on the nature of Caribbean social structure; Lloyd Braithwaite's rich and insightful study of social stratification in Trinidad; numerous important statistical studies by Jack Harewood, G. W. Roberts, and others, which lay the foundations for regional demography; Arthur Lewis's seminal work on labor surplus economies and industrialization, even though much was not actually done at the UWI; and Nettleford, Smith, and Augier's pioneering study on Rastafari in Jamaica.[4]

All of this research was propelled by a sense of Caribbean nationhood; a secondary recognition of the need to end, or at least ameliorate poverty; and an accompanying, though retrospectively naive belief in the social sciences as not just tool but limitless source of answers. This phase collapsed after the loss of the referendum in Jamaica in 1961, which led to the demise of the federal project. Demoralization and cynicism prevailed among many academics and students who had been overwhelmingly pro-federation. Some never recovered. And, in the subsequent years, as the promise of independence proved to be chimerical and the safety valve of emigration to the UK was turned off, demoralization at the university was matched in the wider society by a growing frustration and alienation, fuelled by increasing social polarization. As the decade of the sixties grew longer, a new cohort of students and younger academics, inspired by new national and international imperatives, reinvigorated life at the university and, even if building on these earlier foundations, helped redefine the relationship of the intellectual to the wider society.

PHASE 2: COUNTER-HEGEMONIC PRAXIS: 1968–83

The second phase emerged in the face of disappointment with independence; continuation of unjust racial and color hierarchies that had been inherited from colonialism; endemic poverty and growing unemployment, most evident in Kingston and other urban centers like Port of Spain; and an international context that favored popular upsurge, including the growth of North American black power, the radicalization of American young people due to the war in Vietnam, and the advance of the African liberation struggles, particularly in Portuguese southern Africa.

Two vibrant intellectual streams emerged. The first, primarily at the academic staff level, was a form of Caribbean "dependency theory" and was embodied in the formation of the New World Group, first at Mona and then St. Augustine. The second, which gained a far more significant following among the student population, was Black Power. If, generalizing dangerously, it can be said that New World's forte was its energetic debates with the economic policies practiced in the first decade of independence, then Black Power's main success was its frontal confrontation with the persistent social and racial inequalities and the resultant relegation of the vast majority to the margins of society.[5]

Historian Walter Rodney was the embodiment of this period. In his short stint at Mona, before being expelled in the infamous events of October 1968, he managed to achieve two things.

First, he helped to consolidate the notion that the intellectual's role was to serve the people, though it is true to say that the earlier Rastafari study and the active participation of students on the side of federation in the referendum, among other cases, suggest that there were embryonic signs of a wider engagement even before Rodney.

Second, and where Rodney departed from these earlier instances, is that he moved beyond the realm of explanation to put his job and, ultimately, years later in his home territory Guyana, his life on the line. Rodney established the principle that the true intellectual must, if (s)he recognizes injustice, also have to be an activist against it.[6]

Beyond Rodney and Black Power, Marxism-Leninism emerged as an important current, particularly on the Mona campus; however, beyond its radical rhetoric, it bore damaging similarities with earlier schools of behavioralism and positivism. Caribbean Marxism-Leninism, emerging afresh after two decades of Cold War suppression, was never grounded in a deep philosophical foundation. While, undoubtedly, one of its strengths was its orientation toward activism and a healthy notion of *praxis*, there was no corresponding tradition of the elaboration of Marxism to suit the peculiarities of the Caribbean. This weakness was compounded by the glaring absence of a reflective and self-critical epistemological gaze, which would have been the necessary counter to the mechanical and damaging pro-Soviet positions that eventually came to dominate.[7] C. L. R. James, the preeminent Caribbean Marxist thinker and perhaps the best person then able to guide such a process, was, ironically, marginalized. Ultimately and not surprisingly, it was Rodney who carried the debate on the philosophical foundations for a Caribbean radicalism furthest, and it was his party, the WPA,[8] that was able to respond most effectively to the post-Grenada challenges, though the damage, at least in part wrought by a shallow grasp of theory, had been done.

Indeed, arising from the trail blazed by Rodney, we can look at the seventies as the decade in which the academic, especially the social science academic, emerged as national political activist. Almost uniformly, this was the case throughout the Anglophone Caribbean.

In Trinidad and Tobago, the Black Power movement in its active phase of street demonstrations was guided by the National Joint Action Committee (NJAC), whose leader was Geddes Granger, a former president of the guild of undergraduates at St. Augustine. On that campus, Lloyd Best, a leading member of the New World Group, formed his small but intellectually influential Tapia House movement. Less successful was historian James Millette, whose

United National Independence Party (UNIP) flourished only briefly. In Guyana, the aforementioned WPA attempted, with some success before Rodney's brutal assassination in 1980, to bridge the historic divide between the Indian and African segments of the population. Other important intellectuals who joined the WPA included former Mona economist C. Y. Thomas, Andaiye, Rupert Roopnarine, and Eusi Kwayana, icon from the earlier nationalist struggle. The Workers Party of Jamaica (WPJ), while never accumulating significant electoral support, remained an important intellectual presence in Jamaican politics for more than a decade. An entire generation of young people at Mona, including myself, was influenced by the militant praxis of Trevor Munroe, Rupert Lewis, Don Robotham, Derek Gordon, and others.

Perhaps the real legacy of that effort is to be seen in the University and Allied Workers Union, which has expanded far beyond its original foundation to become one of the largest unions in the country. Of greater national significance in Jamaica was the impact of left intellectuals—many of whom had honed their political perspectives at the UWI—on the PNP regime of the 1970s. Persons like Arnold Bertram and Winston Davidson, who rose to senior positions in the Manley administration, had been radicalized in the years following the Rodney expulsion. Others, like George Beckford, Michael Witter, Louis Lindsay, and Norman Girvan, were established academics who influenced—though with limited success—the regime's economic policies.

But the instance in which the radical academic was most influential, and in the end most devastating, was in Grenada, where Bernard Coard became deputy prime minister of the People's Revolutionary Government (PRG) between 1979 and 1983. He and his wife Phyllis, who also played a significant role in the Grenada revolution, had taught at both the St. Augustine and Mona campuses before returning to Grenada in 1976.

But the project of the academic as activist and the left that emerged around it collapsed in a twofold movement, first, with the electoral defeat of the Manley government in 1980 and then, decisively, with the bloody debacle of the Grenada revolution and the immediate U.S.-led invasion in 1983. The resulting intellectual climate has been a vacuum, or more appropriately a state of ennui, far more profound and stultifying than that which emerged after the Federal defeat two decades before.

PHASE 3: THERMIDOR: 1983–PRESENT

The brutal killing of Maurice Bishop and his associates in Grenada in 1983 and the invasion severely undermined the credibility not only of individual intellectuals but of intellectualism and its methods. Despite the stated Marxism of many of the leading protagonists, the new Caribbean left had failed to elaborate and sustain a serious philosophical conversation on the nature of Caribbean existence or its future direction. The decades since then have been a period of profound crisis, though it deserves sub-categorization. Thus, the heart of the storm was the period 1983–90. The last eight years have witnessed a counter-flow when the basic features of crisis and defeat still predominate, though with important signs of recovery.

1983–90

In Jamaica many thought that, after the defeat of the Manley regime in the 1980 election, "deliverance" would come and the country would return to the halcyon days of growth of the 1960s. In Grenada, similar hopes of imminent wealth and nirvana emerged and were shattered[9] after the 1983 so-called "rescue mission." While there are counter-factual trends that require close scrutiny—the economic success of the smallest islands and dependent territories, and the continuing anomaly of Barbados, to mention two—if we look at the socio-economic results of the last fifteen years, the conclusions for the region as a whole are dismal. Poverty and inequality have grown in Jamaica. The infrastructure of a country that was able to host the Commonwealth Games in 1966, but could not do so today, has declined exponentially.[10] Guyana, despite earlier signs of recovery after Forbes Burnham's death, is now once again in a state of economic stagnation and mired in an increasingly dismal spiral of racial hostility. Trinidad, while by no means another Guyana, is consumed by questions of race and a rising crime rate not un-reminiscent of Jamaica.[11] And the relatively successful Windward Islands now struggle for survival[12] in the face of unfair and seemingly uncaring terms of trade for their bananas, imposed by the faceless institutions of a new economic order.

At the UWI, the pendulum has swung dramatically from a point at which a critical mass of students and academics were concerned with issues of transformation to one in which the vast majority of students seem obsessed with certification and career, while many academics have retreated from the public sphere and focus on consultancies and salary increments. This is said not in order to mean-spiritedly berate, for the market is a powerful thing, mouths have to be fed, and people will do what they have to do in order to survive. But the need for intellectual engagement, for explanations and proposed solutions to the vast array of social problems, is ever more pressing even as the intellectuals are in retreat.

Someone must remain to ask the question as to what the market really is and why it is so powerful.

Someone has to rethink the broad models of development, question the assertions as to what is normal, and boldly propose alternatives.

Someone has to pose the issue as to what standards of behavior are acceptable in public as in private life.

Someone has to face governments and openly raise issues of corruption where those may be appropriate.

Someone has to speak out when large countries simply use brute force to take out leaders of smaller countries and install them in prison cells, as the United States did in Panama, no matter what we may think of the guilt or innocence of the particular leader.

Someone has to speak out for small, defenseless states in a world dominated by large, unimaginably powerful mega-blocs.

Someone has to speak truth to power.[13]

At the UWI, in this phase of Thermidor and its accompanying ennui, the windows and spaces for the relevant conversations on all of these issues, which do, ultimately, affect the price of cheese, are, at best, half closed. This is less a case of official proscription than an instance of academic self-censorship and a timid acquiescence to the status quo.

I recall a conversation four years ago with two colleagues from St. Augustine when I was told, in the friendliest terms, that I was a dinosaur because of my interest in political theory. This was unnecessary in the new world that was emerging, they told me. What was needed was pretty much straightforward. The terms for doing business were already well established. What the Caribbean required was more managers and better systems in order to get ahead with the task of making profits. I wonder what they would tell me just four years later, after the meltdown of the Asian economies[14] and closer to home the collapse of the financial sector in Jamaica and the gas riots and the rapid decline of social cohesion in both Trinidad and Guyana.

My response today, I think, would be consistent. We are obviously in urgent need of managers of all kinds. A quick glance at the chaos[15] on the roads in Jamaica would seem to confirm such a conclusion. But there is an even more urgent imperative to think about what is going on in the Caribbean in this new world order; to question why neo-liberal formulae have worsened the situation of the poor not only in Jamaica, but in much of the "developing" world; to argue as to why it should be obvious that tiny mountainous Dominica should compete on equal terms with flat, relatively vast Honduras in the production of bananas, or whether there are simple, easily accessible alternatives that can be adopted without widespread immiserisation, or why it is that governments are forced by transnational agencies to follow policies of privatization even when the privatized bodies, as with urban transport in Jamaica, are far less efficient than the public system ever was.

For difficult questions cannot be relegated to matters of implementation. They lie in the field of intellectual inquiry.

What has happened since 1983—though, thankfully, there are important signs of revival[16]—is that the harsh, saline climate of Thermidor has eroded the intellectual foundation of the university. Its role as iconoclast has been undermined, often by default, as a result of inactivity from within; and if we do not consciously arrest this, what will remain will be a collection of buildings, an army of students, but no intellectual center. Many people will be very happy with this, but for many others it will signal the beginning of the end of a Caribbean project. For without an intellectual conversation, an intellectual opposition, and an ongoing process of questioning, the soul of the university is lost. And if we cease questioning, we relegate ourselves to being passive recipients of intellectual aid; to accepting instructions from foreign consultants who will only too happily take pay in order to tell us how we should live. A university imbued with a sense of philosophy and inquiry is not, from this angle, a luxury, but a necessity.[17] In this twilight hour the university needs to recapture, and in so doing reinvent its soul of inquiry and of activism, which emerged in its first two decades, both appropriately modified to the needs of a new time and a new generation.

6. Black Power Forty Years On (2014)

> Do you know what it is to have a revolution?
> —Dennis Brown, "Revolution"[1]

Looking back across these forty-something years, what is most striking about the Caribbean Black Power movement is the steepness of the curve of its rise and fall and yet the significant impact that it has had on subsequent social and political events in the region. In the narrow definition, Caribbean Black Power flourished for a mere six years. Inspired in name by Stokely Carmichael's 1966 rallying cry in Mississippi[2] and really taking flight with the demonstration, riot, and events surrounding Walter Rodney's expulsion from Jamaica in 1968, Black Power rose to a crescendo in the 1970 "revolution" in Trinidad and Tobago and then was rapidly eclipsed with the crushing of the National United Freedom Fighters (NUFF) in Trinidad. The rise of the New Jewel Movement (NJM) on a Marxist-Leninist footing and the Grenadian revolution of 1979–83 can be viewed as tragic epilogues to this period. There is, of course, a longer genealogy that reaches back into the history of resistance by people of African descent against Caribbean societies built on stifling race and color hierarchies and is captured in the history of the Universal Negro Improvement Association (UNIA) and Garveyism, the Negritude movement, Rastafarianism, and the numerous riots, protests, and demonstrations that punctuated the century after emancipation. Yet there is always the evident danger of conflating the specifics of the movement with the general history of resistance, which, inevitably, will obscure its contribution to the longer process.

Another critical dimension, too often missed by the existing, if limited commentaries on the period, is that it was a far more pan-Caribbean movement than any of the contemporary participants genuinely understood. Thus, while one could arguably make connections between the emerging movement in the Anglophone Caribbean, with its evident linkages to the 1969 Sir George Williams University protests in Montreal and with ready-made connections through the New World Group[3] and the student and faculty of the University of the West Indies, similar organic connections did not exist with the Dutch Caribbean and there were only limited linkages to the U.S. Virgin Islands and Bermuda, to mention two other instances. Yet the movement emerged and flourished for a time in all these jurisdictions and beyond.[4]

To appreciate its scope, then, one has to move beyond the specific concerns that fed the Caribbean movement in order to locate it within the broader global wave of resistance of the late 1960s. From such a purchase, Black Power was the peculiarly African Caribbean response to an international revolutionary *abertura* that was captured, *inter alia*, in the Czechoslovakian Spring, the student uprisings in Mexico that were suppressed brutally preceding the Olympics, the tumultuous, revolutionary French student and worker strikes, the Tet offensive in Vietnam, the flourishing of the peace movement in the United States and Europe, and, of course, the North American Black Power movement, all focused around that remarkable year, 1968. From this perspective, the rise of the Caribbean movement was only part of an irrepressible wave of anti-systemic insurrection, questioning the authority of dominant states and systems and threatening, though unsuccessfully in the short run, to overturn them. Such moments, as Immanuel Wallerstein et al.[5] propose, are rare. While national and international events conspire to produce on a more regular basis the conditions for local revolt, it is a rare moment when there is a global alignment—the 1848 European revolutions being, in Wallerstein's accounting, the only prior example. It is this overarching zeitgeist of the times that must necessarily be introduced into the calculation to grasp the moment. The anti-systemic moment of 1968, as virtually a force of nature, battered traditions, tossed social mores around, and demanded that individuals caught up in the maelstrom take a position on one or the other side of the ramparts. I can best try to explain this with my own little narrative as a high school student coming to maturity at the cusp of the moment.

I was fortunate, indeed privileged to live for extended periods in three nodal points in the Caribbean, looking at the region from the perspective of the consolidation of a radical politics, beginning with the Rodney events of 1968[6] in Jamaica. I grew up and went to high school in Jamaica and was in sixth form in 1968 during the period of Walter Rodney's exclusion and the subsequent riots. I went to University in Trinidad and Tobago—my mother's country—as an undergraduate in late 1970 and stayed until graduation in 1973. This was the period of the state of emergency that followed the mass demonstrations and their aftermath,[7] when radical politics, despite the defeat of the street phase of the Black Power revolution, continued to have significant momentum in the Eric Williams–led twin-island state. I returned to Jamaica in 1973 and spent the crucial years from then until 1980 as a graduate student at UWI Mona and later as television producer at the Jamaica Broadcasting Corporation (JBC) and partisan in favor of the Workers Party of Jamaica (WPJ) and Manley's People's National Party (PNP) during its radical, democratic socialist phase.[8] And, at the invitation of the People's Revolutionary Government (PRG), I lived in Grenada from 1981–83, returning to Jamaica only weeks before the collapse of the Grenada revolution in October 1983.

Jamaica

I begin around 1968, my first year as a sixth former at Jamaica College (JC), one of the premier high schools in Kingston, in order to suggest the outlines of what was, if only in retrospect, a prerevolutionary situation. October 16, 1968, marked the occasion when the Guyanese historian Walter Rodney, who had been attending the historic Black Writers conference in Montreal, was declared persona non grata and excluded by the government from returning to his home and job at the University of the West Indies (UWI) Mona campus. It tossed us schoolboys and girls headfirst into the hurricane of Jamaican politics. As its immediate prologue, Emperor Haile Selassie of Ethiopia had visited Jamaica in 1966 and part of his itinerary had taken him to Jamaica College. This close-up of the man revered by so many ordinary Jamaicans, but more so the sheer numbers and enthusiasm of the many Rastafarians who followed his every move, exposed us to Rastafari as not simply a religion but a mass movement.[9] Rodney's banning as he was on his way back to Jamaica from attending the Black Writers' Conference in Montreal, suggested that the Jamaica Labour Party (JLP) government led by Hugh Shearer was arbitrary and able of committing what seemed to us to be extreme calumny in its condemnation of Rodney and the students as dangerous subversives.[10] The tear gas attacks on the students who marched in support of Rodney and the subsequent attempt to paint them—particularly those from other territories—as anarchists and terrorists elicited tremendous sympathy among students and young people like me.

We moved overnight from partial Black Power sympathizers to avid supporters. A year later in upper sixth form, a small group of us would leave school without permission to support university students who had occupied the new Creative Arts Centre at the UWI, arguing that its aims and purposes were not sufficiently oriented to black and African themes. Our little group eventually published a cyclostyled news sheet entitled *LIJ Youth Move*.[11] We had read somewhere that the Amharic word *Lij* meant "sons of one mother," and this was our symbolic way of announcing our own blood brotherhood, albeit inadvertently reflecting the deeply gendered character of both our enterprise and the times in general. The content, as I recall (I have not been able to rescue an intact copy), varied between articles attempting to recover a lost African past, reflections on poverty in Jamaica, and calls to revolution expressed in fairly incendiary terms. Awareness of its publication and distribution was cause, I learned many years later, for an item at a board meeting of the school, and my parents were called in to warn them of their 16-year-old son's "dangerous" turn.

The Jamaican Black Power movement took the form of an intense popular process of consciousness raising. Students demonstrated against what they considered to be colonial-minded principals, some of whom actually banned the Afro hair style in their schools. There was also a proliferation of pamphlets, led by the iconic *Abeng* but including *Black Man Speaks*, *Bongo Man*, and many others, among them LIJ.

Undoubtedly, the most important vehicle for consciousness raising was popular music. If rock steady—the beat of the "rude boys," with its slow, deliberate, rhythm—was a portent of a broader, mass rebellion, then reggae, its far more famous successor whose history is almost parallel to the rise of Black Power, was from its origins rebel music.[12] Bob Marley and the Wailers' 1969 "Fire Fire (Babylon Burning)" epitomized the new mood in its prophecy of the cleansing destruction of Babylon by fire: "Fire, Fire, Fire Fire, Fire Fire they have no water / Babylon' burnin', Babylon burnin', Babylon burnin', they have no water."[13] This and scores of similar 45 rpm recordings became the clarion calls for a generation from varying social backgrounds, ranging from inner-city poverty to upper-middle-class comfort and privilege.

The remarkable feature of this phase of Jamaican politics, however, is how this broad river of young people dedicated to a cause (even if the cause had not been sufficiently defined) chose, for the greater part, a channel that led into the mainstream political party system. By 1972 it was the youth, many inspired by Black Power, who had propelled Michael Manley up from his lower profile as a trade unionist and son of Norman, to become Joshua, the charismatic leader who would march 'round the walls of Jericho and defeat the heathen in the 1972 elections.[14] Thus, aside from the profound street act of October 1968, Jamaican Black Power took the form of a broad, multi-faceted hegemonic process, of newspaper publishing and distribution of street-corner and backyard "reasonings," of the utilization of popular music as a means of social and political education. Its ultimate effect was both profound—the election of a government and leader who could only have won because they promoted the cultural and some of the implicit political aims of the popular movement—and also compromised, as the party itself, the vehicle of the victory, was deeply divided between a commitment to the new politics and a rootedness in a traditional, relatively conservative two-party system that, then as it does now, dominated the country's politics.

Trinidad

I graduated from JC in the summer of 1970 and, despite receiving a letter of acceptance to Columbia University, decided to read for a degree in social sciences at the UWI campus at St. Augustine in Trinidad and Tobago. The reasons were twofold. Trinidad was my mother's homeland and, growing up in Jamaica, it was a part of my own background that I felt I needed to understand. More importantly, word of the Black Power demonstrations had reached me just about the same time that I had to make decisions as to which college to attend. In my mind there was no question, as Trinidad was the venue where the real action was taking place. I landed at Piarco International Airport in September 1970 as a 17-year-old with a thin veneer of militancy derived from my sixth-form experiences of marginal involvement in the publication of a newspaper, membership of a Rasta-oriented school band, and three weeks of teaching literacy in the Jamaican countryside that summer.

I came to a country in the middle of a revolutionary crisis. The leaders of NJAC had been imprisoned since April, but all over the place were second-level leaders, supporters, and followers of the mass movement that had taken over the streets in the preceding months. The movement had not been cowed but with the state of emergency had entered a new and more dangerous phase. Within a few months of being on the St. Augustine campus, I had been introduced to the *Anarchist's Cookbook*,[15] a truly subversive publication with instructions in manufacturing dangerous things. One evening I had been invited and visited some "brothers on the block" in Belmont on the outskirts of Port of Spain, who were talking insurrection and seemed to have close connections with others who actually had guns in the hills to the north of the city. Later I would discover that they were not just talkers, but very serious. This was the beginning of the National United Freedom Fighters (NUFF) that carried out limited guerrilla action in various parts of Trinidad and Tobago between 1971 and 1974. NUFF[16] was a small splinter group from the mass movement that had gathered force between February and April of 1970, but it also reflected the extent to which the movement had moved beyond the parliamentary fabric of Trinidadian society and shifted focus to the more fundamental questions of state and power. As a post-1970 pamphlet of the National Joint Action Committee (NJAC)—the leading Black Power organization—put it succinctly: "Conventional Politics or Revolution?"[17] The People's National Movement (PNM) government was attempting to recover authority in the wake of an army rebellion that had failed, and in the context of an urban, black population, many of whom, particularly among the young, were fully open to the possibilities of insurrectional politics. When a group of students (among whom I was a mere freshman participant) held a march in support of the detained NJAC leaders, we later discovered we were under intense surveillance. A policeman who was also a student on campus brought us a picture with neatly penned-in arrows and numbers pointing at me and a number of other marchers. He told us to be very, very careful. Trinidad Black Power operated within its own cultural and political confines. In the same way that the street phase of the movement was initiated during the 1970 carnival celebrations, Trinidadian social life never abated during the state of emergency, with fetes continuing sometimes until dawn, in order to avoid the curfew.

The Black Power movement, however, never brokered the unity between the divided African and Indian elements of the society that it aspired to achieve as one of its main and laudatory goals.[18] As a young Jamaican student without the same cultural patterns of constraint applied to Trinidadian society, I remember being advised by friends on both sides of the ethnic divide that too much friendliness might be inappropriate and that Indian girls were off limits. Yet, with all the communally imposed constraints, small (and, especially in urban areas like St. James, Curepe, and Tunapuna, sometimes significant) numbers of Indian Trinidadians were deeply involved in the movement.

Trinidad Black Power never recovered the momentum it had on the streets in early 1970, before the state of emergency was declared. The decision of NUFF to wage guerrilla warfare was more a reflection of the extent of alienation among the young than it was a concerted and serious attempt to capture state power. But by its engagement in armed warfare, NUFF intensified state repression against more peaceful mass organizations like NJAC and left trade unionists like George Weekes in the Oilfield Workers Trade Union (OWTU) and Joe Young in the Transport Union (TIWU). At any rate, the various factions were unable to forge a working alliance that might have countered the traditional base of the PNM; and despite the belated attempt to do so through the United Labour Front,[19] by 1973—with the Arab oil crisis and the spike in the price of petroleum internationally—the popular foundation for the movement was mortally wounded as the Trinidadian state moved into a decade of rising incomes, state-sponsored jobs, and cost-of-living allowances that acted as a successful palliative against radicalism of whatever stream.

Back to Jamaica

Returning home to Jamaica in the seventies to pursue graduate studies at UWI Mona, I encountered an entirely different situation. The radicals were in power, but then again they were not. I recall as if it were yesterday a meeting of the "anti-imperialist forces" in Cookhorne Lane in 1973 hosted by Ben Munroe of the South West St. Andrew Citizens Association (SWSACA). Representatives came from among Mona students, the People's National Party Youth Organisation (PNPYO), a Maoist faction, the Youth Forces for National Liberation (YFNL), the embryonic Marxist-Leninist Workers Liberation League (WLL), the Marxist but never clearly defined Movement for Social and Political Consciousness (MSPC), and the neo-Trotskyite/neo–C. L. R. Jamesian Revolutionary Marxist Collective (RMC). The proliferation of names and organizations alone—very few if any of which existed three years earlier—suggests the mushrooming of radical ideas that had taken place in the mere three years of my absence.

At the entrance of the dark lane off Spanish Town Road was our security detail—a single young man armed with a "bucky," a hollowed-out bicycle frame that was now the improvised barrel for a shotgun. Just after the meeting started, we heard the sound of automatic gunfire. It certainly was not the primitive weapon of our security detail and the meeting dispersed as everyone ran for cover, scaling the fence of the yard and heading up Waltham Park Road, or seeking cover wherever seemed adequate. What saved us that dark night was that one of the PNP comrades rang their party headquarters and Tony Spaulding, then minister of housing and a leading figure on the left of the party, sent his personal security team, which, properly armed, dispersed the invaders in short shrift. This early indicator turned out to be the truest warning of the violence that was soon to come.

Michael Manley, in his somewhat hesitant and uncertain attempts to undermine the colonial undergirdings of Jamaican society, was entirely unprepared for outright class war. The history of this period is yet to be told in a thorough, scholarly manner. My own experience suggests that the burnings and lootings—a sort of early ethnic cleansing practiced against partisan opponents—were first unleashed by the social and political opposition.[20] At first it was met with determined resistance and, aided by the state of emergency, Manley won the 1976 election with an increased mandate over that of 1972. However, following the 1976 victory, when open urban warfare was combined with economic destabilization, it proved to be overwhelming for the fledgling movement. Manley plunged from the heights of political success in 1976 to massive electoral defeat in 1980, though even then he was able to retain a solid 41 per cent of the electorate, despite months of incessant violence, a prostrate economy, and at least eight hundred dead in the streets.

The 1980 election took place in late October; by January, along with twenty other newsroom and current affairs workers, I had been kicked out of my job at the Jamaica Broadcasting Corporation (JBC)—the sole television station. The new Edward Seaga–led JLP government accused us of partisanship and kicked us out of our jobs, illegally, as it was later adjudged in court. Seaga was right in his perception that there was little support for his party in the newsroom, but in dismissing the entire staff he had breached the statutory requirement that the station should provide a regular stream of news and current affairs. We were later to be compensated, though in the economic situation of a rapidly devaluing Jamaican dollar, it amounted to very little.

Grenada

I was unemployed until June, when I got a message from WPJ General Secretary Trevor Munroe that the People's Revolutionary Government in Grenada wanted me to help develop their work in the media. I dropped everything and left for St. George's. Salary wasn't a question, terms of employment not an issue. The revolution called and I left. Grenada was something new. The youthfulness of the movement, even from a Jamaican perspective, was palpable. Maurice Bishop and Bernard Coard, the top leaders, were in their thirties. The next tier of leadership was largely in its early twenties. The existence of a radical state power without a powerful reactionary opposition seemed almost unreal and intoxicating coming from the near civil war trenches of Jamaica. There was much that was going on in the new situation that was positive. The work in education and the formulation of a new curriculum for primary and secondary students was rich and ahead of much of the Caribbean.[21] The annual budget debate, carried out through popular discussions surrounding the economy that took place across the length and breadth of the island, was rich and still provides a template for alternative approaches to a more participative economic democracy.[22]

However, there was a darker side to all this. I remember a political education meeting in 1983 chaired by Maurice Bishop at his home, when I mooted that I might be going back to Jamaica to pursue graduate studies. Someone said, jokingly, "Comrade, it is easy to come to Grenada, but not so easy to leave. Remember we control immigration." Of course it was a joke and one that I later discovered was oft-repeated to visiting supporters of the "revo." It nonetheless reflected the reality that after 1979, power and almost absolute power belonged to the People's Revolutionary Government (PRG). The United States had genuinely not anticipated revolution in Grenada,[23] and in the face of Caribbean resistance to their intervention had no concerted plan as to what to do. Further, there were the bigger geopolitical problems of Iran and Nicaragua, with both of these revolutionary overthrows occurring in the same year.

This temporary window of opportunity enhanced the PRG's virtual monopoly and helped encourage various abuses of power. Long before the crisis of 1983, there was the excessive detention of so-called "counters" (counter-revolutionaries) and the brutalizing of some of them by senior officers. While the number of persons detained during the tenure of the PRG is disputed, there is little doubt now that many instances were unwarranted.[24] There is a certain logic to governments that come to power by insurrection, and that is that they must protect themselves against imminent counter-insurrection. Certainly among the leading failures of the PRG was the failure to recognize that—in a country in which their support had been built on popular opposition to Eric Gairy's authoritarian tendencies—if support was to be consolidated, it would have to be on a foundation of enhanced democracy and not a new authoritarianism supposedly justified by the act of revolution.

The New Jewel Movement (NJM) also evolved a particularly rigid and mechanical version of Marxism-Leninism, very evident in the stolen party documents that still reside in Washington, D.C.[25] The NJM recognized that, with less than one hundred thousand largely rural people, Grenada did not have a proletariat. A conscious proletariat was seen to be a prerequisite for socialism. So, since socialism was desirable, the PRG would have to build a proletariat, which meant building factories—a daunting task at best, in a country with a working population of less than fifty thousand persons. This mechanistic, one-size-fits-all, building-block approach to politics and socialism signaled the doom of the nascent process. It is inappropriate here to reprise the crisis of 1983[26] except to say that the death of Maurice Bishop and his associates at the hands of some of his closest comrades, closely followed by the U.S.-led invasion, signaled not only the end of the Grenadian revolution but the rapid demise of an entire political movement that spanned the region and that had been born some fifteen years earlier in the moment of popular efflorescence that followed Walter Rodney's banning from Jamaica.

By Way of Conclusion

Caribbean Black Power was a movement for radical change of the social and economic system in the Caribbean. It borrowed critical elements from American Black Power, in some of its symbols and styles as well as the militancy that came to be identified with the mature North American movement through formations like the Student Non-Violent Coordinating Committee (SNCC) and later the Black Panther Party.[27]

Caribbean Black Power, however, possessed an autonomy rooted in indigenous movements for black self-assertion, such as Rastafari, and was sparked by a new generation of radicalized youth who keenly felt the failure of the states

across the region to fulfill the immense expectations invested in the nationalist and independence movements, including an end to racial privileging, real
economic and social improvement, and a more meaningful, more democratic
politics.

Caribbean Black Power existed in the world of the sixties and seventies, a
time of unprecedented international uprising. Thus the icons of that era—Che
Guevara, Ho Chi Minh, Huey Newton, Angela Davis, and Malcolm X—were
all inscribed on its masthead, along with other images of Marcus Garvey and
Haile Selassie, Trinidad's (and Grenada's) Tubal Uriah "Buzz" Butler, and of
course, the iconic figure of their generation, Walter Rodney.

However, among its many flaws, Caribbean Black Power was a male-centered movement, evident in the paucity of females among the leading personalities of the era and their virtual absence at the top leadership levels of the
various organizations throughout the Caribbean territories. Women were everywhere present in the "struggle," but they were almost everywhere subordinate to male leadership.[28]

It also borrowed substantially the styles, strategies, and tactics of its own
generation of insurgents—the Black Panthers, and the French and Mexican
students—in notions of frontal confrontation, of guerrilla warfare, of revolutionary overthrow as primary moves in any political engagement, as opposed
to the more moderate notions of struggling for trade union rights, universal
adult suffrage, and general elections that occupied the attention of an earlier
generation. The idea that all of these tactics, each deployed appropriately depending on overall national and international conditions, could be woven into
a more complex and nuanced political strategy, was largely alien to the generation of 1968. This political immaturity, and indeed naiveté, was the Achilles'
heel of the movement. It contributed to the failure of the Trinidad contingents
to overcome minor differences and build a potentially winning coalition; the
failure of the Jamaican movement to consolidate as an autonomous political
force; and the egregious failure of the Grenadian movement (albeit in its post–
Black Power Marxist-Leninist garb) to maintain political unity at all costs in
the face of daunting international opposition from the United States and conservative countries in the region.

Finally, the impact of the Black Power movement on the course of the region
is, at best, ambiguous. On the one hand, the overt and exclusive hierarchies of
color that characterized the colonial and immediate post-independence eras
have largely retreated. The discriminatory employment of lighter-skinned persons in banks and businesses, which Acton Camejo for instance saw in his
early seventies study of Trinidad,[29] is no longer immediately evident. But has
this changed the more fundamental underlying reality of ethnic minorities

dominating Caribbean economies? The answer is undoubtedly no. The Black Power movement heralded an era of black pride and identity, most evident in the Rastafari movement, which gained worldwide popularity in the seventies and into the present era. But the irony of the moment is that, while wearing the once denigrated dreadlocks hairstyle[30] has now become a fashion statement, skin bleaching in inner-city communities in Jamaica has proliferated, with practitioners arguing that lighter-skinned persons have better chances at employment and even attracting a mate.[31]

And at the macro level of Caribbean political economy, it is sobering to note how the more things change, the more they remain the same. In October 1980 the Michael Manley government, which came to power on the wave of the Black Power movement, was defeated in elections in part because of the strangulating effect of one of the earliest IMF structural adjustment agreements that it was forced to implement.[32] Four decades later, in December 2012, another PNP government, headed by a black Jamaican woman from humble, rural origins—Portia Simpson Miller—was entangled in negotiations with the IMF in order to hammer out an agreement that some suggest will inevitably undermine her popularity and that everyone recognizes will impose new hardships on the backs of the long-suffering Jamaican working people.

7. Lloyd Best, "The People," and the Road Not Taken in 1970 (2003)

I dream myself of participating in a massive Caribbean sou-sou. This is something understood by the whole population except for the governments who are intimidated by the propagandists of the IMF, and the economists, who are brainwashed by Ricardian economics into canvassing patterns of accumulation relevant only to England in the 19th century. Starting small as did the New World, we can aim ultimately to tie this sou-sou to the more pressing needs of the population in housing, education, farm improvement, financing of business and the like. The concept of 'casa money' can be modi-fied and extended to provide a margin to purchase the service of lawyers, agricultural economists, engineers, architects and all the other skills required to get the communities moving on their own resources, instead of waiting for Washington, New York and London to send money as our phoney develop-ment plans are advocating.
—Lloyd Best[1]

One Obscure Anecdote

The epigraph to this chapter is from Lloyd Best's "Whither New World?" I use it because, in compact fashion, it encapsulates everything that he has stood for: a deep concern for his country, always defined in a regional, rather than narrowly insular sense; an intellectually rigorous and consistent approach to scholarship; and an abiding respect for the innate creativity of the Caribbean people. This last feature in particular, segues into the purposes of this essay, which is an attempt to excavate the Bestian approach to that most difficult problematic: the appropriate relationship between leaders and followers, par-ticularly in those rare moments of unprecedented popular upheaval. The main suggestion is that Lloyd was among the few in his generation who consciously explored the existence of the problematic; and, though his tactical approach was in the final analysis found wanting, his proposals remain highly original and a fertile source of ideas for those who will be involved in the next round of popular engagement.

I want to start with a small obscure anecdote. Ivor Oxaal, in his little book on the 1970 Black Power revolution, *Race and Revolutionary Consciousness*,[2] notes a conversation in Britain with C. L. R. James, in which he asks what James thought about Best's decision not to join forces with Geddes Granger and the NJAC mainstream. James, as reported by Oxaal, responded with more than a little of the wagging finger. The reportage, for its authenticity, is worth quoting at length:

> When I had seen James on a previous occasion I had remarked, "Mr. James, history hasn't quite caught up with you yet, but she's running hard." James, seated on his dusty sofa below the inevitable print of Picasso's *Guernica*, answered with bright conceit: "I can't complain, Mr. Oxaal; can't complain." That was before April 21. My last visit found him in a different mood. The popular movement had been suppressed; his friend and former colleague in the 1966 Farmers and Workers Party, George Weekes, was in prison. What about the Tapia House Group, I asked. His reply was outspokenly critical. There had been a genuinely popular revolutionary movement in Trinidad, he pointed out. The duty of those who sought basic change, he implied, was plain: it was to join the movement in however humble a capacity.[3]

Oxaal subsequently traveled to Trinidad during the period of the state of emergency to do research on the book and met Lloyd from whom he, purportedly not to hurt the latter's feelings, withheld the bad news that James had been unreservedly critical of him. (Of course, Oxaal then published this anecdote in his book, making it available to Best, James, and his entire readership!) But, to continue the story, Lloyd's response was then solicited:

> I finally got together with Lloyd on Sunday. . . . Well, what about it, I asked; why hadn't Tapia joined the mass movement in its Black Power phase? His answer was, basically, that through its community activities, and links with other community organizations, particularly in the South, Tapia hardly considered itself divorced from the Trinidad masses. Tapia too, was being pressured by the regime. Tapia's chairman Syl Lowhar—the seemingly shy Guyanese seated next to me—had just gotten out of prison after having been detained in solitary confinement. So far as NJAC was concerned, that sounded good in principle, but the organization had been so chaotic, and the inexperienced new leaders possibly insecure over retaining their own status, that Tapia would have been able to contribute very little in any case.[4]

The significance of this is far greater than it might at first appear. While Lloyd did play a role on the fringes of the popular movement as a commentator, journalist, and later leader of the Tapia House movement, which was by no means insignificant, his absence from the center of the action, deprived the movement of his technical perspective on economics and more crucially of his unique, deeply democratic perspective on the relationship between leadership and the people. My own memory as a student at UWI in 1970–73 is perhaps useful. We had tremendous respect for our teacher Lloyd the academic, but thought of Best the political activist as a somewhat disconnected figure: a little too intellectual, a little too distant from the real movement of the people. All of us felt that he had an important role to play, but there was something missing. Evidently, Oxaal shared this perspective:

> Still, Lloyd Best, Denis Solomon and the others in the Tapia circle were too talented and dedicated to a social transformation to be debunked as "elitists." But Tapia House did not seem to be the right methodology for spawning local self-organization throughout Trinidad. Why had it made such limited inroads? On the face of it the scheme for multiplying such community centers seemed beautifully attuned to the neighbourhood milieux in Trinidad with their residual "nigger-yard" and steelband practice-yard traditions. Or were we—the middle class intellectuals who claim to understand Trinidad—constructing our prognosis on the basis of a fatally incomplete, utopian, concept of the revolutionary potential of the masses?[5]

While Lloyd's absence from the centers of decision-making may not have changed the course of the 1970 events one way or the other—these things are inevitably highly speculative—I suggest, however, that the virtual absence of his perspective meant that there was little or no resistance to the ascension of traditional charismatic, authoritarian, and centralist notions, which thrive in the ether of Caribbean politics and which merged quite happily with ideological assertions of the vanguard. This latter development would, of course, lead to damaging effect in the collapse of the Grenadian revolution more than a decade later, in 1983.

NJAC and Lloyd

So what were the differences between NJAC and Lloyd? Was it an ideological divide? There were certainly differences between NJAC's more race-centered positions and Lloyd's "indigenous thought" approach, but I suggest these were not substantial enough to warrant a distancing of the two trends. Both approaches shared a reflexive hostility to foreign domination; both were rooted in some notion of Caribbean authenticity accompanied by a cultural revolution in values and new approaches to living. Were they related to a clash of "doctor" politicians, in which Lloyd, the senior doctor and indeed teacher of many of the NJAC leadership, would be asked to enter the alliance as a junior partner, in an unacceptable role reversal? I have no doubt that this is part of the story. If one reads Winston Suite's comments in Ryan and Stewart on the monopolistic nature of the NJAC leadership, there may be more than a little reason why Best, with his fiercely independent perspective, might have sought to distance himself from NJAC, as well as reason why NJAC itself might not have been enthusiastic in having Best as a rival pole of power. It is worth quoting here from Suite: "C. L. R. James had a saying that you cannot organize a party autocratically and expect it to operate democratically, and that applied not only to NJAC but also to many other organizations. I am contending that NJAC did not create February 26, did not create any revolution, and that itself was an error. . . . The revolution did not belong to any one group or any one individual."[6] Since the appearance of Paget Henry's important book *Caliban's Reason: Introducing Afro-Caribbean Philosophy*,[7] one is also encouraged to search beyond narrowly defined structural or even ideological explanations to understand that political decision-making is powerfully influenced by the ego, and that an understanding of that ego's formation and cultural context is of the utmost importance.

Even so, I would suggest that this would only provide a partial explanation for the rift. The real answer, I suggest, is to be found in profoundly different conceptions of leadership and its relationship to the popular base.

If Suite's approach is to be given credence, then, on the one hand, NJAC lauded the people but believed and practiced traditional forms of strong leadership, while envisioning the organization as a sort of proto-vanguard:

> The leader of NJAC had a sense of messianic mission; he hears a voice from within; he identifies himself with everything as though revolution is not a drama. It was always "he did this" and "he did that" . . . NJAC behaved as though the movement was its own. It was said (by Kambon) that other people were not excluded. That is not true, and if you were invited to have any say, it was probably on their terms. They wanted you to do whatever they wanted to be done; they did not want you as an independent entity. It was an open secret that a state of emergency was coming, and we tried our best to prevent certain things from happening; but we were powerless to do that. I am saying that a lot had to do with the style of leadership.[8]

Best, on the other hand, had a profound distrust of middle-class leadership, as suggested in this Tapia pamphlet, written at the height of the popular upsurge:

> Revolution is not achieved simply by feeling the fraudulence and the brutality of the regime and reacting against it. Revolution, that is to say, fundamen-

tal change, is achieved when we also see so clearly through the regime that we can take the steps required, not to replace it with another tyranny, but to displace it with a better order. . . . This is not to deny that a time will not come when guns and violence may be necessary to overthrow those who have dispossessed us, in the last resort, by guns and violence. We know this very well, and our strong sympathies with current revolt arise from precisely this understanding. But we know, too, that the revolt must be reinforced by its own thought, must be informed by its own ideas. This blend between thought and action must be organic—which is quite a different thing from merely imposing plausible sounding "technical solutions." That procedure can only lead to the Strongman, the Maximum Leader.[9]

It was not the popular movement that Best feared, it was its inchoateness and the evident danger that unscrupulous leaders could take advantage of this: "The present crisis, with its threat of utter breakdown and chaos, shows disturbing signs of taking just that turn. For Tapia to join the revolt in the role of 'technical advisor' would mean a betrayal of our integrity and convictions. It would help to create precisely the kind of power structure to which we are fundamentally opposed."[10]

The alternative, outlined at this urgent moment in brief strokes, was a popular forum, to raise the political consciousness of the people and simultaneously undermine the political base for authoritarian leadership:

Our job is to continue to sketch perspectives for the entire nation and to engage in the community activity for which we are equipped. All our activity is public and no one is debarred from participating. Our members are also free to participate, wherever they will. If we do what we can honestly and well, the time will soon arrive when a broad "cross section" of the nation will be able to agree on the next step. At that point, thought and action will have achieved proper harmony, both within and between groups. And it will be power to the people.[11]

Lloyd Best and Garth White

Was this perspective one that had evolved primarily in relationship to the looming crisis, as Trinidad moved inexorably to a state of emergency? My suggestion is that this was decisively not the case. The origins of Best's positions on leadership, activism, and the relationship to the popular base can be found in a series of debates that took place in *New World Quarterly* involving Best, Garth White, Ivan Van Sertima, and others in 1967, long before the 1970 Black

Power revolution and just ahead of the Rodney riots in Jamaica. White in particular, reflecting a certain urgency in the mood of young, urban Jamaicans that would lead to the streets in a few months, severely criticized the New World Group for what he considered its armchair activism:

> What about New World? The days of sipping tea and airily contemplating "high issues" is past. It is now a question for survival for that same majority of people whom New World by positing social change as one of its aims should try to aid. We are told that "New World Group is an instrument of radical change in the entire Caribbean" (New World Pamphlet). The qualification was made that New World could only serve this end in the realm of ideas. There is to be no association at the level of the New World Organisation with other instruments more activist in orientation. . . . Some people argue that it is too early for action. Every revolutionary knows the danger of acting too soon. But anyone conversant with the politics of the situation, knows that this may very well be due to the inactivity of the intellectuals. They should have been in the field a long time ago if their concern was change. . . . Although New World constitutes perhaps the only articulate opposition to the classical policies of governments of the region, insofar as it is only at the level of speech that it is willing to act, it may be better to shut up![12]

White's answer to seeming intellectual complacency, interestingly, was not advocacy of a vanguard, or similarly centralist organization, but the immensely novel idea in its own right of the intellectual activist merging and becoming one with the people:

> But what is the use? It occurs finally, that perhaps mobilization is looked at in one way—as a call to arms. That certainly is not the only interpretation of mobilization. The other meaning—that of actively becoming one of the people and not in any patronizing way—cannot perhaps be understood by New World people. . . . Of living like the people and however slowly, rising with them, positively in this upward movement, also perhaps, cannot be comprehended.[13]

Best's response in "Whither New World?" does not so much frontally confront White's call for active involvement as it counterpoises an alternative mode of activism. It evolves through two phases: in the first, he underlines the importance of democratic organization as critical in the building of a new society and redlines the danger of one-man leadership of the traditional Caribbean variety:

> It is in being able to appreciate the circumstances of the other man that we

find the trick of building a democratic movement which is able to commit people not only to take power—which we could probably do now if we
wanted—but to put their shoulders to the wheel and reconstruct the country
after. The movements which come into office by trumpeting the new men of
destiny ("with the plan") soon find themselves confronted by "Napoleonci-
tos," who, too impressed by their importance to identify and work to remove
the causes of other men's opposition, become "damn vexed" and anxious to
chase opponents "hellout."[14]

In the second phase, he posits an alternative modality of popular engagement
in which the intellectuals act as a forum or tribune to stimulate popular consciousness and gestate new political institutions:

> In this context, the way in which New World can reform the role of the
> intellectual classes and intellectual institutions is by stating what it knows
> to be true whether or not this angers "the government" or wins us popular-
> ity and support. . . . What is more, when they go into the field, there is no
> guarantee that the various political organizations they will found will all go
> the same way. The achievement of New World will then be to have spawned
> a number of political movements with some common consciousness of the
> Caribbean condition. That, I might add, is a real "alternative." But groups like
> New World will still be needed to defend the community against the new
> orthodoxy.[15]

The last sentence above should be given special note, for Lloyd here envisions
New World not at all as an instrument to take power, but a sort of gadfly on
the body politic, a permanent opposition and source of new ideas in the face of
possible new bureaucratic clerisies.

Independent Thought

This position is fleshed out in mature form in Best's classic statement "Independent Thought and Caribbean Freedom," the purpose of which extends far
beyond the narrower question of leadership. Best engages in a wide-ranging
critique of Marxism, Western positivism, and Third World developmentalism.
Three themes can be underlined for our purposes. First, there is a danger in
Marxism, though present in all modes of "evangelical" thought, of doctrinal
authoritarianism. This approach leads to the death of democratic popular
movements and that undermines the emergence of a relevant Caribbean body
of thought:

The Marxists have been learning that we cannot approach the building of
a better society with prepared positions—or at least, with positions so fully
prepared that they lead us to suspend our discrimination as to context. But
the cost of the lesson is already high—for individuals, for nations and for
the world. The evangelistic character of the doctrine has helped to promote
quasi-religious confrontations both within societies and between them. This
crusading has, in turn, provided an excuse—if not a cause—for rival political
systems to restrict freedom and to resort far more to coercion than to political persuasion.[16]

The second is that social change must begin in a fundamental rethink of the
Caribbean condition from top to bottom:

By now it may have been possible to define that what I am arguing is that
social change in the Caribbean has to and can only begin in the minds of
Caribbean men. If we are to act for change, our philosophers and theorists
have first to understand how we relate to ourselves and to the wider world in
which we live.[17]

The third is that the act of rethinking is the first phase in the creation of a new
kind of Caribbean political movement:

One half of our intellectual classes is apolitical . . . The other half is clamour-
ing to lead the people. Like so many brave Bustamantes, their burning
ambition is to march before the masses. Confronted with the question as to
how, where and when, their answer is a stony silence. They too, one fears,
are merely idling their resources away in impractical rhetoric. It is being proposed here that being who we are, what we are and where, the kind of action
to which we must be committed is determinate. Action in the field, if it is not
to be blind, presupposes theory. To acknowledge this, is to set ourselves three
tasks. The first (task) is to fashion theory on which may be based the clear
intellectual leadership for which the nation calls and which it has never had.
The second is to conduct the enquiry on which theory can be soundly based.
This is what may be called, in the jargon of my original trade, the creation of
intellectual capital goods. Thirdly, we are to establish media by which these
goods may be transmitted to the rest of us who are otherwise engaged . . . to
use power effectively and wisely, we must, before we have gotten it, largely
have agreed with other men (or persuaded them) about what the issues are in

social change. In other words, it is the terms on which we have gotten power which will determine our ultimate use of it. So that the politics of the Trojan Horse, of the Vanguard Party, of the high priests who will seize power and then liberate the people, might well be the politics of conservation. In this respect it is of the same genre as that of men who now join the going regime in order to beat it, who accept procedures they claim to oppose in order to gain positions from which later, they hope, they will be able to change the rules. . . . We are well advised to abandon these dubious strategies. To change the world it is not enough to announce our intention to do so when we get power.[18]

Finally and critically, it is the intellectual exercise of rethinking and restructuring the way we live, from top to bottom, that will lay the basis for the alternative society, not the proverbial act of insurrection in itself:

> We have also, it seems to me, to demonstrate the sorts of changes we are aiming at by starting to live them now . . . so far as that is possible. Which admittedly, may not be very far. . . . To shift the focus into our mode of living, as an instrument of social change is to imply that real change is a comparatively slow process. It results from the patient and purposeful building which each of us undertakes in the personal sphere. It takes time and many rounds of fresh initiative to transform an individual breakaway into a social movement. I hasten to add though that I am not arguing for the Finland Station, neither am I advocating the inevitability of gradualness. Change is not at all inevitable. And besides, there are occasions in history when a quite radical break from the past is feasible.[19]

What Best attempts to accomplish, with significant headway if not complete success, is a seamless praxis in which the democratic methodology adopted for the investigation and rethinking of the Caribbean condition becomes, in itself, the template for the mode of functioning of the new political project. The act of theoretical investigation, in which the intellectuals are merely facilitators, not heroes or keepers of the book, serves to compress the distance between manual and mental labor. The intellectual, not only in his method of engagement but in his very way of living, becomes the embodiment of the new modality. The relationship between leadership and led is radically transformed, if not erased.

Indeed, and somewhat ironically in light of how this chapter begins, if one is to find the closest bedfellow to Best, it is probably the C. L. R. James of "Every cook can govern," or in his reading of the role of the people in the Hungarian uprising, where he lauds and validates their autonomous and independent activity. Where Best, however, differs with James is the space he gives to the local, the particular, as opposed to the broadly ideological and predetermined, in the argumentation and formulation of the popular theory.

This perspective, as earlier suggested, remained on the fringes in Tunapuna, as it were, and did not work its way into the heart of the popular movement, leaving its default: Strong central leadership with a charismatic leader. When the NJAC version of this failed in the peculiarities of the Trinidadian matrix to yield political power, the even more centralist and exclusive Marxist-Leninist version took over, with "success" to the north in Grenada.

Conclusion

So, was Best wrong to have distanced himself from the movement, or was James right that Best should have joined it in any capacity possible? Somewhat disingenuously, I want to suggest that they were both right in some respects and wrong in others.

Best failed to recognize what Gramsci elsewhere refers to as the shift from a war of position to a war of maneuver.[20] The popular upsurge after February 26 changed the normal rules of the game. The people were in the street and demanding new strategies for taking power and new approaches to the organization of society. The muse of history had, with typical irony, placed the movement ahead of its careful preparation, the proverbial cart before the horse. In such a conjuncture, James is right that there was little alternative but to enter the movement in however humble a capacity.

No one can say what Trinidad would have looked like with a Best playing a more central role in the popular movement, but we are clear as to what his marginalization meant. The absence of perhaps the most talented economist of his generation was one thing; more critical, I suggest, was the absence of a well-developed and persuasive approach on the role of the people in "popular" movements. The result was the default domination of middle-class leadership and centralism.

In conclusion, however, it is necessary to reiterate that Best was also absolutely right: what was required in that rare moment of the loosening of social and political integuments was a different kind of movement, turned bottoms up, in which Caribbean people begin to contemplate who we are; in which, through a protracted process of education and discourse, the people are brought to the fore, in which we lay the basis and give meaning to the classic

Jamesian phrase "every cook can govern." To this extent Lloyd was far ahead of his time.

But the enigmatic question remains to be posed: might he not have closed that temporal distance between his ideas and real time by a more organic involvement with the revolutionary movement in those heady days of 1970?[21]

Postscript

This chapter was first written as part of a panel sponsored by the Mona-based Centre for Caribbean Thought,[22] in a collective tribute to Best, as we celebrated his work at his testimonial conference. It also included papers by Rupert Lewis, Paget Henry, and Tony Bogues. The panel was subsequently expanded by the conference organizers to include an interesting paper by Kirk Meighoo, which argued, inter alia, that Lloyd's oeuvre was apposite to that of the Caribbean radical tradition. Indeed, Meighoo suggested that Best was closer to V. S. Naipaul and, more startlingly, the progenitor of modern conservatism, Edmund Burke, in his philosophical perspectives.

On the matter of Naipaul, aside from their shared iconoclasm, it is hard to discern the points of intersection. Best's entire life is characterized by an innate optimism in the capabilities of the Caribbean people and their capacity, if given the opportunity, to conceptualize and implement alternative and better ways of living. It is precisely the absence of this faith that characterizes Naipaul's painful and arduous engagement with the region of his birth. There is an absence of faith in the people, especially Naipaul's "negroes," though acerbic judgments are not by any stretch restricted to them.

For Naipaul the very geography, in its tropicalité and humidity, conspires to make the region, indeed the entire netherworld of the south, an area of darkness. Best, on the contrary, in "Caribbean Thought and Freedom," "Size and Survival," and in the very substance of his praxis, valorizes the Caribbean people and searches for the institutional means, the "politics" that will allow their creativity to find expression.[23] It is not that Naipaul's sharp eye and scathing prose do not capture truths about the West Indian condition, but that he fails to see beyond the immediate, and is therefore unable to grasp the possible.

The similarities with Burke are even more difficult to appreciate, and I await the full publication of Kirk's paper to see and contend with his argument. I suspect, however, that an approach to understanding this somewhat disturbing association may in part be found by comparing recent Caribbean political histories. During the question-and-answer time after the panel, at least three persons from the floor showed sympathy with Kirk's perspective and expressed a critical disdain for the rest of the panel, who were perceived, I imagine, as hard-core Caribbean radicals, despite varied presentations.

In subsequent discussions with Tony Bogues we both felt, though we could not fully explain it, that there was something peculiarly Trinidadian about this response. An equivalent audience at Mona in Jamaica, might not have agreed with our varied arguments, but the reflexive hostility to a radical perspective would not have possessed the same intellectual weight. This may in part have to do with the course of Jamaican political economy over the past twenty years. In this post-radical period, many of the ideological and institutional precepts of neo-liberalism have been adopted as gospel, yet the limited benefits are far outweighed by the sacrifices that the majority of the Jamaican people have had to endure. There is thus a widespread skepticism directed at the market and its corresponding sources of power.[24] In Trinidad, I suspect that oil and gas wealth and the complications of ethnic politics may have served to dampen, at least among intellectuals, the discrediting of the elsewhere moribund neo-liberal agenda.

But there is also another dimension having to do with reclaiming the no-menclature of "radical." Listening to Kirk and to the few comments from the floor, it was evident that the thrust of the criticism was directed at the check-ered history of Caribbean Marxism-Leninism and its sordid demise in the ashes of the Grenadian revolution.

If, however, the Caribbean radical tradition is considered as possessing a much longer and richer genealogy, going back to Berbice and Morant Bay, to Toussaint, Bogle, and Butler, to James, Elma Francois, and Garvey, then a com-pletely different approach is possible. At the heart of such a reinstated radical-ism would be three features: a determined resistance to empire; the willingness to speak truth in the face of power; and a consistent stance on the side of the poor, the exploited, and the disenfranchised. If these indeed are irreducible, then not only does Best stand on the side of Caribbean radicalism but is to be located close to its very soul.

8. Cuba from Due South (2012)

in 1962 a blue
mountain peak showed
a green horizon
to the unsuspecting eye.
standing spyglassed
staring blindly,
thought I'd see a dull grey line
tinged with red and barbed around/
the picture framing
captive portraits/
hiding from the sunlight/
ideologically bound.

the Caribbean green
surprised my eye
and set my mind
to thinking.

did the New York
Times twist the
Cuban line around?
were the refugees
from Trench Town's
equals or refuse
from Batista's hi-life
heroes of the torture
chamber, green backed
snakes of a long-lost
hunting ground?

In 1975, Marti's
children came back
into sight . . .

Fidel the workers
greet your
friendship/ those
who read between
the lines/ the unemployed
call out your name each day
on Kingston's boiling sidewalks
board meetings watch
our people rise
and plan their mutual fall in fear.[1]

I start this narrative dangerously and furtively, with my own poem, written in 1975 at a moment when the Michael Manley government was approaching the pinnacle of its engagement with Cuba. It was published four years later, as part of a collection in 1979, the year before the defeat of Manley's People's National Party (PNP) in the bloody general election of 1980. I say dangerously and furtively because it is always risky business to critique your own work, even if more than three decades separate you from the original composition. Yet, in searching desperately for material to illustrate this chapter, I was pleasantly surprised, aside from its literary (de)merits, how well it reflected my own evolving worldview of the Cuban revolution and my attitude as a partisan in its support, as it probably still does those of a generation of now aging Jamaicans.

Jamaica lies ninety miles due south of Cuba. Yet, as middle-class high school students growing up in the sixties, Cuba had been largely excluded from our mind's eye. When Alexander Bustamante won the 1962 general elections, defeating Michael's father Norman Manley at the polls, he declared unambiguously as he led us into independence that "We are with the West."[2] What this meant, in the anti-communist atmosphere following the U.S.-backed Cuban exile defeat at the Bay of Pigs, was that we were going to decisively distance ourselves from our closest geographical neighbor, despite the long tradition of cohabitation that has existed between the two Caribbean islands.

Cuba has always loomed large, if just over the horizon, in the Jamaican imaginary. When the Spaniards fighting a desperate rearguard action in the seventeenth century against the English invaders finally fled, it was to the well-defended, far more important and secure colony of Cuba to the North.[3] When in the nineteenth century Cuban independence fighters sought refuge, many came south to recuperate and rethink strategy for further engagement with the Spanish colonialists. Jose Martí lived for a time in exile in Jamaica, as did the outstanding General Antonio Maceo. Indeed, Maceo's mother, Mariana

Grajales, declared "the Mother of Cuba" by the prerevolutionary mayor of Havana in 1957, spent her final sixteen years in Kingston, where she was mourned at her funeral by many of the more than 1,500 Cuban exiles who lived in the city and beyond it.[4] It was these exiles who had brought their tobacco planting techniques to Jamaica, significantly enhancing the quality and cachet of Jamaican cigars.[5] Yet, certainly from the Anglo-Caribbean perspective, the most important aspect of the relationship was not the southward migration of Cubans, but the northward movement of West Indians to work, primarily in the Cuban sugar industry. Tens of thousands of Jamaicans, Barbadians, St. Lucians, and others, facing poverty at home, migrated to Oriente and other points, many never to return. They carried with them West Indian Creole languages, unambiguously British surnames like Hutchinson, Johnson, and Lewis, and a love for the game of cricket. On a visit to Barbados in the nineties, Fidel Castro is reputed to have stopped at a local cricket game and commented that cricket may be the sport that can unite the Caribbean. Perhaps he was reflecting on his childhood in the east of the island, where Anglo-Caribbean ways and the game of cricket are still alive and well.[6]

Yet, from my perspective as a youngster at the dawn of Jamaican independence, Cuba might as well have been in a different hemisphere. Yes, there were vibrant clubs in the east of the city with names like Copacabana and Adastra, and bands like Carlos Malcolm and the Afro-Jamaican Rhythms pumping out a new version of the ska beat heavily influenced by Cuban rhumba.[7] And everyone talked about Fidel Castro and his bearded guerrillas who had taken over Havana and driven many into exile, a few of whom washed up on Jamaica's shores, as many Cuban exiles had in the past. But beyond what seemed to be a few eccentric letters in the press, there was little apparent understanding or sympathy for Fidel's movement. Or so it appeared. Beyond Jamaica College, Hope Pastures, Mona, Half Way Tree, and the other boundaries of my comfortable middle-class existence was another world in which Fidel and Los Barbudos, in the few years of their ascendancy, had already attained iconic status.

Claudius Henry

In 1960, barely a year after the triumph of the Cuban Revolution, Claudius Henry, leader of a significant Rastafarian church with many supporters in the poorest slums of Kingston, wrote this letter to Fidel Castro, carried here only in part:

> Dr Fidel Castro, Cuba's Prime Minister.
> Dear Sir, this serves as a medium to inform you that we the undersigned

members of the back to Africa movement here in Jamaica is informing you on behalf of our leader Rev CV Henry RB, with 20, 000 members, are now organizing a government known as the lepers government.

Hence we wish to draw your attention to the conditions which confronts us today as poor, underprivileged people which were brought here from Africa by the British slave traders over 400 years ago to serve as slaves.

We now desire to return home in peace, to live under our own vine and fig tree, otherwise a government like yours that give justice to the poor. All our efforts to have a peaceful repatriation has proven a total failure.

Hence we must fight a war for what is ours by right. Therefore, we want to assure you Sir, and your government that Jamaica and the rest of the British West Indies will be turned over to you and your government after this war which we are preparing to start for Africa's freedom is completed and we her scattered children are restored. . . . We have the necessary men for the job. Since you cannot know Sir, without our information, the black people of Jamaica are with you and your government one hundred percent and desire to see Jamaica get in your hands before we leave to Africa.[8]

Less than six months after this letter was written, a small group of Jamaican and African American guerrillas, led by Henry's son Ronald, confronted British soldiers in the hills above Kingston, but were quickly outmaneuvered, arrested, and charged with treason. Ronald and his cohorts were found guilty of treason felony and executed; Claudius's life was spared, but he served a long prison sentence.

Henry's letter to Castro remains of immense interest beyond the failed strategy and tactics of his movement, because written into it is this iconic projection of Fidel Castro and the Cuban revolution into the imaginary of poor and black Jamaicans.[9] Claudius Henry's Rastafarian church, with its African identity and back-to-Africa ideology, was not asking Castro to join with them in a project of repatriation; rather, Fidel was being urged to assist and facilitate a revolution that would allow Afro- Jamaicans to depart this cursed land of "Babylon" forever. The notion that Castro would then rule over Jamaica and, beyond her, the British West Indies, was in recognition, perhaps, of his difference as a white Cuban, but simultaneously an honor bestowed on him as the staunchest defender of the poor. This notion of Fidel as guardian of the underprivileged is a subliminal though constant theme beyond the cacophony of official anti-communism and *anti-Fidelismo* that dominated the media and the Jamaican worldview in the immediate post-independence era. Thus, one of the best-known recordings of the renowned Jamaican band the Skatalites, with the mad genius Don Drummond leading on trombone, is titled "Fidel Castro."[10] And in the 1972 classic Jamaican film *The Harder They Come*, when Ivan (the fictional name for the real-life character Rhygin), wounded and wanted for shooting a policeman, is trying to make his escape, he is advised by his friend Ras Pedro to stow away on a boat to Cuba, where he will receive a positive welcome. The book with the same title by Michael Thelwell, unconventionally written following the appearance of the film, captures the dialogue, beginning with Ras Pedro:

> "Anyway him get a work pon a ship whe sail go Cuba. Im say you will get a big welcome dere." He could see that Rhygin was examining the proposal. It was the best chance that had come along. He was relieved to see a slow smile creep across his friend's face and into his eyes. "Yes, yes," he said beaming, as the possibilities struck home, "revolutionary to raas. Yes Pedro, mek we do it! An I could get treatment for me shoulder too."[11]

This blossoming realization on Ivan's part that Cuba might be a place of solace and recuperation, if only he could reconfigure and reinvent his act of individual violence into that of revolutionary gesture, speaks eloquently to the hidden text of Cuba as ultimate defender of the poor and line of last retreat for the downtrodden and rebellious.

Better Must Come

It was into this already quite elaborate script that the real Cuba parachuted when Michael Manley and the PNP came to power in 1972 under the heady social reformist slogan "Better Must Come." In one of his first major international appearances, Manley attended the Fourth Non-Aligned Summit in Algiers in 1973. Castro, a seasoned non-aligned figure, had offered Manley a seat on the Cuban plane to Algiers and he accepted. My mother,[12] who at the time was Michael's personal assistant, remembers the trip and the meeting with Castro as one of the high points of her career. Fidel was the gracious host and he, Manley, and a small group talked for most of the transatlantic trip about Jamaica's social and economic problems, the Cuban efforts to educate all her citizens up to the secondary level, and myriad matters of common interest. By the end of the Summit, Castro and Manley were not just allies but close friends.

Cuba no longer occupied the binary of either mythical icon or pariah, but entered the landscape of Jamaican politics. The first doctors came to assist clinics in rural areas where few Jamaican doctors wished to practice. Cuban construction workers started to build high schools and tertiary-level institutions in Jamaica. My first (and some might argue my last) experience of honest, hard labor was spending Sundays as a volunteer worker helping to build the Jose Martí Secondary School on the outskirts of the old Jamaican capital of Spanish Town. The school still stands near the Central Village roundabout and continues to take pride in its unique work-study curriculum, modeled on the Cuban pattern.

Since these early beginnings Cuban technical assistance to Jamaica, the Caribbean, and the world has, of course, grown exponentially. To mention just a few instances: some 1,500 doctors (116 from Jamaica) have been trained in Cuba, mostly on full Cuban government scholarships; over 1,300 Cuban nationals are working in some 22 Caribbean countries in fields as varied as medicine, engineering, sports, culture, and basic education; and Operation Miracle, which gives free surgery for cataracts and glaucoma, has treated over 33,000 people in the Caribbean and over 750,000 worldwide.[13]

Angola

The next phase of the narrative carries us from Jamaica to Southern Africa in the middle of 1975. Agostinho Neto and the People's Movement for the Liberation of Angola (MPLA) had led Angola to a bitterly fought independence from Portugal, but were faced almost immediately with significant violent resistance from Holden Roberto's National Front for the Liberation of Angola (FNLA) in the north and Jonas Savimbi's Union for the Total Independence of Angola (UNITA) in the south. In August, Savimbi, in Michael Manley's words, "made his pact with the devil"[14] and joined forces with apartheid South African troops in a determined dash to decapitate the MPLA regime and capture the capital Luanda. Cuba, in response to a request from Neto, responded by transporting troops across the Atlantic, many of the planes making their last refueling stop in Barbados. The South Africans were already 500 miles into Angola when they encountered the first regular Cuban troops in Benguela and Malange on November 14, 1975. Recognizing the quality and professionalism of the Cuban resistance, the South Africans hesitated and then retreated across the border into South-West Africa (now Namibia). The Cubans, in effect, played a critical role in saving this newly independent black African country from a future of thralldom to racist South Africa.

Manley, then prime minister of Jamaica and whose fate would become intimately intertwined with this moment, suggested the significance of the event in his book *Struggle in the Periphery*:

> It is impossible to overestimate the significance of this Cuban action. You
> have to go back to the days of Alexander the Great to find a parallel where

so small a country by feat of arms has affected so profoundly the balance of forces on a continent. If South Africa had installed Savimbi as its puppet ruler, it is safe to say that Rhodesia's Ian Smith would be firmly in control to this day. By now Zambia might have fallen, Namibia would be a lost cause, Botswana throttled, Tanzania and Mozambique impossibly isolated. Certainly Tanzania could not have lifted the yoke of Amin from the necks of the Ugandan people.[15]

The effects on Jamaica, as intimated, were also profound. Manley estimates that it was the Jamaican decision to support Cuba, rooted in a long-held solidarity with the anti-apartheid and liberation movements, that led decisively to U.S. intervention, destabilization, and ultimately electoral defeat of his PNP government.[16] The effect on the streets of Jamaica was equally profound. The Studio One session band the Revolutionaries produced a memorable 45 rpm record in 1976 simply titled "MPLA."[17] A subsequent long-playing album included other singles with African Liberation themes and sported the classic portrait of Che Guevara with his black beret and single star. The association of Cuba with the oppressed and exploited, who in Jamaica were invariably black and which had dated back to the dawn of the Revolution in 1959, was further rooted and cemented by the Angolan action. Cuba, Africa, liberation, and Fidel were all constituent elements of a narrative that predominated among significant swathes of the poor and dispossessed in Kingston and across Jamaica.

However, it was never the only narrative. Deep reservations persisted and continue today on the nature of Cuban democracy and on the harshness of daily life, particularly from the perspective of the unavailability of consumer goods in Cuba. In the lead-up to the 1980 elections, at a time albeit when anti-communist sentiments were on the rise, 58.3 per cent of the people in Kingston felt that Cubans were too involved in Jamaican affairs. While 53 per cent felt Jamaicans had nothing to fear from Cubans, a full 45 per cent felt there was something to fear.[18] When the then Cuban ambassador to Jamaica, Ulysses Estrada, responded undiplomatically to statements made about him by the opposition JLP and the daily newspaper the Gleaner by openly criticizing them, some 53 per cent of the people polled felt that he should be sent home, as opposed to 32 per cent who felt he should stay.[19]

There has therefore been no automatic acceptance of revolutionary Cuba in Jamaica and there is certainly no consensus on the Cuban political system. Indeed, one might argue that the spontaneous support that has accumulated for Cuba exists autonomously of local assessments of the Cuban political system. The existence of a single party, the spartan discipline of the ration system, and a controlled media are all opposite to the Jamaican social and political space, with its polyphonic individualism, sharp political contestation, and history of repeated, if often flawed, democratic political succession. In such a context, the persistence of the perception of Cuba and Fidel as bulwarks of solidarity on behalf of the poor is even more remarkable.

Michael Manley's Funeral

Michael Manley died on March 6, 1997, and his burial was witnessed by a throng of tens of thousands in National Heroes Park in Kingston. This story, however, is not about Manley but the arrival of Fidel Castro. Here is how the Gleaner's reporter described it in detail:

> However, apart from the former Prime Minister, for whose funeral they ar-
> rived, the day undoubtedly belonged to Cuban President Fidel Castro. Figur-
> ing initially in a security blunder which saw his car passing the main entrance
> to the church, Castro emerged a giant in the eyes of the Jamaicans present. .
> . . The Cuban President looked rested and fresh-faced. The imposing figure
> of the man exuded an aura which brought tears to the faces of the many
> Jamaicans present at yesterday's funeral service. The man whom many con-
> sider to be detached and aloof was not immune to the cheers and the signs
> of welcome as he turned to face the expectant crowd and raised his tightly
> clenched fist in the air, an action which elicited shouts of "Viva Castro." . . .
> When the Cuban leader arrived at the National Workers Union (NWU)
> on East Street, excited onlookers continued to praise him, calling him "the
> leader who is the only living Don," the "man who refused to bow" and "the
> rough neck boss."[20]

I choose Castro's overwhelming reception at the Manley funeral, but more so these final three comments from anonymous Jamaicans, to capture the essence of the Cuban, and more particularly Fidel's, place in the Jamaican imagination. For as I have suggested, it is not the Cuban social order that is of primary sig-nificance, nor is it at all the political system in itself, but rather the sense of au-dacity, of resistance of "facetyness"[21] to power that Cuba represents and that is of interest to the Jamaican street. David Scott[22] has suggested, using Foucault's insights on care for the self,[23] that the Jamaican *ruud bwai* or street gangster of the sixties, in his style, dress, language, and deportment, was a classic embodi-ment of resistance to power. Then, utilizing Scott, the Jamaican "massive"[24] has reinvented Cuba (and Fidel as her embodiment), as the ruud bwai writ large. For in a world with one overwhelming superpower with unimaginable nuclear and conventional forces, what greater solace can there be to the poor and downtrodden but the existence of a David state, embodied in an individual and one whom in manner and style is incorrigibly West Indian to boot, that looks Goliath squarely in his face and spits in his eye?

9. Grenada, Once Again: Revisiting the 1983 Crisis and Collapse of the Grenada Revolution (2012)

Remembering Grenada

The twenty-fifth anniversary in October 2008 of the tragic killing of Maurice Bishop and his associates and the subsequent invasion of Grenada, followed closely by the release on September 5, 2009, of Bernard Coard and the six remaining prisoners convicted of his murder, has been cause for a flurry of new conferences, papers, letters, and communiqués on the Grenada revolution and its tragic demise. Among the most outstanding were the conference and remembrance activities on the anniversary at the University of Toronto;[1] the April 2009 conference on the legacies of radical politics in the Caribbean at the University of Pittsburgh; Rupert Roopnarine's[2] reflective paper delivered at the Pittsburgh event; and Shalini Puri's panel[3] at the 2009 CSA conference, along with her graphic presentation of memory and the revolution first presented in Toronto.

Following the September release of the Seven, things picked up pace. Thankfully, many of the letters on the ubiquitous websites and email circuits, particularly those written by Grenadians, suggested wariness with the recriminatory monologues that have been typical of many reflections on the tragedy. Wendy Grenade's "Beyond the Legal Chapter: An Opportunity for Rebirth," for instance, suggests that the release of the Seven provides the opportunity for a genuine and open discussion on the strengths and weaknesses of the revolutionary period and calls for the assertion of humanitarian, socialist, and democratic principles for the future.[4] In a similar vein, Patsy Lewis's intervention distinguishes the reaction of Grenadians from those of other West Indian nationals who attended the 2009 CSA panel. She suggests that Grenadians have moved further along the road of reconciliation, while others seem to have been suspended at the traumatic moment of crisis in 1983.[5] Most tellingly, layperson Randal Robinson's letter to the Methodist Church's newsletter, suggesting genuine happiness over the release of the Seven, strengthens Lewis's conviction of a deep current of reconciliation on the island: "This day will be a bittersweet one for us Grenadians, but if we don't learn to forgive we will all perish through hate and there is no place in Heaven for haters."[6]

Countering Conventional Wisdom

Understandably, all commentaries did not comply with this tone. Jorge Heine, for instance, who had written one of the early forensic studies of the collapse of the revolution, wrote in his short piece "The Return of Bernard Coard"[7] that the "dual leadership" formula of the Central Committee (CC) was "utterly impractical and unworkable" and, in opposition to the common perspective that Coard and Bishop held distinct and contradictory ideological perspectives, that "no differences existed among the party leadership as to the pace or general direction of 'The Revo.'" These observations I entirely agree with and shall return to look at in more detail anon, but it is with Heine's substantial claim as to the fundamental cause of the crisis that I part company. He suggests that the entire joint leadership proposal was a ploy, as he puts it, "merely one additional move in Bernard Coard's long-term strategy to gain full control of the party and state."[8] In relation to the underlying causes—the impetus for Coard's actions—Heine proposes a "feeling of resentment" that the young Bernard had inherited from his father, Frederick Coard, who had written a book entitled *Bitter-sweet and Spice: Those Things I Remember*, in which he reflected on the fact that as a civil servant he was subordinate to people less qualified than himself. Heine proposes that this led to resentment and, by a process of transference, the son came to feel the same way about his seemingly perpetual number two position in revolutionary Grenada:

> The son identified with the father. Both bureaucrats to the core, who loved
> statistics and files, the colonial civil service was to the father what the party
> was to the son. The complaints by father and son about their fellow clerks
> or party comrades are also similar. The father's frustration is that he never
> made it to the very top of the colonial civil service, the officer of comptroller
> of income tax. Thirty years later, for Bernard Coard, the prospect of spending
> the rest of his professional life in the relative obscurity below the very top of
> the political structure, doing the legwork for somebody else, was surely un-
> bearable. To live in the shadow of Maurice Bishop, whose father was a martyr
> of the anti-Gairy struggle and who had once employed Bernard's father as a
> clerk, was unacceptable, as was working under somebody he considers his
> intellectual inferior.[9]

Heine's proposal is highly tendentious and eminently contestable. I am not equipped to delve into the claims of inherited psychological states and will leave that aspect of his argument for the experts to consider. However, the equation of the elder Coard's lowly status in the civil service with his son's number two position in the New Jewel Movement (NJM) begs an immediate response. From his return from Jamaica in 1976 until his resignation from the CC in 1982, Coard enjoyed inordinate influence in the party and, after the March 13, 1979, revolution, in the state. This was in part the result of a special and peculiar symbiotic relationship between Maurice and Bernard that was palpable and often noted in various commentaries. In what was a de facto form of joint leadership, they divided labor according to their respective talents and maintained a genuinely fraternal relationship between each other. Thus, Roopnarine in his paper recollects speaking with Maurice at the first conference in solidarity with Grenada in St. George's in November 1981. Just before leaving the event, Maurice pulled him aside and said: "If ever you come and I am not on the island, talk with Bernard. Talking to Bernard is the same as talking to me."[10] Claremont Kirton, then a senior economist with the People's Revolutionary Government's (PRG) Ministry of Finance, told me in an interview in the eighties that "I worked with both of them and each used to tell me, if I submitted documents to one, then ensure that the other had a copy. I had no reason to believe on the basis of what I could see that there was any kind of tension at all between them."[11]

I recall meeting Maurice for the first time in Jamaica in 1977 when he and Bernard were seeking support from the Jamaican government, and subsequently, though without any success, from the Cubans. They were ebullient and almost romantically optimistic about their hopes for success in their struggle against Eric Gairy. What was most evident, though, was the closeness between them. There was a distinct casualness that suggested friendship in their conversation and a naive willingness to share what seemed to me at the time very dangerous details of the covert aspects of the anti-Gairy struggle.

Coard, evidently, was no bureaucratic subordinate to Maurice. On the crucial decision to strike on March 13, Bishop was against it, but when the majority of the Political Bureau, including Coard, voted in favor, he supported the action wholeheartedly.[12] Maurice accepted Bernard's fine eye for detail, superior grasp of economics, and, for the most part, political judgment. Bernard, and indeed the entire party, understood equally that Maurice, while considered weak from organizational and theoretical perspectives, possessed a quality that was more valuable than any of these. He was the person with the common touch, with the ability to move crowds, to convert the PRG's policies into words that everyone could grasp, and the timing to use them appropriately. He was the charismatic leader and everyone seemed to understand this. Both enjoyed tremendous prestige within the ranks of the NJM; but if one were asked who in 1983 commanded the greater respect, I would have to conclude that it was Coard. This in some respects was inevitable. After March 13, Maurice had an immense responsibility for state and diplomatic work. Bernard had the Ministry of Finance, but with his meticulous organizational abilities he was able to manage this and also play the leading role in party organizing and building. Thus Coard's popularity grew among party cadres, while Maurice's consolidated and blossomed in Grenada as a whole and beyond.

On the question of longstanding conspiracy, I suggest that the Achilles' heel in Heine's and most of the conspiracy-based arguments is exposed when asked to explain how Maurice became so marginalized within his own party. One school, led by Fidel Castro, proposes that Coard and his clique were able, by subtlety and subterfuge, to eke out majorities in the CC and in the military leadership and this is how they eventually ousted Bishop.[13] This notion of a narrow majority primarily at the level of the leadership is a misrepresentation. In reality, when the crisis ripened, the overwhelming majority of the NJM was in opposition to Maurice, as was the leadership of the People's Revolutionary Army (PRA) and also the rank and file. This, I suggest, is because, unlike the rest of the population, they were privy to the twists and turns of the joint leadership discussions, voted, in the main, in favor of joint leadership of the party and had collectively come to the conclusion that Maurice had disrespected the party by breaching a solemn promise. Herein lay the root of the tragedy of October 19; for if the NJM had been divided and the PRA split, Maurice would have rallied the loyal sections to his side and, with the populace overwhelmingly in his favor, the jig would have been immediately up for Coard and the recalcitrant minority. But with a united party and behind them a united army facing the largely unarmed and now hostile population, the door was open for dangerous and deadly solutions.

As an aside to the notion of conspiracy, I recall an incident in August 1983 during my stint with the Ministry of Mobilization following Maurice's return from what would be his final visit to the United States. He had given a triumphant anti-imperialist speech to an adoring Brooklyn crowd at CUNY's Hunter College,[14] belying the view expressed by many subsequent commentators that his U.S. trip represented some sort of attempt to modify the PRG's previously uncompromising approach to the Reagan regime. On the instruction of the Political Bureau (PB), Selwyn Strachan, at the time minister of mobilization, called on me as coordinator of worker education classes to play the hourlong videotape of Maurice's Hunter speech at every class, as it was an excellent speech in defense of the revolution and showed the Comrade Leader at his best. A month later divisions would become apparent; two months later Bishop would be killed. This suggests that Strachan, arguably at the time the third most powerful man in the country and someone who would spend the next twenty-six years of his life in prison convicted and accused of killing Maurice

Bishop, was in August 1983 actively promoting him! This is a powerful piece of evidence and I am remiss, out of a desire to take my own story out of the narrative,[15] in not having used it in previous writings, for it throws significant amounts of sand in the engine of the conspiracy idea.

In preliminary summary then, in response to Heine's portrayal of Coard as being resentful of his second-best status as deputy leader, I advance the simple contention that there is significant evidence of a very comfortable and, one might argue, fulfilling relation of mutual sharing of leadership between both men, certainly up until late 1982. This questions (though in itself cannot dismiss) the notion of a power grab based on venal, long-term, psychologically fuelled factors. In relation to conspiracy, I advance the evidence of Strachan's position on promoting Maurice in August and ask for consideration whether the entire party, bar a literal handful, was duped by Bernard Coard's magic, or whether the overwhelming suit of majority votes in the party opposing Maurice on pivotal decisions suggests a different, more complex story that needs to be told, beyond the tattered notion of a longstanding conspiracy based on the will to power.

The second comment that I wish to contest is that of Barbadian lawyer and political activist Robert "Bobby" Clarke. In a sketchy letter,[16] though significant for its reflection of commonly held perspectives, Clarke makes a number of assertions, three of which are worth mentioning:

1. *Bernard Coard was not made deputy prime minister by Maurice Bishop's government but by an announcement made by his wife Phyllis on the radio.* This argument is new to me and I cannot recall seeing evidence of it in any of the numerous Grenada documents stolen from the country as spoils of war by the U.S. military in 1983. Taken on its own, it is preposterous. The NJM was an aspiring Leninist party that, as tragic events would prove, actually believed in the notion of democratic centralism as the best way to organize a party to lead a revolution. Phyllis Coard was on the CC, but she was not a member of the all-powerful Political Bureau (PB) and simply did not have the kind of influence to get away with such a maneuver. She would have been roundly condemned and the results of the enquiry would have surfaced in the captured and extensive party minutes.

2. *The OREL Conspiracy Proposition.* The pre-party Organisation for Revolutionary Education and Liberation (OREL), which Bernard Coard helped to guide before the revolution and which included key proponents of joint leadership like Liam "Owusu" James and Ewart "Headache" Layne, was never dissolved into the NJM but remained as a conspiratorial clique, guiding the plot and eventually displacing Bishop for Coard. This is also a part of Fidel

Castro's[17] argument, but it is equally fallacious. Again, there is simply no evidence of OREL in any of the minutes or the numerous microfiche documents. Elsewhere I have argued that on Grenada's physical and demographic scale, it is impossible to hide a conspiratorial organization for four and a half years of revolution in which virtually everything was public and social. Inhabitants of larger small countries like Jamaica or Trinidad, with populations in excess of a million are beyond a certain minimal threshold for an easy grasp of the phenomenon that it is impossible to keep an organization secret for very long in a micro-state with roughly 100,000 inhabitants. This applies not only to the OREL contention but to the general theory of a longstanding conspiracy. Further, the overwhelming demand on time which the party and revolution imposed on leading individuals would have made it virtually impossible for front-line cadres like Coard, Layne, James, Leon Cornwall, and John Ventour to maintain a parallel set of meetings, minutes etc. The OREL argument, I suggest, is simply not true.

The subset of this contention, however—that Coard maneuvered people onto the CC so that his people were on board and Maurice's were ousted—needs also to be addressed. While on first glance persuasive, the pattern of promotions and demotions ultimately belies this argument. Layne, James, and Ventour, formerly members of OREL, all found their way onto the PB after the revolution, while longstanding militants like Kendrick Radix and Vince Noel were demoted. But on closer examination, it was the chairman of the PB—Maurice Bishop himself—who was in charge, and he never once expressed doubts about this process. Indeed, on closer examination, the pattern is simply not consistent. George Louison, who had risen fastest in terms of state and party responsibilities, was never a member of OREL and ended up on Maurice's side in the final dispute; among the members of the PB who had been severely reprimanded by Coard at an earlier date for showing militaristic tendencies was Ewart Layne, an ex-OREL member and one of the final Seven convicts; and also among the Seven and in favor of joint leadership in the crucial September meetings were Selwyn Strachan and Hudson Austin, who were with Maurice from the foundation of NJM and definitely not part of OREL.[18] Louison himself, hostile to Coard and the other prisoners until his death, put the nail into the coffin of this argument in an interview with me in the eighties, when he said, "I think that over the years there were certain people who earned their position on the CC and there were certain people who could not function or pull their weight in the last days."[19]

3. *Bishop was ideologically different from Coard.* Clarke asserts that Maurice's position "differed completely in that the Grenada Revolution should take the path of a combination of Marxist economics and Caribbean based cultural philosophy."[20] Bernard Coard, on the other hand, was "influenced by his mentor Dr. Trevor Monroe [Munroe] of the Workers Party of Jamaica a devout Stalinist at the time,"[21] and Munroe "advised [Coard] on all the actions he should take to bring about a USSR style government."[22] My own residency in Grenada between 1981–83, consultations with Maurice Bishop on the editing of the weekly newspaper the *Free West Indian*, meetings with Bishop, Coard, and Strachan on planning the worker education classes, and subsequent extensive reading for my PhD thesis of many of the available documents on the Grenada revolution, lead me to the conclusion that there were few if any substantial differences on critical ideological matters between the two. Both had been nurtured in the Black Power and anti-war movements of the sixties—Coard and Bishop in Britain, Coard subsequently in Trinidad and Jamaica, and Bishop in the cockpit of action in Grenada itself. Both had subsequently passed through that transitional phase between 1970 and 1975 when a significant part of a generation of radical intellectuals shifted from various Black Power streams to an equally varied potpourri of "Marxisms."[23] Both had settled on a particular version of the doctrine that we might call, for want of a better coinage, "Caribbean Marxism-Leninism"; and the available evidence suggests that, on the key markers of ideology, theory, party strategy, and government policy, there were no discernible differences between them before 1983.

Caribbean Marxist-Leninists cannot simply be folded into "Stalinists," though they were subject to potentially dangerous authoritarian tendencies that derived in part from ideology but also from indigenous regional traditions of authoritarianism. From this perspective, to describe Trevor Munroe as a Stalinist or, even more startling, a "Pol Potist" is as wrong and equally mechanical as was Munroe's highly flawed praxis as applied by the WPJ. Stalin was a product of one of the worst forms of state oppression in the nineteenth and twentieth centuries—Czarist Russia—and he became its even more terrible alter ego. Despite the WPJ's propensity for dogmatic interpretations of Marx and its failure to gain political traction in Jamaica, to equate Munroe with Stalin is a travesty and a failure of imagination in not sufficiently understanding Caribbean politics and its inhabitants on their own historical foundations.

The irony is that Coard, Bishop, and Munroe were all part of the same post-independence, radical Caribbean middle-class intellectual stream. Neophytes in Marxism, the overarching problem is that they had all launched into the big league of revolution while attempting to master instruments that they had barely begun to comprehend. When crises overtook them, rather than seeking creative solutions the answer was sought in exegesis—the doctrinaire adherence to scripture. The peculiarity of the Caribbean turn to Marxism of the intellectual generation of the early seventies, then, is its immaturity and the dangerous implications that this held for popular movements that were advancing at a faster pace than were their intellectual leaders. This approach is more fertile ground for an enquiry as to the collapse than the worn notion of a "moderate" or "cultural" Bishop versus a "Stalinist" Coard.

Much work, however, still needs to be done on the WPJ's involvement in the Grenada events. There is a view held in Jamaica and elsewhere, and evident in Clarke's comments, that the WPJ was the intellectual and ideological mentor—the *éminence grise*—of the NJM. This was not the case; there was WPJ involvement, but again, a more complex picture needs to be painted. Coard had read Marxism-Leninism with a Workers Liberation League (WLL)[24] study group during his sojourn in Jamaica from 1973–76, and was therefore very close to the Jamaican party. An interesting footnote to this is that when Trevor Munroe, who was seeking to win port workers away from the traditional unions and organize them in the University and Allied Workers Union (UAWU), was attacked and seriously injured along with a group of students and union workers on the Kingston waterfront in 1974, Bernard Coard was physically present. He narrowly escaped injury by being further away from Trevor, who was the main focus of the attack.

This story, to my knowledge, has never been told and I speak from personal experience. I travelled to Grenada for the first time in July 1981 as a request from the PRG to come and help build the media there. After the 1980 Jamaican elections, the entire news and current affairs department at the Jamaica Broadcasting Corporation had been made redundant by the newly elected right-wing Jamaica Labour Party (JLP) government, which had considered us adversaries in the hotly contested 1980 election campaign. George Louison visited Jamaica in March 1981, and among his requests was that Maurice and Bernard wanted me to come and work. I packed my bags and left in July, without a contract and quite willing to work for free if that were the arrangement. I was somewhat surprised to discover that I had both a rented house that I shared with another WPJ comrade *and* a salary. This was a far cry from the bleak future that I faced in Jamaica as an unemployed television producer in a country with one government-owned television station and a hostile government that had just kicked us out of work. There were seven WPJ comrades in Grenada when I arrived, with an additional two coming sometime after. Four of us worked in the media, two in the commercial sector and one in the Ministry of Justice. Aside from the Cubans, whose numbers (boosted by hundreds of construction workers on the airport) far exceeded other "international workers," WPJ comrades were the largest group and the only one to my knowledge with an organized cell. We participated fully in the life of the "Revo," attending rallies, conferences, budget debates, etc., and all members of the group interacted regularly with the leadership of the PRG, though this was more in the nature of tiny Grenada than any special favor extended to us.

What was immediately evident was that the Grenadians had their own distinct organizational standards and a keen sense of national pride. During the Julien Fedon Maneuver a friend had loaned me a green army jacket, which I was wearing with some pride on the steps of Butler House when I was spotted by Ewart "Headache" Layne, then a colonel in the PRA. He approached me and discreetly indicated that, as an international comrade, it would be damaging to the revolution if I were photographed in even a partial army uniform. I removed the jacket immediately.

It is difficult to know the details of party-to-party relations beyond the material in the minutes reproduced in the Grenada Documents, Grenada Papers,[25] and the original papers and microfiche documents in the National Archives in Washington, D.C. However, this much is evident. In the weeks leading up to the October crisis Trevor Munroe did visit Grenada, as did leaders of other "fraternal" parties, including Michael Als from Trinidad and Rupert Roopnarine from Guyana. What Munroe said and what effect this might have had on the NJM leaders is difficult to discern, but I suggest that the crisis had its own dynamic, rooted in the tension between the two logics mentioned above. The WPJ almost certainly supported the idea of joint leadership, but it was not their invention and any notion of the WPJ giving directions to the NJM simply fails to understand Grenadians in general and the enhanced sense of pride and self-determination that blossomed with the revolution.

As to which side the WPJ stood with, I recall a poignant moment on October 19—the day of the killings on the Fort. I had returned to Jamaica to pursue doctoral work at the University of the West Indies on the political economy of the revolution. News of the crisis had traumatized Jamaica but it was particularly acute for me and the few Grenadians on campus, including my close friend and later wife Patsy Lewis. I had gone down to the WPJ office on Lady Musgrave Road, because I knew that there would be a close monitoring of events. News of Maurice's death was not yet confirmed when a female comrade on the WPJ Central Committee emerged and said quietly, "Maurice is dead. The CC is in charge." For my part, there was just a deep and bottomless sadness. For at least a year, I was unable to put pen to paper to write about Grenada. Gradually, with Patsy's help, I emerged from depression. Over time I started to do research, and the act of writing became cathartic. I finally finished the thesis *Social Formation and People's Revolution: A Grenadian Study*[26] in 1988.

In summary then, in 1983 the WPJ sided with the NJM's Central Committee on the matter of joint leadership, though its influence on the peculiar dynamic of events was, I suggest, limited. In the sweep of history, however, it paid the price for this as the party and many of the other left-leaning groups in the Caribbean failed to survive. I propose that while the WPJ did not instigate the joint leadership proposal, their support for the majority on the NJM CC gave the latter greater confidence in the decisions that had been taken and thus contributed significantly to the hardening of positions and the slide that eventually led to the collapse of the revolution and the discrediting of radical politics in the Caribbean for a generation or more.

Alternative Explanations

Having tried to counter some of the flaws that seem to be reemerging in the new round of debate, it is only reasonable to propose even the outlines of an alternative explanation. If Coard was not power hungry, whether via Freudian or Nietzscheian explanations; if OREL was not planning to overthrow Bishop; if Bishop and Coard did not have measurable ideological differences; then why was he placed under house arrest and subsequently executed in the most brutal, militaristic manner? I have tried to explain this twice before, in my doctoral thesis and in my book on Caribbean revolutions; but time provides new information and a new generation demands that old truths be restated. I restate my argument as a series of theses.

AUTHORITARIAN SOCIAL FORMATION

At its fundamental level, the crisis of 1983 was rooted in traditions of authoritarianism and arbitrary rule that the Grenadian revolutionaries inherited from Eric Gairy and the colonial regime that preceded independence. Gairy, in his hostility to local elites and desire for effective power, abandoned many of the tenets of liberal democracy including notions of habeas corpus, individual security, and free and fair elections. The British, despite the active opposition of tens of thousands of citizens, granted independence in 1973 in full knowledge of Gairy's predatory capabilities and what he was likely to do if given greater autonomy. Indeed, it is Gairy's arbitrary rule, fixing of elections, and terror, particularly from 1972–79, that undermined his initial legitimacy and laid the foundation for popular support for extra-constitutional activity.[27] The NJM, therefore, came to power with an ideological predisposition that disparaged "bourgeois" constitutional electoral government, but also in a social and political moment in which these forms had already been savaged by Eric Gairy. Nonetheless, it is the failure of imagination[28] of the NJM leaders as a whole not to recognize that, after having promised early elections at the birth of the "Revo," the longer they held on to power without restoring democratic rights and freedoms, the more they came to mirror the regime they had toiled so hard to overthrow. An early election, say in 1981, when anti-Gairy feelings still ran high, would undoubtedly have been won by the NJM, would have undermined internal opposition to the regime, would have blunted the effectiveness of U.S. and regional conservative opposition to the process, and would have given the PRG breathing space to consolidate its authority as it strove to complete the program of infrastructural development. Elections, however, are uncertain things and inevitably hold the possibility of defeat. The straightforward lesson derived from the Grenada tragedy must be that revolutionary and reforming regimes must be prepared to lose. If democrats believe that the people ultimately are sovereign, then they must be willing to concede governmental power when the voters are fed up with them, return to the hustings, and live to fight another day.

This, some might argue (quoting Lenin, perhaps), is a form of parliamentary cretinism and fails to take into account the overwhelming power of capital, the poisonous nature of the media, the machinations of the CIA, etc. As in Allende's Chile in 1973 or Sandinista Nicaragua, these all work together to ensure that reforming regimes are isolated, excoriated, and never return to power. All of these are substantial points, but the stark alternative is to hold on to power in the absence of the perceived wishes of the majority, which must, in the end, lead to the erosion and destruction of any notion of popular rule.

THE ROLE OF VANGUARDISM

The vanguard party, or "small group of highly trained and committed comrades leading and guiding,"[29] was a critical element in the success of the March 13 overthrow, but afterward became its dialectical opposite. In 1973 and 1974, when the newly formed NJM was able to put a significant part of the population on the streets and help shut down the country in opposition to independence under Gairy, it was still unable to remove him from power. The party was capable of bringing people into the streets but did not possess the capacity for clandestine work, nor did it have a military capability. In the new, more repressive conditions that emerged after independence, both of these were critical requirements for political survival and, with the erosion of free and fair elections, were vital for possible military victory over the regime.[30] Both of these features were incorporated after 1975 and served the party well as it built a small but effective armed force and planned for the possibility of insurrection. At the same time, NJM vanguardism led to a rapid fall in the number of active cadres and a highly hierarchical, top-down system of command, both inimical to popular democracy and empowerment. Inevitably, too, the NJM became a somewhat schizophrenic organization, with full members reading Marx and seeking to build a "real" Marxist-Leninist party while the popular base remained largely ignorant of all this, supporting the party mainly because of its history of standing for popular causes.[31]

In hindsight, the best solution after 1979 would have been a rapid transition from a clandestine "vanguard" structure to a mass organization, allowing all supporters meeting minimal requirements to join. This would naturally have to be accompanied by elections to posts in the party at all levels, conventions, and all the paraphernalia of democratic mass parties. This to the Grenadian "Leninists" and their wider Caribbean compatriots was heresy, but consider what would have been the result of a joint leadership dispute that went before a convention with—based on the crowds the NJM was able to mobilize from its birth—ten thousand party members. Coard would have had his fulsome say and so would Bishop. Which one of them could oppose a decision for joint leadership, carefully considered, if the vast majority of that ten thousand supported it? Which one could have even considered calling on the PRA for support if the overwhelming majority of the ten thousand party members, and quite likely the majority of the soldiers, felt that it was a bad idea?

This is wishful thinking, of course, but it is sobering to consider that such a discussion was entirely off the agenda of the party for four and a half years, only to be raised by Bernard Coard in the dying weeks of the revolution, when he proposed that there should be popular involvement in the selection and promotion of members to the party.[32] Finally, the small and narrowly constituted nature of the NJM was having a terrible toll on the health of its membership. Faced with the daunting task of running a state, maintaining an army, building a revolution, projecting tiny Grenada onto the diplomatic stage, and building the party, by 1983 most of the leadership and many of the members were groggy, sick, or demoralized from overwork and sheer exhaustion. This as a factor in the final demise cannot be overstated, for it undergirds the evident lack of judgment that prevailed among all the leadership in the final days.

RETHINKING THE CUBAN CONNECTION

What brought Grenada sharply into the crosshairs of the United States was its extraordinarily close relationship with Cuba. The Cubans played a central role in the building of the airport, new housing construction facilities, medical care, and the education of hundreds of Grenadian professionals, among many other gestures that went far beyond the boundaries of generosity.[33] Most urgently, the Cubans provided critical military support in the form of small arms and equipment in the uncertain days after Gairy's overthrow and the months and years that followed. In exchange, Grenada gave Cuba and her strategic ally the USSR diplomatic solidarity, most egregiously by supporting the Soviets in voting against the condemnatory UN resolution surrounding the 1979 Soviet invasion of Afghanistan.[34] This was a dangerous game, as it served to focus unnecessary attention on Grenada and strengthen the view of the hawks in Washington that, in a military standoff, Grenada would be a reliable and valuable asset for the Soviets in the middle of a presumed American sphere of influence. This was intolerable to the resurgent right under Ronald Reagan and underlined their expressed fear as to what the airport meant. As Assistant Undersecretary of Defense Dov Zakheim said after the invasion: "It mattered little whether the airport at Point Salines would be used primarily as a tourist facility, as the NJM claimed. It was the potential that the airport offered to the Soviets that worried American analysts."[35]

In retrospect, it is difficult to see how the PRG would have survived without a modicum of military assistance, and Cuba was the only regional force able to provide it; but a more tactical diplomatic relationship with Cuba might have blunted the arguments of the U.S. policy hawks. The vote on Afghanistan certainly was entirely unnecessary. Would the Cubans have stopped assistance to Grenada because of an abstention on this issue? It is unlikely. In the end, this is a moot question, as the murder of Bishop so egregiously tore down the last defenses against invasion that the subtleties of diplomatic maneuvering were made redundant.

CRISIS AND COLLAPSE: COARD'S RESIGNATION FROM THE CENTRAL COMMITTEE

If longstanding conspiracy, secret cells, and ideological differences are to be ruled out of the equation, then the crisis of 1983 can best be understood as a series of vignettes, each causally connected to the previous and each contributing to an accumulation of uncertainty and misunderstanding that was eventually irrecoverable.

The first stage was the October 1982 resignation of Bernard Coard from the Political Bureau, Central Committee, and Organizing Committee (OC), though he retained his public positions as minister of finance and deputy prime minister. Coard claimed that he was tired, that his influence had intimidated other comrades, and that they would now have a chance to develop. More pointedly, he outlined that the CC was "slack"[36] and that, in order not to have personality clashes with its chairman Maurice Bishop, he would rather resign.

What undermined the carefully developed synergy between Coard and

Bishop to the point that Coard felt he would rather withdraw than clash with the leader? I suggest elsewhere that this was part of a divergence that had been present from the taking of power in 1979, in which two logics competed against each other.[37] One was the logic of the vanguard party, in which collective CC decisions, arrived at by democratic discussion and then applied downwards in an authoritarian manner (democratic centralism), prevailed. The other logic was that of the national, charismatic leader, in which the leader typically is responsible only to himself and the crowd. Through the years in opposition Bishop adhered faithfully to the notion of democratic centralism, most strikingly illustrated in the previously mentioned decision to seize power. But as the months and years wore on, the influence of the second logic became overwhelming. It was he and not the NJM who the crowds saw as the embodiment of the "Revo." He was the individual who more often than not interfaced with heads of state and prime ministers. While the party remained the creaky, increasingly overworked, but necessary instrument that held everything together, to the general population of Grenada it barely existed. The very exclusivity, clandestine nature, and secrecy that had served it well in the preparation for insurrection was returning to haunt it.

Bishop was also prompted by his new Cuban associates, particularly in the diplomatic and military spheres who, in elevating their own particular experience of a single powerful leader almost to a law, encouraged him to act independently without reference to the party. This was the clear cause of the spat in mid-1982 (to my knowledge, the first between Coard and Bishop) when military comrades who should have attended an Organizing Committee (OC) meeting, chaired by Coard, were told that they were instead to attend an army meeting under Bishop's direction.[38] Yet Coard's absence from the leadership in this period seemed to have done nothing to assuage the tension between these two competing logics.

Faced with Coard's resignation, the CC, now entirely under Bishop's leadership, in response to Coard's reference to slackness sought not to rapidly increase membership by loosening entry requirements but to place the party on a more rigid Leninist footing, by increasing study times, tightening membership requirements, and intensifying disciplinary measures for supposedly recalcitrant comrades. Plans were also put in place to project the image of the leader more effectively in public events and in the media—undoubtedly the basis for the aforementioned directive to use Maurice's Hunter College speech in worker education classes. Thus in late 1982, under Bishop's sole leadership but with the full assent of all the CC members, vanguardism was intensified while simultaneously the tendency to imbue the leader with a heroic national profile was accelerated by the party itself.

THE NATURE OF THE CRISIS

The revolution was approaching a crisis early in 1983. The U.S. military maneuvers of March 1983, in which elements of the U.S. navy carried out activities in the Atlantic off the coast of Barbados, was for the first time met with a lukewarm response from Grenadians. A subsequent party survey of support for the NJM and PRG in some workplaces came out with frighteningly low figures,[39] which suggested significant disenchantment with the process. My own experience teaching worker education classes (primarily Caribbean and Grenadian history)[40] in a number of workplaces during this period reinforces the contention that support was tepid, though I had no basis to assess whether it had decreased over time or had always been low. I taught classes in the nutmeg factory in Grenville, to the road building crew on the Eastern Main Road, the Grenada Electricity Company workers, and civil servants in the Ministry of Finance. In all instances, attendees were polite and I developed over time an easy camaraderie with many of the participants. But many others, particularly in the ministry, did not attend, and among those who did there was a handful who were clearly hostile to the idea of spending an hour each week talking about Caribbean history and politics. At the time, it struck me that for a country in the midst of revolution, the atmosphere was far less militant than I had expected, indeed far less militant than the average trade union meeting that I remembered in Jamaica. Blurred by the intercession of a quarter century my own perceptions may be skewed, but they are echoed in the documents of the CC, where the dominant opinion, including that of Maurice himself, felt that the party had come close to losing its mass base.

This perspective was conveyed to a meeting of the entire party in July, in which the state of the deteriorating links with the people was raised.[41] In keeping with its earlier positions, the CC used the opportunity to blame party comrades for indiscipline and called again for a further intensification of Leninism as the only required solution. This time they were met with solid opposition from the members, led by the women, who argued that they were doing the best for the party and sacrificing care and attention to their children in the process. Members demanded and succeeded in getting the CC to reconvene and review its assessment. When the CC reconvened on August 26, there was extensive debate followed by the sobering conclusion enunciated by Chairman Maurice Bishop and noteworthy for its effect on the course of subsequent events: "We are faced with the threat of disintegration."[42]

Jorge Heine, Gordon Lewis,[43] and others have argued in effect that the revolution was going well in 1983 but that elements in the Central Committee argued that it was doing badly in order to promote their solution of joint leadership, effectively to elevate Coard and demote Bishop. This argument is predicated on the notion that Grenada had recently obtained IMF loans, many of the infrastructural programs were advancing, and that when the Point Salines airport was completed it would lead to significant improvements in the country's economy. This assessment is largely true, though it misses the effects of the international economic downturn of 1982–83 and the resultant fallout of loans, which even then had started to adversely affect employment. But the cutting edge of the crisis was not the economy, but rather the effective collapse of the party and the implications therein for the collapse of popular support and the revolutionary base. This was a point understood by the entire leadership and enunciated by Bishop above all. It required creative solutions; but the one that was eventually sought was fatally flawed, exacerbated the latent tension between the two logics of the party and of the leader, and eventually contributed to the catastrophe of October 1983.

THE JOINT LEADERSHIP DEBATES

On September 16, 1983, the Central Committee of the NJM reconvened to consider the crisis that, under the chairmanship of Maurice Bishop, it had previously recognized in August. Liam "Owusu" James started the meeting by criticizing Maurice's leadership style and calling for a new model of joint leadership, marrying the qualities of the two men, Coard and Bishop. Unlike the earlier meeting there was no unanimity. After much discussion, nine voted in favor; Bishop, Unison Whiteman, and Hudson Austin who had arrived late abstained; while George Louison voted against.[44] Bishop was obviously wavering and expressed the view that the masses might interpret this as a power struggle in the revolution. Despite the vote, however, he was asked for time and granted it to consider the implications. Nine crucial days elapsed until the party general meeting on September 25.

What happened in that period is difficult to piece together. I recall being asked seemingly out of the blue, by two party comrades in the corridors of the Ministry of Mobilization on Lucas Street, what I thought were the qualities of a leader. I found it odd and do not recall what my answer was, except that they seemed pleased with whatever it was I had said. I was preparing to head back to Jamaica at the time of the full party meeting on September 25 and recall hearing, from my house next to the St. George's lagoon, muffled sounds from the gathering further up the hill in Butler House.

The meeting itself appeared to be a decisive turning point. Bishop at first expressed his reservations couched in the notion that there was a distinction between the Party's Leninist perceptions of what a leader should be and that of the masses, who, he mooted, tended to build up a cult around a single individual. In this, he was expressing in his way the tension between the two logics, of the party and of the leader. Then, member after member spoke from the floor, overwhelmingly expressing support for joint leadership, but also love and respect for Bishop and Coard. Maurice was clearly overwhelmed and conceded to the views of the majority. The meeting ended with embraces between the two now joint leaders and the singing of the Internationale. Later, members of the CC gathered at Maurice's house for what seemed like completely convivial drinks and reflection.[45]

It is important to pause for a moment and take stock of the events up to this point. Aside from Maurice Bishop, only Louison and Whiteman on the CC had expressed reservations about the policy of joint leadership. The party members were overwhelmingly in favor and Bishop himself was genuinely swayed by the show of solidarity. Had he not been scheduled to travel the next day to Hungary with both Whiteman and Louison—the two leaders most opposed to the proposal—as part of his entourage, things might have turned out differently. I am certain that both worked to convince him that he should change his mind. However, the decisive moments occurred on his way back from Hungary, when the plane stopped over unexpectedly in Cuba. Maurice met with Fidel Castro and something emerged from that meeting which changed the mood entirely. Bishop's personal security chief Cletus St. Paul is reputed to have called Grenada and threatened the overall head of security that blood would flow on their October 8 return.[46] In response to this ominous threat, Coard did not go to the airport and meet Bishop as was the custom and indeed did not see him for four crucial intervening days.

On October 12, rumor hit the street that Phyllis Coard and Bernard[47] (in that order) were trying to kill Bishop, heightening tensions and leading to the first physical clash, when a militia group in Bishop's community St. Paul's sought to mobilize in defense of their leader and one member was shot. When the party, now in full emergency mode, met on September 13 to consider the source of this damaging rumor, Bishop denied knowing anything about it. He was immediately followed on the floor by Errol George, the second person in his security unit, who testified that the rumor had been given to him by none other than Bishop himself. When asked to respond to George's report, Maurice refused to answer. There was deep emotional distress and many comrades started to cry.[48] It is at this moment on September 13 that the integument between Maurice and the party was severed. From here onward, the overwhelming majority of the vanguard were convinced that their adored if still only human leader—who, despite his reservations, had stuck with the party over its desire to improve the profile and substance of leadership—had betrayed them in the worst possible way. For not only had he seemed to be retreating from the joint leadership agreement, but had opened the door to division and actually caused bloodshed by what they perceived to be his dangerous and unprecedented rumormongering. This is the setting within which the CC took the precipitous measure of detaining Bishop, which brought the inner-party conflict—without any prior warning—to the people for the first time and rang the death knell of the revolution.

The critical factor at this juncture, I underline once more, is not the overwhelming support of the masses for Bishop; this was a relative constant throughout the process. He was the leader and was revered then as he is in death today by many Grenadians of a certain age and beyond. Who, after all, to the man in the street, were these interlopers who were mere shadows in the wake of the great leader? What is critically new is the unity that now prevailed in the party, and by extension the PRA, whose officer corps was composed almost entirely of party members and candidates. Without the people, the NJM could not rule; but Maurice equally could not easily assume power in the face of a fully mobilized PRA and a party convinced that he had betrayed their trust by reneging on his own solemn commitment of September 25. This is what I have referred to as the "gridlock of events"[49] with each in its own moment contributing to a traffic jam of consequences, leading beyond these to his release on October 19, the decision to capture the fort, the clash with the troops sent to retake it, the capture of Maurice and his small contingent, and their bloody execution.

CONCLUSION

To attempt therefore to move beyond conventional wisdom and try to understand the crisis, I suggest that three critical decisions need to be brought to the fore:

1. *The fatal choice of joint leadership.* Joint leadership was not something entirely alien to Grenadians. Bishop and Unison Whiteman had been joint leaders when the two movements JEWEL and MAP merged in 1973 to form the NJM. Coard and Bishop were in effect joint leaders, though informally so, at the time of Gairy's overthrow. There were therefore some resonances in recent Grenadian history. But the time for such an approach had been eclipsed by the transformation in Bishop's role and standing after the seizure of power, and by the very nature of the NJM, which in its mechanical approach to the vanguard severely restricted membership and thus damaged its organic connections with the people. The average Grenadian who revered Maurice but knew little or nothing about the party could not be expected to understand that out of the

blue, for no apparent reason, Coard was now to be elevated to equal rank with Bishop. This, some have argued disingenuously, was an internal party matter and did not affect the profile of the state. Such a fine distinction could be expected only from persons who were fully aware of the party and its relationship to the state; this was by definition known only to senior party members. In the end, the perception was inevitable that Coard was being promoted, while Bishop's sole leadership of both party and state was being reduced.

2. *Reneging on joint leadership.* Those responsible for opening up suspicions and hostilities on the trip to Hungary and on the way back in Cuba must take their full share of the blame. Whether it was Fidel Castro, George Louison, or Unison Whiteman, or all three and others unnamed, the question must be asked in retrospect, what were they thinking? Anyone who attended or was given reports of the September 25 meeting, the show of solidarity and the sense of relief when Bishop consented to the sentiments of the majority, should have thought twice about the implications of convincing Maurice to renege on his initial agreement. This could only have been met by hostility and the closing of ranks, which is exactly what eventually happened. Was the plan to execute a military coup with the support of Cuban construction worker/militia-trained contingents, as Ventour and Coard[50] intimate writing from behind bars? This is a possibility, but would a seasoned tactician like Fidel Castro and the other members of the Cuban leadership have advised Bishop to resist the agreement on joint leadership if they knew exactly how united and determined the party was at this moment? I suspect not, supported by the fact that the at best lightly armed Cuban construction workers would have been heavily outgunned by the PRA with their artillery, light armored vehicles (BTRs), and heavy machine guns. The only feasible context for a military victory by Maurice over the Central Committee, supported by the Cubans, would be in a context where the party was divided and a significant section of its members and their comrades in the military had supported or been won over to Bishop's side. This was never the case. One distinct possibility is that Whiteman and Louison convinced the Cuban leadership that the party was an insignificant force and/or that support among its membership and, crucially, in the military was split. This is a consideration, as it would be a means of boosting their own image, when the alternative point is mooted that you have no support whatsoever in the party beyond your own small contingent. I shall return to this argument in the postscript.

3. *The decision to hold power after the popular rebellion.* The CC had one final option when they became aware that the crowd had freed Maurice from house arrest. They could have called it a day. Indeed, Bernard Coard had made it clear that he was packing and preparing to leave. This would effectively have ended NJM rule in Grenada, though whether Bishop would have been able to piece together a new party and resume power, in the fluid situation in which the United States had already begun to mobilize its forces in and around Grenada, is moot. It might however, have avoided the worst possible outcome, the terrible events on Fort Rupert. Had Maurice headed to the Market Square, mobilized a general strike, cut off power, and called for the resignation of the entire leadership, this new Maurice without the party might have had a fighting chance to succeed. But when the crowd headed for the fort, entered the compound, stripped female soldiers of their clothes and weapons, and threatened NJM members present, the die was cast for a military confrontation.

Over the past quarter century I have thought long and hard about the Grenada revolution, about my time in that wonderful little island, and about those sad and tragic days of October. I stand in utter revulsion to the all too real image of soldiers putting Maurice Bishop, Jacqueline Creft, Fitzroy Bain, Norris Bain, and their supporters up against the wall and riddling them with bullets. Whether Maurice's supporters had fired first and were responsible for the deaths of the four soldiers who were killed in the approaching BTRs or not, all conventions of war assert that combatants, once hostilities have ceased, have the right to be treated humanely. The execution of Maurice Bishop thus put the final nail in the coffin of the Grenadian revolution. The U.S. invasion, despite the fierce resistance from the PRA and elements of the militia,[51] was its inevitable coda. The story of what happened, however, is still to be fully told; and as a partial result, what I consider to be old misunderstandings keep recurring. I have tried to address these and to rethink and restate what I know to the best of my ability for a new generation and a completely different world.

Postscript: The Turn to Fort Rupert

Much has been made of the many commentators on the events of October 19, including myself, on Bishop's decision on the way to the crowd in Market Square to turn toward Fort Rupert.[52] The common wisdom, as intimated here, is that had Maurice and the group who freed him gone to the square to meet the very large throng waiting there, he would have lived. The military would have found it difficult to fire on an unarmed crowd, as was the case when they had come to force his release only moments before at his home in Mt. Weldale. From this tactical place amidst his natural mass support base, he would have been able to follow a variety of tactics, including, most potently, calling for a general strike, as was the case against Gairy in 1974. Why the decision to confront the military by going to the fort? Did Bishop, Vince Noel, Unison Whiteman, Einstein Louison, and the others who led the group (Einstein in particular, George's brother and the only senior PRA officer to break with the CC) expect that the show of popular force would divide the army and give them at least a fighting chance of success? If this were the case, the tactics followed once the fort was occupied should surely have been aimed at appeasement, discussion, and an attempt to win over potential converts who were wavering among the troops, militia, and party cadres who were present. Instead, the opposite was the case: soldiers were forcibly disarmed; female soldiers in particular were treated badly and at least two were stripped.[53] Party comrades who were present were forced to lie prostrate and were told that they would soon be "dealt with." Meanwhile, a small contingent of armed men led by Bishop's press secretary Don Rojas travelled the short distance to Grentel, the telephone company located on the Carenage, and gave instructions that all telephone lines be cut to the homes of CC members and the other St. George's military installation at Fort Frederick.

This is powerful evidence to suggest that Bishop and his closest supporters had made the clear decision that a military solution was the only possibility. The implications of this are clear. The Party and PRA in turn were fully aware of the events on the fort and it was now a matter of survival. Having conceded to the Crowd at Mt. Weldale, they were unlikely to concede again, as in their minds it was a matter of life and death. But did Maurice genuinely think that a largely untrained group of people off the streets of St. George's could bring the small, but reasonably well-trained PRA, with its BTRs and light artillery, to its knees? Bernard Coard and John Ventour, writing from their time in prison, suggest that at this stage Bishop and his supporters were depending on Cuban support. The 800 Cuban construction workers—a sizeable counterforce by any measure—in typical Cuban fashion were all trained militia and were prepared to be mobilized into a battalion led by Cuban officers, who were present in Grenada to train the PRA. If indeed the Bishop-led group expected such a force to rally to their side, it would explain not only the turn to the fort but also the uncompromising behavior once it was occupied. It might also explain the fact that once crowds had started to come onto the streets before October 19 and the CC sought to negotiate terms with Unison Whiteman, they were met with the sole response, "no compromise."[54] So why didn't the Cubans mobilize? I suspect, to return to a point made earlier in the chapter, that whatever discussions that occurred in Cuba (any Cuban participation is vehemently denied by the Cubans to this day) was predicated on a split party, or at minimum a split army. The Cubans understood that the united PRA was a small but committed force and certainly a match for a lightly armed Cuban militia. The likelihood of the decimation of their own units when it was known that they would face the PRA at full strength would have caused the Cubans to pause, thus settling the balance of military forces for the tragedy that was about to unfold.

PART THREE

Jamaican Journeys

10. Reinventing the Jamaican Political System (2001)

The new year began with a bang. On one particular Sunday in late January, these were among the leading stories in the *Gleaner*. The first, under the nonchalant headline "Higglers selling prescription drugs on the streets: Open-air pharmacy on the sidewalks," went on to note: "The illegal trade has left the health sector baffled about how so many different kinds of prescription drugs could have found their way on the street side, and concerned about the health risk involved in the abuse of these drugs."[1]

The second, under the photograph of a single telephone pole with a spider's web of hundreds of wires leading away from it, was, with more than a touch of irony, entitled "Wired Up": "This is one of many illegal wire connections in Majestic Gardens in the Kingston 11 area. The Jamaica Public Service Company estimates that there are 50,000 illegal wire connections island wide. Majestic Gardens is an inner-city community, but illegal connections are found in various forms in suburban and rural communities."[2]

The third, on page three, blared the decidedly more pedestrian headline "Thousands of drivers using expired licenses." The new computerized system for issuing drivers' licenses had encountered a number of glitches; these, a Mrs. Ferguson of Inland Revenue indicates, would soon be ironed out, but then she continues to raise the more burning problem of the proliferation of illegally issued licenses:

"We are talking about illiterate drivers," Mrs. Ferguson admitted.

She said drivers who have "bought" their licenses and avoided the standard examinations can hardly be singled out as long as their original documents were signed by legal authorities and they passed the reading test.

"If there is collusion at the depot, there is nothing we can do about that," she explained. "If the person can read, the department cannot tell whether the license is bogus."[3]

The fourth, on the front page, was the increasingly familiar story: "Gun Battle follows boy's abduction: Seven-year-old Jovayn Miller abducted. Abductors demand $10 million ransom."[4] In this instance, the good news was that the boy was later found and returned to his family unharmed.

Finally and also on page one, this now traditional, though also increasingly antiquarian report of the political clash, in this case intra-party, appeared under the head "Charles, Broderick in heated brawl": "The police confirm that they had to break up a stone and bottle-throwing incident in Summerfield Clarendon Friday night, involving Pearnel Charles, JLP caretaker for the Clarendon north central constituency and Dr Percy Broderick former JLP Member of Parliament for that constituency."[5]

These five incidents illuminate the state of lawlessness, anarchy, and drift that typifies Jamaica at the turn of the century.

My last visit to the Institute for Research in African American Studies at Columbia was in 1994, at which time I presented a paper entitled: "The Political Moment in Jamaica: The Dimensions of Hegemonic Dissolution."[6] The paper proposed that following the retirement of Michael Manley from public life in 1993 and the reelection of his People's National Party under the new leadership of P. J. Patterson, the island was approaching a social and political crisis point. The main suggestion was that Jamaica was in a state of hegemonic dissolution: "The old hegemonic alliance is unable to rule in the accustomed way, but equally, alternative and competitive modes of hegemony from below are unable to decisively place their stamp on the new and fluid situation."[7] In the absence of a populist organization to take the lead and carry events in a more radical direction, and in the context of an international conjuncture that did not seem to provide a permissive opening for radical action, three potential options were mooted. The first was the option of an increasingly authoritarian government, "within or outside the constitution";[8] the second was the possibility of a democratic renewal across the breadth of the Jamaican social and political terrain; and finally, following Marx, was an option described as the "common ruin of the contending classes," or widespread deterioration in the fabric of civil society and the state. In the seven years that have passed since then, this "strange, eventful history"[9] is unveiling an alternative that is altogether none of these, though it appears to include elements of them all.

The New Situation

The Zeeks riots of late 1998, in which thousands of nominal PNP supporters brought Kingston to a standstill in protesting against the detention of their "don," or area leader, and the April 1999 gas price riots, during which the entire island was under a state of siege from protests following budgetary increases in the price of gasoline,[10] signaled a new phase in the old situation. The decision by besieged police officers to ask the detained Zeeks to quiet his own crowd graphically indicated their recognition of the relative autonomy of the dons and of the downtown "massive."

Globalization and neo-liberalism, in drastically reducing the size and reach of the state, have undermined its critical power, which derives in part from the ability to distribute scarce resources. Simultaneously, new opportunities in the international illicit drugs market provided formerly loyal political enforcers with independent sources of wealth. Long before the 1998 crisis, the dons had begun to assume quasi-statal functions as disbursers of social benefits and, in the absence of a reliable and trusted police force, as law enforcers.[11]

Yet, even now, the process is incomplete. Though following the Zeeks events there was talk of an alliance of dons across traditionally antagonistic party lines, and while it is true that a truce of sorts has held in the inner city for three years, the party divisions have not altogether been erased. Thus, in the gas price riots of the following April, Zeeks's decision not to block the roads in downtown Kingston provided critical relief for Patterson's Government in its politically most vulnerable zone. Tactically, this was a brilliant move, for it both asserted Zeeks's autonomy and strategic importance and simultaneously sent the message that he was still "PNP," though now more an important ally than operative of the governing party. If this were at all in question, Patterson's visit to Zeeks's stronghold in Matthew's Lane immediately after the riots to thank him for his support should leave no doubt as to the not-so-subtle shift in power relationships. The Jamaican state is still in charge, but the cracks are opening up. Governments still rule, but increasingly require the tactical support of these area leaders.

The complexity of the present moment is evident in all this, for the devolution of power to warlords who gain wealth from illegal drugs and the substitution of the rule of law to the rough retributive justice of the streets, is an evident indicator of the collapse of the political and the approach of the Hobbesian "war of all against all." Yet, is there not a democratic kernel in the popular mobilization of people outside of the restrictive confines of middle class–led political parties? Is there not a certain laudable autonomy that derives from the shrinkage of the pervasive and bloodily divisive patronage networks of the seventies and eighties? None of this potential can fully bloom so long as authoritarian dons run these communities along the lines of feudal fiefdoms, but it would be remiss not to see the implicit potential for a democratic renewal in the collapse of clientelist politics.

The more evident feature, however, is the growth of the authoritarian trend. This is manifest in the police force and in the formation of a new crime-fighting group, the Crime Management Unit (CMU), under Senior Superintendent

Reneto Adams. Following a new round of particularly heinous crimes, the CMU was set up in the middle of 2000 as the latest special squad to combat violent criminals.[12] Adams's unit has already gained special notoriety for its viciousness and scant regard for procedure. In the most recent incident, seven young men were killed in a shootout in a house in Braeton, a lower-middle-class suburb southwest of Kingston. The police claimed that the victims were wanted in connection with, among other crimes, the brutal killing of a head-master of a local primary school. The police assertion that they approached the house and were fired on was hotly denied by citizens from the community. Firsthand reports of grieving neighbors and family members who heard the shootout suggest the degree to which notions of the rule of law have been abandoned and hint at a growing groundswell against the formal representatives of the system:

> Residents find cold comfort in relating the blood-curdling first-person reports of screaming youth, mercy pleas and explosions which dominate their conversations in the day, and their dreams at night . . .
> "I heard 'Gallus' (Andre Virgo) saying the Our Father prayer. He was crying and begging for his life. Then I heard a barrage of shots and he went silent," a neighbor said.
> "Mi hear an officer sey 'Weh yu a do bwoy? Try run?' and him seh 'No, officer, how mi fi run and yu a beat mi,' and then mi hear pure explosion and nothing else," another neighbor said.[13]

Any assumption, however, that these acts are carried out by rogue elements in the police force, without the support of a significant body of the citizenry, would be mistaken. In 1991 Carl Stone's polls showed a 56 per cent support for vigilantism in the adult population, while Harriott in 1994 found that among Jamaican police officers there was a similar support of some 54 per cent.[14] If there was any lingering doubt that support for summary justice exists in the very highest echelons of government, it would have been dashed when Justice Minister K. D. Knight—in an intemperate reference to violent gunmen and no doubt spurred on by repeated, highly publicized acts of wanton violence—blurted out in early January that they belong in the morgue. Indeed, it is fair to assume that in the face of repeated incidences of brutal and wanton violence, even as there is a growing and vocal constituency for justice and fair play, the constituency demanding law and order by any means necessary is also con-solidating.

The weakest tendency in all of this is that of democratic renewal. There is a significant increase in community organization. For instance, Munroe records the increase in the number of registered youth clubs from 596 in 1989–90 to 727 in 1996–97.[15] And there is a laudable return of elements of the middle class to political activism, evident in the formation of human rights groups like Jamaicans for Justice and the UWI's Faculty of Social Science's initiative to educate citizens in the inner-city community of Craig Town. But there has so far been no indication that these disparate tendencies might coalesce into some kind of new social movement. Indeed, with the gutted trade union movement struggling for its survival and a new round of immigration undermining nascent community organization, the likelihood of the emergence of new political formations in the short run is limited.

Certainly, from the perspective of the initiative of the PNP regime, there has been very little that can be considered as supportive of a new democracy. In the early years of the Patterson regime, there was an explicit trend to make government more open and politics more accessible to ordinary people. Thus, the important Values and Attitudes conference of 1994 brought hundreds of delegates together and sought to tap broad national opinion on the ways to address and overcome the evident deterioration in manners and civic responsibility at the social and individual levels. The prime minister's own "Live and Direct" meetings, in which he established face-to-face contact with people at the community level, was also a part of this period, as was the local government reform initiative out of Arnold Bertram's ministry. But, particularly since the cataclysmic financial-sector collapse of 1997,[16] these have receded across the policy horizon.[17]

With the eclipse of these initiatives is emerging the silhouette of a largely unimaginative regime presiding over a decade without any real growth[18] that, in deciding to underwrite the profligacy of the banking sector, has placed an enormous yoke of debt around its own neck and that of this and future generations of the country's citizens. The structural adjustment policy of high interest rates, further enhanced to deal with the fallout of the financial sector, has served as a blunt instrument to reduce inflation, but more damagingly has facilitated, in the context of an already skewed pattern of distribution, the transfer of wealth from the poor to the rich. Thus, the UNDP's 2000 Human Development Report sought to single out Jamaica along with Brazil and Guatemala as among the countries with the greatest income inequality, where the top fifth's share in national income is more than twenty-five times that of the bottom fifth.[19] The outcome of these policies, alongside the decline of any positive democratic initiatives in an already sharply divided community, has resulted in greater alienation, the feeling that the government does not care, that individual ministers are corrupt, and that the ship is rudderless.

Thus, even positive administrative moves, like Minister Peter Phillips's road repair and rebuilding efforts and the attempt to resuscitate a public urban transport system,[20] have so far had little discernible impact. The peculiarity of the PNP's third term is this: not everything that has been done has been misguided, nor has everything collapsed. The 1999 *Survey of Living Conditions* asserts that mean consumption has increased, there have been statistical improvements in education, and the health status of the population has remained stable; however, on the negative side, there has been a noted stagnation in housing development. When the sample was asked whether their personal economic situation had improved from that of five years ago, 55.4 per cent of all respondents said it had improved or remained the same, while only 44.6 per cent said it had worsened.[21] On its purely statistical performance, aside from the damning failure to grow and the hard inequality indices, it can be credibly argued that the government's performance, in a generally difficult situation, could have been much worse. The regime has certainly not presided over a total demise of the island's infrastructure, evident in the previously mentioned road-building program, the upgrading work on the two international airports, and the proposed new trans-island highway.

What then accounts for the anomie and drift in which solutions to the endemic violence appear as elusive as ever, where the sense of lawlessness and disorder pervades every sphere of life? What accounts for the dissatisfaction, where in December, the JLP for the first time in seventeen years nosed past the PNP in national public opinion polls and then defeated the governing party's candidate in a by-election in one of the PNP's safest seats in North East St. Ann?[22]

Many reasons can be put on the table for disenchantment and political dissatisfaction. Growing, blatant, and manifest income inequality is obviously one. The feeling that government does not care, that it has looked after itself, has become too fat, and operates at a bureaucratic level without reference to the popular base is another. There is also the simple factor of having been in power for the unprecedented length (for modern Jamaican politics) of twelve years. An entire cohort of new voters was six years old when the JLP was last in power. For them there is no memory of the authoritarian "one-manism" of the Seaga regime of the eighties. All their frustrations about unemployment, their real experiences of police brutality, and sense of alienation from an apparently uncaring society are focused on one known reality: the third-term PNP government.

But in order to further understand the present moment, we need to return to the notion of hegemonic dissolution, the disconnection by significant sections of the population from a formal order that they no longer feel any loyalty toward, that they perceive to have disrespected them repeatedly, and that is no longer able to provide many with the modicum of a decent livelihood.

At the economic level, the world built around remittances, the barrel, and Moneygram[23] has grown exponentially. Swathes of the island are now completely dependent on this avenue for survival. At the community level, the dependence on the don for social welfare has grown exponentially. At the level of justice, the disconnection from the formal justice system takes two forms: for those living in the downtown ghettos, the justice of the dons is increasingly more available and reliable. For those living in fortress-like middle-class townhouse complexes, a similar reliability is to be found in the justice and efficiency of the fast-response guard services. So, even in the context of some statistical social and economic reprieve, the disconnection from official society and the law has intensified. This, incidentally, is characteristic of many prerevolutionary situations, though a case is not being made for Jamaica being at this stage yet.

The Turn in the Global

The "election" of George Bush, in a deeply flawed electoral process in which he received fewer votes than his opponent Al Gore and would, by all indications have lost on a careful recount of the decisive Florida vote,[24] signals a new and dangerous moment in the neo-liberal globalization project.[25]

Like every stock market bubble before it, the particularly long ten-year boom, fuelled by the fanciful optimism in technology stocks, has burst.[26] In the harsh glare of the morning following the collapse of Nasdaq and then the Dow Jones, the weak fundamentals of the U.S. economy are once again on display for all to see. In an insightful article in *Newsweek*, Fareed Zakaria points out the growing U.S. current account deficit in which, in 2000, the United States spent $435 billion more than it earned, a figure roughly equivalent to 5 per cent of its GDP.[27] The United States, argues Zakaria, has sustained its profligate consumption habit because countries with "spare cash" have found it appropriate to invest in U.S. stocks and bonds. However, if, due to falling confidence, even a fraction of this infusion of resources were to stop: ". . . it could produce a spiral of problems: a falling dollar, which produces rising interest rates, which weakens stock prices and further slows the economy. Practically every time an advanced country has run a large current account deficit this vicious cycle has emerged."[28] In favor of the possibility of such a vicious cycle is the fact that this correction is occurring at a time when the Japanese economy is doing badly, the Asian economies have not yet recovered from the crisis of 1987, and the

German economy is slowing. Against this likelihood is the hegemonic position of the United States as the sole surviving world power and the peculiarity of the dollar as a world currency. Thus the United States is the only nation that pays its foreign debts in its own currency, significantly enhancing its ability to pay its way out of crisis.[29]

There is, therefore, no certainty that the vicious cycle will be the only option. Zakaria, however (in what, to be fair, is only an op-ed piece), fails to sketch the outlines of a broader and more dangerous secular crisis facing the OECD economies. Whereas in the period 1950–73 the OECD economies as a whole grew at an average annual rate of 4.3 per cent, in the period 1973–95 this shrunk dramatically to an average of 2.4 per cent. This was accompanied by a parallel contraction in the rate of growth of private consumption from 4.3 per cent in the earlier period to 2.6 per cent. The relative contraction in the rate of increase of final demand has led to a decrease in the propensity to invest in fixed assets. Thus, fixed capital formation, which grew at an annual rate of 5.7 per cent in the 1950–73 period, grew by only 2.1 per cent from 1973–95.[30] This secular decline in growth, consumer demand, and the demand for fixed capital has contributed to the exponential growth of investible funds without a clear productive "home." Thus, as Shutt suggests: "Inevitably this coincidence of a continuing steady growth in investible funds with slowing demand for both fixed investment and working capital meant that a significant proportion of such funds were channeled into speculation—that is, into assets that held out greater prospect of gain from capital appreciation than from earnings yield."[31]

If this fundamental reality is used as a point of focus, then much in recent global economic policy can be discerned. The WTO project, for instance, can, through this lens, be understood as an attempt to find a means of kick-starting the Western world by opening up new markets and somehow stimulating stalled consumer demand. And yet, by shifting wealth from the wage sector to capital, neo-liberal economic policies have, if anything, exacerbated the problem. For, while more markets have been liberalized and while the marginal productivity of capital has improved, failure to stimulate growth and the shift in the distribution of wealth means that there are fewer consumers able to exercise effective demand for the increased production of goods and services. Therefore, with mountains of idle cash and insufficient productive enterprises to invest in, there is the even greater possibility of speculation to put this cash to "work." The result has been the proliferation of a variety of strategies, from the privatization of governmental assets, to junk bonds, to futures markets, to derivatives, and the promotion of so-called emerging markets. The outcome of what is essentially a massive speculatory bubble, based not on production and growth but the artificial inflation of stock prices without foundation, must ultimately, as Shutt bleakly suggests, lead to a correction of epic proportions:

> All the [new financial] devices . . . are ways of artificially boosting the rates of return on investment in response to unrelenting pressures to push them ever higher. Theoretically, of course, this problem might be resolved if these forces were somehow to abate, so that the market rate of return could fall to a more readily attainable level. However, history suggests unambiguously that the only way this can happen under a competitive market system is by means of a destructive "crash" rather than an orderly retreat to lower returns. . . . Hence a sober assessment of these various financial stratagems must surely conclude that, for all the undoubted ingenuity of the financial manipulators, it can only be a matter of time before the forces of gravity reassert themselves and the reality of systemic financial failure must be faced.[32]

The implications for the developing world in such a context are both well known and well documented. Countries caught in the quagmire of indebtedness find themselves in a permanent cycle of structural adjustment. Primary goods exporters, traditionally "price takers," have now become "policy takers"[33] as well. The policies of "opening up," export orientation, and privatization that they have been forced to adopt have not, for the most part, led them onto autonomous paths of growth, but rather:

> These countries must forever "export themselves out of debt," no matter that they are competing with a dozen other countries exporting the same coffee or cocoa—or shoes and shirts. No matter that domestic food production is declining, as export agriculture is favoured over food crops and natural resources are pillaged for instant returns, with long-term damage to the environment. The export of commodities, both primary and manufactured— because labour intensive manufactures are the new "commodities"—is a way of exporting cheap labour. . . . The increasing volume of these developing country exports have assisted the United States to maintain the long boom of non-inflationary growth in the 1990s. This is the one sense in which "globalization" has increased wealth—in a unidirectional way. . . .[34]

For countries like Jamaica, then, caught in the fakir's stare of neo-liberalism, the primary policy question has been how to follow the rules of the game more thoroughly, how to make the state "lean and mean," how to find that elusive niche and how to take full advantage of the purported comparative advantage with the economic wealth and well-being that should naturally follow. The dismal result has been a collapse of the productive economy, the exacerbation of the gap between rich and poor, the impoverishment of the countryside, a massive export of talent, the undermining of the state, and, in some instances, an all-class crisis or process of hegemonic dissolution.

Above all, there has been a patent failure at the governmental level, from the "loyal opposition," and from most leading intellectuals and representatives of civil society to heed lessons perceived by Michael Manley[35] two decades ago: that capital follows its own logic of accumulation; that powerful nations set the rules and look after themselves; that economically powerful states are always the advocates of open markets even when, as with the infant United States, they were premier defenders of protectionism in earlier phases; and that it is therefore absolutely necessary to begin the debate on alternative futures against and beyond the false horizons of neo-liberalism.

There is, of course—present bear market aside—no certainty that a cataclysmic crash will occur. Unprecedented growth (barely understood as a phenomenon) along the lines of the fifties and sixties could come again and so effectively utilize the capital overhang as to undermine a devastating correction. But if there is any substance in the foregoing analysis—and the general unease with which leading Western commentators view the present bear market would tend to support this[36]—then the need for an entire rethink of the Jamaican agenda is not only necessary, but any delay in doing so would verge on the criminal.

Thinking Outside the Box

The postwar system based on competitive parties dispensing scarce benefits and led by heroic leaders is moribund. The populist party, whether in its nationalist PNP garb or its private sector–oriented JLP form, is dying. The results of the St. Ann North East by-election suggests the degree to which Patterson's PNP, which was elected to power eight years ago with genuine popular support, has lost credibility. In the absence of a genuine alternative, popular support, in the Jamaican tradition, will flow in the direction of the default alternative, the JLP, though it would not be surprising if the overall turnout at the next general election were the lowest in Jamaican history, as disenchanted voters stay away from the polls in droves.

If the present situation can at least in part be accounted for in the alienation of people from politics, then what is urgently required to correct the dangerous drift to the rocks of nihilism and authoritarianism is a popular renewal. The ideal alternative would be a new, democratic federation of local and grassroots organizations that would unite a critical mass of Jamaicans around a politics based on participation, inclusion, and transparency. Such pure forms, however, seldom present themselves. An alternative, in keeping with the country's two-party tradition, might well be a critical alliance of well-thinking men and women across party lines that would allow them to maintain their vestigial party loyalties while beginning the conversation that will lead to a new formation.

Such a national alliance might evolve into a government of national unity, but the danger in that possibility is the reassertion of politics from above, without the limited safeguard of an opposition in waiting. Such an outcome would not only prolong the politics of the last half-century, but possibly entrench an even more dangerous monopoly, when what is desperately required is a new popular politics from below.

The first task on the agenda of such a formation would have to be a constituent assembly of the Jamaican people at home and abroad. The year 2002 marks the fortieth anniversary of Jamaican independence. What more important milestone to begin the debate around a new social contract, this time discussed and ratified by the people, than this important date! The notion of "abroad" is particularly stressed in this formulation, as roughly half of all Jamaicans live overseas. They are "taxed," as it were, by their remittances to their families on the "rock," but they have no representation. The slogan of Jamaicans overseas must be the classical one of "no taxation without representation." Any new contractual arrangements must include the input of the diaspora and must make constitutional arrangements for its inclusion beyond the conclusion of the initial debates.

The constituent assembly would not be a one-off meeting, but would involve a series, perhaps hundreds of meetings in Browns Town and Above Rocks, Brooklyn and Brixton, to discuss alternative agendas and ultimately to mandate delegates to a national convention to debate and ratify a new constitution. Issues on a possible agenda should not be preempted, but if the experience of the last forty years suggests that there needs to be a thorough democratic reform of the political system, they might include:

1. The appropriate constitutional arrangements to undermine the constituency-based spoils system and the ruthlessness endemic in a winner-take-all election. This might include discussions around proportional representation to partially or completely replace the first-past-the-post system, the question of term limits, the matter of the recall of non-performing representatives, and the entire question of the transparency of elections, with particular emphasis on electoral funding arrangements.

2. The devolution of power from the center to the communities. This process in a de facto sense has already begun, as the patronage system has receded. To the extent that people have real local control, the process of reconstructing community can genuinely take hold.

3. The political inclusion of overseas Jamaicans in any future electoral arrangement, whether by transparent overseas voting procedures or otherwise. The obverse of this is the development and fostering of powerful lobbying groups in the main immigrant centers. The strength of the overseas Jamaican and Caribbean community can only be manifest to the extent that there is active organization at the community level with close ties to natural allies in the African American community and among environmentalist groups, organized labor, and elsewhere.

4. The unprecedented extension of democratic procedures into all spheres of government, including: a. A publicly elected commission to oversee the operations of the police and the military. b. The opening up of the budget debate to the nation by a discussion at the grassroots level months in advance of the preliminary budget and the election of mandated delegates to a national budget debate. c. The further extension of the principle of democracy and accountability into key national institutions, such as the election of direct delegates to the Public Accounts Committee to sit alongside members of the house and similar directly elected representatives to sit on the Committee of the Ombudsman and one of the Contractor General.

5. The initiation of a debate around national social and economic imperatives. These must no longer be subject to secret negotiation by international agencies with no responsibility for the survival of the Jamaican people. Thus, a national food policy that would ensure a strategic agricultural sector, educational and health policies that would have twenty-year plans, subject to variation only on the basis of democratic decision-making, would all be high on the agenda.

6. The beginning of a conversation on the role of international capital and its character. Such a debate cannot begin after a crash when it is too late, but must raise some of the critical issues mentioned in this paper with a full recognition that capital and the market is not only far from benign, but is, as we speak, in deep crisis, with profound implications for the future of the world.

7. The proposal of a federation of the Caribbean peoples. The island-by-island sovereignty of the 1960s is as moribund as its accompanying political system. The Caribbean is our natural region, geographically and culturally. It is here that we need to look for the forms of solidarity and cooperation that will give us more meaningful space, allow us to develop while taking better advantage of economies of scale, and allow us to play a more coherent role in world affairs.

There is no fear to be found in a federation based on democratic principles, in which power is devolved to the grassroots and in which cooperation is based upon principles of respect and the search for mutual benefit.

To many, these proposals may seem far-fetched and tendentious. They are meant to be. For too long we have played it safe by restricting ourselves to thinking only within the box. That box, the stultifying paradigm of neo-liberalism, is now in tatters. We need to begin thinking outside of it. It is therefore as appropriate as any to end on a quote from Kari Levitt, who has recently sought, in a similar vein and spirit, to address the elements of a program for the Caribbean and all developing countries beyond the failed neo-liberal paradigm: "You may dismiss this wish list as idealistic. Perhaps so, but it is certainly more realistic than the assumption that the world can continue on its present path without courting disasters more terrible than any we have yet visited upon ourselves. Without dreams, nothing is possible. Without hope, there is no future."[37]

The collapse of Jamaica in its present form, whether by slow burn or more rapid denouement, may be closer than we think. Jamaica, I submit, shall be democratic or not at all.

11. Imagining the Future: Rethinking the Political in Jamaica (2006)

Beyond the Season of Adventure

In the closing pages of *Season of Adventure*, his powerful novel of the postcolonial Caribbean, George Lamming makes a stunning about turn. Suddenly and without warning, the author appears to abandon the storyline and speaks directly to the reader. Powell, the bête noire of the narrative, murders Vice President Raymond. In a long soliloquy, the author admits that Powell is his half-brother. Until the age of ten, they lived together, but then their lives diverged. The author enters a life of scholarship, education, and privilege, while Powell remains in the world of the tonelle, of the drum, of the traditional culture. Finally, our author admits his deepest fears that Powell's murderous act was related in some way to his desertion of his brother and of their shared peasant roots: "I shall go beyond my grave in the knowledge that I am responsible for what happened to my brother. . . . For I have never felt myself to be an honest part of anything since the world of his childhood deserted me."[1]

Season of Adventure appeared in 1960, a full two years before the beginnings of Anglophone Caribbean independence, yet Lamming's prescience fully grasped the dilemma that would emerge in the postcolonial era. The solidarities of the anti-colonial moment, of a single purpose, a single mother as it were, are replaced by the uncertainties of political responsibility in a world whose parameters of power and privilege remained substantially unchanged. Were the new postcolonial leaders, who had been given their mantle of authority, based precisely on their distance from the Powells of this world, capable of reaching out to the denizens of the tonelle and bridging the divide across which their very privilege was built? Would even the radical reformists, like Lamming's new leader Kofi James-Williams Baako, find the wherewithal to rise above their cultural horizons and psychological centeredness and address frontally the dire social problems of the broad populace? *Season* ends inconclusively, for Lamming is not entirely convinced that even Baako, with his rhetoric and style, can transcend the limitations of his own training.

Four decades later, Lorna Goodison writes about her island, describing it as a "Swimming Turtle":

Black rubber tire smoke
Belching from its breath
And machete chops
And gunshots on its carapace

Goodison's conclusion, perhaps the necessary indulgence of the poet, is the terse but plaintive shout: "Cry out O terrapin."[2]

Forty years after the measured uncertainty of Lamming's prose, we have the frantic lifeguard appeal of Goodison's poetry. What is the true measure of this short journey of independence and what do the mileposts tell us about where we really are?

Failed State or Tunnel's Light?

There are two competing views about the state of Jamaica in its fifth decade. On one pole, the pessimists invoke the notion of a failed state with the nightmarish images of the Hobbesian war of all against all, the Yeatsian mantra that the center cannot hold and things fall apart. Undoubtedly, there are features of the present moment that give grist to this particular mill. The murder rate in itself, accompanied by the remarkably low threshold required to commit murder; a pervasive sense of incivility in all social spaces; frequent incidents of barbarism on the roads, in the prisons, and in the home, all support this view. Yet surely, the keen observer must make the distinction between the truly failed instances and the state that is merely in crisis. In the former, the normal facilities associated with civilization such as reasonably functional utilities, a basic security force as a final resort, a system of law, and a working economy have all ceased to exist. This might describe Somalia or, for a certain time over the last decade, Sierra Leone. But it is hyperbole and bombast to suggest that Jamaica, with all its known warts, even with the multiple "gunshot wounds over its carapace," is close to any of these instances, involving the utter abandonment of the civil and the absolute reign of fear.

On the other pole of perception are the optimists, who invariably point to light at the end of the tunnel. The statistics, they argue, suggest that things are improving. If only we tighten our belts a little more, boost the reserves to that crucial comfort level and hold strain on all the macro indicators, then investments will flow, real growth will resume, and good times will follow. The statistics, while certainly not all heading in a favorable direction, do suggest that there has been some movement in recent times. Poverty indicators have generally improved; unemployment, with some reversals on the way, is marginally down; and there has been growth, however anemic, which is better than none at all. Unfortunately, this is the moment when Disraeli's famous quip that there are "lies, damned lies, and statistics" must, perforce, be exhumed. Marginal movement is better than no movement at all; yet incremental changes, if they lead to the complacent assumption that we were on the road to some sort of East Asian miracle, would be deceptive at best and dangerous at worst.

The basic requirements for an East Asian–style takeoff are decisively missing in today's Jamaica. Many commentators wrongly assume that the success of Singapore, Taiwan, South Korea. et al. was predicated on some prior insight into the advantages of neo-liberalism with its entire baggage of privatization, downsizing, marketization, and the like. Nothing could be further from the truth. Almost to the letter, most East Asian "tigers" followed the Japanese route to success, which required an intimate cooperation between the private sector and the state and an equally close if unwritten contract between these two entities and the broad mass of the citizenry. The latter contract in particular, was achieved through a complicated process of give and take. In Taiwan and South Korea extensive, one might even say revolutionary, land reform programs preceded the phase of rapid growth. This laid the foundation for more balanced urban and rural development and simultaneously, gave large swathes of the population purchasing power and access to capital, creating a significant market for goods and laying the foundation for an indigenous entrepreneurial class. Closely following this was an unprecedented human investment in education, housing, and health services, and, perhaps most critical of all, the emergence of labor regimes that assured relative job security. The combination of these prior investments in what is loosely referred to as human capital, together with the existence of a Confucian culture in which unquestioning loyalty is given to the benevolent father, lay the foundations for a social pact that allowed for high savings, low consumption, and high productivity. This ultimately led to rapid economic growth and the Asian miracle that is so often lauded, but so often for the wrong reasons.

Jamaica, I submit, is not even on the same playing field. Decades of structural adjustment and belt tightening have undermined the little trust that might have existed between the state and capital on one hand and both to labor on the other. Free-trade policies, if largely imposed from the outside, have eroded agriculture, and along with it the once-vibrant rural culture. Investments in education and health, while by no means entirely wasted, have been insufficient to redress the structural problems in these vital sectors. Most critically, not only is there no social pact commensurate to the experience of East Asia, but the society is moving in an opposite direction. The crucial statistic here is migration. The massive and continuing outflow of people is the surest indicator of dissonance in the Jamaican social space. Jamaica, over the past two decades, despite the heralded benefits of remittances, has lost, according to a recent IMF study, more than 13 per cent of its entire GDP to migration.[3] This alarming statistic does not even try to calculate the social damage incurred in the collective loss of the most active, educated, and talented citizens at the peak of their careers. The toll of absent fathers, mothers, Sunday school teachers, role models, and caregivers is immeasurable.

Hegemonic Dissolution

If not failed state or light at the end of the tunnel, what then describes Jamaica today? In 1994 I offered the notion of *hegemonic dissolution*[4] to illuminate an earlier phase of the phenomenon that I still think largely describes the state of the nation.

At the political level, the loyalty that was an integral part of the old patronage networks (what I refer to as the pact of 1944)[5] had been eroded over time. The ability to grant largesse was undermined by the downsizing of the state. Party enforcers, particularly in so-called garrison communities, became more autonomous from the party leadership due to newer independent sources of financing through drugs, protection rackets, and the like. The state's role as an employer had weakened as privatization gained momentum and poor people, the clients in Carl Stone's system of patron-clientelism,[6] were less dependent on it as they went forth to establish new trading circuits in the Caribbean and beyond. The middle classes too, as a source of employment and role model of social progress, became less important, as relatives, legal and illegal, gave many among the poor new, independent resources for survival via the ubiquitous barrel and Moneygram.[7] More critically, the social mores of postcolonial Jamaica, rooted in an Anglico-Methodist morality and a Creole nationalism—best exemplified in the slogan "Out of Many One People"—no longer satisfied, nor did it provide the reflexive touchstone for national unity.

Twelve years later, I think that much in this assessment still holds true, with at least one crucial adjustment. Kingfish[8] may have disrupted some networks, and various peace initiatives in violence-prone communities have been laudable, but the overarching structure of violent and semi-autonomous communities, verging on becoming states within a state, remains largely intact. The breakdown of social cohesion, by its nature a far more difficult symptom to calculate, I nonetheless suggest has proceeded apace. Far more quantitative and qualitative work needs to be done, but the spaces to search for the relevant signals include the rate and particularly the character of murders, the rate and character of domestic violence and violence in schools at all levels, and in the most overt expressions of popular sensibilities in the popular music and the dancehalls. If one listens carefully to the dancehalls in particular—and it is not difficult to do so—then it is evident that the volume of anti-establishment lyrics has been turned up to full watts in the past decade. More so, despite the existence of countervailing trends, the proliferation of "shotta" lyrics and other expressions glorifying a certain kind of violence, is, even if given the most optimistic, metaphorical reading, important as a symbolic indicator of a new turn.

The critical adjustment is that in my 1994 analysis there is a clear underestimation of the durability of the state, its institutions, and its integuments. The assessment made then of "the collapse of the political project" has simply not happened. The political project, if understood to mean the parties, the state apparatus, and its institutions, is alive and well, albeit less powerful and rampant than it was a decade ago. The present moment, therefore, is characterized by an invidious standoff, in which the people, broadly defined, are more disconnected from the old national project, while the political, as exemplified in its institutions, remains battered but relatively intact. This is, perhaps, accounted for in the fact that the popular disconnection has taken the form of a cultural revolt, a physical leaving of the national space, a psychological and individualistic de-linking from the formal economy of government and private sector. If this popular revolt had taken an institutional form, i.e. the proliferation of alternative anti-systemic parties and movements, then Jamaica today might be looking at a prerevolutionary situation. Or alternatively, if the political institutions had collapsed or become increasingly moribund, then the genuine option of the "failed state" might have been a closer description of contemporary reality. As it is however, the present moment takes the form of an impasse, in which the formal exists alongside the informal, the police co-exist alongside legal and illegal protection agencies, gated communities and gated hotels seek to wall themselves off from the presumed hordes without, and violence proliferates at the margins. Such a state may experience episodic economic growth, but this is unlikely to be sustained. Periods of advance will inevitably be followed by periods of retreat, as profits are taken and exported or individuals choose to export themselves. In such a space there is, essentially, no entrenched commitment to the common ground, no sense of an intergenerational imperative to stand and build, no need to save as everything is in the here and now, and hyper-consumption is therefore the only rational choice.

A World of Uncertainty

All of this is compounded by a world of uncertainty that surrounds our swimming turtle in the Caribbean pond. Much of the local debate on globalization, the New World Order, and the like takes a form in which Jamaica is portrayed as the lone bystander on the side of the tracks as the rushing train flashes by. The options are posed as either standing back and vegetating while the future progresses nicely, or hopping onto the fast track of the globalization train where good things await. In this admitted caricature, there is no critical reading of the tentative and fraught nature of globalization itself. It is my proposal, though unfortunately there is little room for elaboration, that what we loosely call globalization is not just a problematic set of policies (though this is the case) but the symptom of a deeper malaise in the entire world system of production. The central problem facing the world economy has, surprisingly, little to do with inadequate production, but, on the contrary, excess capacity and the inability to absorb it. Modern capitalism has managed to produce more and better goods and services than ever imagined in the history of humanity, though it has achieved this while ravaging the environment and without finding the wherewithal to sufficiently expand the demand side of the equation in order to create buyers for its huge productivity. The failure to do this has led to increasingly desperate iterations of production in search of cheaper commodities and cheaper fuel at the expense of the already compromised environment. It has also encouraged the emergence of secondary and tertiary markets in paper options and swaptions, weighing onerously on the body of the productive sector. Most of all, there is the highly publicized rush for the cheapest labor sources—the infamous race to the bottom—which is the ultimate counterproductive move. The shift to the cheapest sources of labor, if imagined globally, may increase output and productivity, but at the expense of global demand, exacerbating the very conditions that initiated cause for concern. This, however, is looking at the problem globally, thinking like a state and not from the perspective of the individual CEO whose primary concern is the board of directors' bottom line. It is to the detriment of the entire world that over the past two decades the business of business has been equated with the business of the state. The urgent need now is to reintroduce the business of the state as a legitimate concern—not the old governmental approach of opacity and hierarchy, but a new one of openness and genuine democracy, both nationally and internationally, in order to effectively face the dire straits that await us around the next bend in the river.

Faced with a moment of hegemonic dissolution in which the glue of the nation is in terminal meltdown, confronted with a highly uncertain global future in which the twin crises of overcapacity and poverty cohabit with the decay of the environment, what are the options for Jamaica, that small turtle in the big pond? In order to escape from the meandering certainties of this particular quagmire, there is first the need to recognize its existence, and second, the need to devise a strategy that will address the fundamental cause—the dissolution of the flawed but relatively effective social consensus, the pact of 1944, that prevailed in the first four decades of independence.

The Way Forward

The problem facing Jamaica is not just criminality; nor is it simply the need for macro-economic belt tightening; nor is it that we have got our educational policies wrong; nor is it that the PNP or the JLP is in power and one or the other must be shunted aside. Many of these may provide a partial explanation of the problem. It is certainly true that no plan for the future of Jamaica can be realistic without a determined attempt to combat crime and violence. It is equally hard to conceive a workable economic model that did not in some way seek to shift patterns of expenditure away from consumption to increased savings. The same applies to education, and it would be a foolhardy analyst who would suggest that a determined educational policy is not central to any model of future development. I submit, however, that the central feature, the one ring to rule them all, is the fact of hegemonic dissolution, the breakdown of an old consensus and the failure to construct a new one.

Consider for the moment Barbados. In 1994, faced with a deteriorating economy and the possibility of IMF-imposed structural adjustment policies, Owen Arthur's newly elected Barbados Labour Party avoided this well-known and socially damaging path by adopting a novel "social partners" approach to national development. The Barbadian model has worked, at least to the extent of avoiding the worst ravages of structural adjustment and returning buoyancy and growth to the economy. Barbados is not Jamaica, however, and the traditions there of national capital, derived from the old settler pattern, are very different from the tradition of the absentee planter fronted by his local attorney, which developed to its highest levels in Jamaica. Equally, the Barbadian working people, with no physical space to expand beyond the boundaries of the plantation, are psychologically very different from the Jamaican experience of free villages and potential escape to the rocky hillsides. A new Jamaican consensus could not look like the Barbadian model, but would have to cut much deeper. It would require compromises on all sides and perhaps an entirely new way of perceiving Jamaica. In the end, however, it would release a wellspring of pent-up energy, presently wasting away or channeled into illegal endeavors. It would give us the best hope of national and collective survival well into the twenty-first century.

The central tasks in such an approach would be to find pragmatic forms of collective mobilization and accompanying institutional arrangements that would:

• forge a national strategy based on a critical alliance between those social forces with an interest in the development of the island space of Jamaica, the region, and its diaspora;

• establish new parameters for economic and political involvement that would give an unprecedented number of people a stake and interest in the project;

• engage in a thorough revaluation and national acceptance of Jamaican popular culture as a central avenue for inclusiveness and unity;

• form the broadest regional alliances to increase the space for international negotiations, economic maneuver, and social living;

• link the diaspora in a tighter network with the local population through the forging of new economic and political linkages; and

• avoid frontal and potentially debilitating confrontation with the hegemonic power, through strategies of regional unity, mobilization of the diaspora, and broader multilateralism.

What then of the fine print of a new Jamaican consensus? I suggest that the basis for a new political compromise would have to begin with a profound historical act of good faith that would indicate to all that the foundations for a new beginning, a genuine social contract was being laid, though more than one and a half centuries late. This would require:

a. *A process of national reconciliation* that would address, fully ventilate, and ultimately exorcise the cataclysm of 1976–80, the specter of which still broods over the country and inhibits any initiative toward national healing. The near–civil war moment of 1980 still haunts Jamaican social and political life. The blood feuds generated in those violent days have fed into the marrow of urban communities and continue to exist in the saliency of "areas" and "zones" of exclusion, long after memory of the era has passed. Any attempt to create a new social pact must, psychologically, put to bed the ghosts of the past. A National Reconciliation Commission would be composed of respected scholars, judges, and citizens drawn from various spheres of life, both locally and internationally. It would be legally constituted and would have as its main task the full disclosure of the causes of the violence of the seventies. It would not seek to prosecute, as, following the spirit of the South African Truth and Reconciliation Commission, its purposes would, in the first instance, be therapeutic. Its hearings and results would be aired and published widely. In its act of revelation without retribution, it would break with the past and set the template for truth and honesty in political behavior in further stages of the new national consensus. The work of a National Reconciliation Commission would precede everything else and its success would be contingent for further progress in the building of a national consensus.

b. *A new, unprecedented, and extensive land reform measure.* Such an initiative would help alleviate rural poverty, slow the rapid migration to the cities and out of the island, and, if accompanied by appropriate food security policies, provide the foundation for new modalities of popular, democratic development.

c. *A Constituent Assembly of the Jamaican People at Home and Abroad*
(CAJPHA). The avenue to a new Jamaican consensus cannot be a single event, but a global conversation on the future of Jamaica and Jamaicans, that can only take place through a series of encounters by representatives and as many people as possible within the island and the diaspora. Such a conversation should not begin with a bureaucratically imposed agenda, as that would imply that it was simply to be a rubber stamp to ratify previously agreed-on points. A genuine consultation leading to new forms of social living would have to begin with the collective discussion of an agenda. However, I propose the following as a few of the possible items on such an agenda:

1. A deeper democracy
2. The closer linking of the economy to the popular culture, including a more urgent and comprehensive approach to the environment
3. The urgent pursuit beyond the Caribbean Single Market of a closer Caribbean union at the level of movement and popular interaction
4. The initiation of a national conversation around the possible elements in a new ethos of being. In honor of Sylvia Wynter's pioneering work, this discussion might be labeled "After Man, Towards the Human."[9]

I now touch briefly on some of the key components in the new approach to the political in Jamaica.

LAND REFORM

The notion of land reform is not new to Jamaica and its history has been rehearsed and critiqued through a variety of disciplines. Yet, despite the numerous programs that have been tried, including those such as Operation Pride that continue today, the true measure of success or failure is to be seen in the stark disparities in land ownership, where 4 per cent of landowners control 65 per cent of fertile, mainly alluvial lands, while the remaining 96 percent farm 35 percent of the lands, mainly on the less fertile hillsides. Alongside this is the reality of fallow land: of the 270,000 hectares of cultivated land, some 83,000 are devoted to pasture, and over the past thirty years the area of land cultivated has fallen by 26 per cent. Amid the inequity and fallow land, the government is by far the largest landowner.

The graphic juxtaposition of idle land and idle hands, the intransigence of rural poverty, the concomitant social disruption of the countryside, and the well-known effects of mass urban migration, all demand a critical reappraisal of land reform.[10]

Any new approach to land reform would have to be conceived within two now well-accepted realities. The first is that the plantation system is at a crucial crossroads. The second is that Jamaica, with the clear history and potential to feed its entire population, has become increasingly dependent on food imports in the last two decades. The gradual phase-out of the Lomé agreement for preferential access of agricultural exports to the European market will make the production of sugar and bananas—Jamaica's two leading exports—almost unfeasible, given present levels of capitalization and productivity. The reason for the maintenance of highly inefficient industries, of course, is the understandable fear of widespread unemployment, worsening rural poverty, and mass unrest if they were suddenly to shut down, though prognostications point to this as the probable short-term result anyway. The other stark reality is the threat that WTO-inspired liberalization of imports poses to the domestic production of food. Trade liberalization undermined local red pea, Irish potato, and onion production and has shifted the fruit and vegetable sub-sector from a trade surplus to a growing deficit. Yet, despite these difficulties, small farmers continue to produce a significant share of Jamaica's domestically consumed food. This congruence of two imminent crises, one affecting the plantation sector and the other small farmers, calls for a strategy that can address both of them. The answer is to be found in a land reform that would shift significant resources from the crippled plantation sector and transfer it to existing and potential small farmers, who would produce both for the domestic market and for export.

Such a policy would have to follow the existing individual or family farm model, should have strict land size ceilings as in the East Asian land reforms, should include inter-generational rights and on-site residence, provide for the land to remain in agriculture, and prohibit sale in large blocs to prevent speculative accumulation.

A broad and substantial reform carried out through a popular and transparent process, with sensitivity to productivity, equity, the environment, and gender and linked to an effective national and regional food security policy, would:
a. halt the articulated drift from the countryside to a life of poverty in the urban

towns; b. give rural people a new sense of pride and proprietorship, belonging and community, reducing the disintegration of the countryside, most exemplified in the prevalence of praedial larceny; c. improve agricultural productivity and food security and potentially lay the basis for new, innovative export thrusts; d: significantly raise the level of consumption in the countryside, creating new, expansive markets for both manufacturing and agriculture; e: serve as a model for a later urban reform, which would use its approaches of democracy, transparency, and inclusiveness to tackle the daunting task of creating community in the cities; f: lay a foundation of trust and goodwill for further extensive debates on the political and social changes required for the next half century of Jamaica's existence; and g: act as a model for bi- and nonpartisan cooperation that can feed through the entire society and initiate a sea change away from tribalism and toward popular, national, and regional renewal.

THE CAJPHA

The second proposal I wish to spend some time on is the convening of a Constituent Assembly of the Jamaican People at Home and Abroad (CAJPHA). Some forty-odd years after the initial drafting of the Jamaican constitution, which decisively did not include popular consultation, and in the face of the dissolution of the social arrangements that accompanied independence, it is time to rethink the way Jamaican people live with each other. The CAJPHA would not only consider and address matters of constitutional reform, but would debate broad questions about the political and economic direction of the country and critically explore the ethos and philosophy that undergirds national life. The actual constitution of the CAJPHA itself, the method of arriving at an agenda and the procedures involved in making decisions would be eminently transparent and democratic and would establish a model for political engagement for other institutions. A possible modus operandi might include the following stages:

1. *The formulation of an agenda.* A genuinely open and non-hierarchical discussion cannot begin with an agenda established by the government, the opposition, or any other single or narrow interest group. On the contrary, an open and transparent agenda can only emerge from an initial round of consultations through face-to-face meetings, the media, and the internet.
2. *A national and diasporic conversation.* Over a specified period, perhaps three to six months, a conversation would take place through all the available instruments of communication around the main agenda items. The emphasis

should be on the actual face-to-face dimension of this conversation, with the steering committee playing a central role. Large assemblies of citizens would be convened in the main population centers, including Kingston, Brooklyn, Montego Bay, Birmingham, Brixton, May Pen, Toronto, Mandeville, and Ft. Lauderdale. These would not preclude smaller meetings in schools, workplaces, villages, and urban communities.

3. *A national and diaspora-wide conference.* The conclusion of the exercise would be a gathering of elected delegates from all the main population centers and localities, and all the critical interest groups. The ratification of delegates would be an appropriate job for the Electoral Advisory Committee in consultation with the emerging network of groups and individuals linked to the Jamaica diaspora conferences. The national convention would be the high point of the exercise—an unprecedented assembly of the people at home and abroad. Ideally, it would agree on the entire agenda of items, but even if agreement were not comprehensive, the exercise would still be of extraordinary benefit. Some of the items would require legislation, and these could be forwarded to parliament for consideration. I suggest "consideration" as opposed to "ratification," as parliament remains the democratically elected and constituted legislative body. The CAJPHA would not legislate but would carry tremendous legitimacy, and elected representatives would want to consider twice before rejecting its proposals out of hand.

4. *The reconvening of CAJPHA once every decade.* One of the central, though rarely discussed weaknesses in contemporary representative democracy is the assumption that the agreement of one generation is to be accepted without question by subsequent generations. In a dynamic world in which access to information and knowledge are changing geometrically, this is an even more difficult notion to digest. The alternative, proposed here, is that CAJPHA would reassemble every decade after its first meeting to once again debate and discuss the terms of living and the agenda for the future.

Among the central debates that the CAJPHA would have to address would be how to deepen democracy. Some of these issues are already a part of the national debate, while others are less well known. I simply mention a few:

1. A popular, annual budget debate discussed through a similar national and diaspora-wide process.
2. The election of designated representatives chosen as part of general elections to sit on sensitive bodies including, for instance, the police services commission, the national contracts commission, and the public services commission.

3. The institutionalization of Carl Stone's older suggestion for a constituency council composed of representatives of all parties.

4. The establishment in appropriate legislation of Carl Stone's proposal of the principle of recall for parliamentarians seen as incompetent or wayward by a majority of their constituents.

5. A policy of affirmative action on the matter of gender representation at all levels of the Jamaican political system.

6. New comprehensive legislation with teeth addressing the matter of money, political parties, and elections.

7. Greater power to local government, extending the positive principles that are now being advanced.

8. Finding ways to incorporate the diaspora into the political and electoral system, including setting aside proportionately elected seats specifically for representatives of the diaspora.

A DEMOCRATIC DEVELOPMENTAL STATE

The third proposal I wish to spend some time on is the matter of broad economic direction. My proposal, elaborated into a phrase, would be for government policy to shift in the direction of the developmental state, along the pattern of Southeast Asia, but that given the peculiarity of Jamaica, the novel element would be to move toward an inclusive and democratic developmental state. My argument in point form:

1. There is as yet no clear alternative to a policy based on growth, but it is possible to take seriously the implications of industrialization and to make choices that do the least damage to people's lives and the environment.

2. In a small island in which the divergence between what is consumed and what is produced is significant, while convergence of these two poles is desirable, there will always be the necessity to export in order to pay for consumption. A strategic and aggressive export policy is therefore essential.

3. The developmental state, not the neo-liberal model of open borders and laissez-faire policies, is the unambiguous example of successful growth and structural differentiation for relatively underdeveloped countries.

4. The specific social history of Jamaica leans away from a politics of elitism and hierarchy. The heart of the argument elaborated here is that any attempt to reconfigure Jamaican politics on a new foundation must be based on democracy and inclusion.

5. A new kind of political and economic relationship needs therefore to be conceived, that incorporates the strategic elements of the developmental state but with an unprecedented and novel approach of democratic inclusion. This state form would seek to level the economic field through extensive land reform. It would be consultative even as it utilized technical talent to search for and elaborate new, strategic options. It would be transparent and provide the requisite information to include the widest circles of the population and private sector in critical discussions surrounding the choice of direction. And finally, it would be accountable, ultimately through democratic procedures but also through the broadest dissemination of all relevant information.

A TURN TO A MORE "POPULAR" CARIBBEAN INTEGRATION

Now, we move to a brief, if thoroughly inadequate word on Caricom, the CSM, and Caribbean integration. I stand here as a committed Caribbean regionalist. It is a matter of belief, though many might argue that in my case it is also a matter of compulsion. Havelock Brewster, rightfully critical of the bureaucratic and statist approach that dominates in the thinking on Caribbean integration, instead proposes a new approach to unity based on "first best" principles of cultural identity, kinship, and unity.[11] This would not negate Caricom or its arrangements but would help determine the ordering and priorities of any integration process.

Brewster proposes as an alternative a different kind of union in which people and movement are given priority over formal institutions and structures.

This more open-ended, yet also more inclusive notion of unity would provide a basis for cooperation in regional "first best" activities—those activities that "from each state's point of view are better pursued regionally, rather than nationally or internationally."

Brewster's approach is compelling because it begins with people. A union based on popular movement, in which small farmers from Jamaica could easily establish homesteads in Guyana or Belize; in which Grenadians could choose to work in the Trinidad and Tobago construction industry as easily as they might in Grenada or St. Vincent, is infinitely superior to one based primarily on the movement of goods, or, as in the instance of the Caribbean Single Market (CSM), on the movement of specified skilled personnel. In similar fashion to which the UWI Mona campus became the fertile womb for elite West Indian unity in the 1950s, genuine Caribbean citizenship and free movement would be the seeding ground for a new, far deeper Caribbean communion as the twenty-first century proceeds.

RETHINKING THE ETHICAL

Finally, I wish to explore the matter of ethos. At the heart of the notion of hegemonic dissolution is the question of culture and values. I am under no illusion that there was any magical moment in the past when all Jamaicans shared a monolithic set of values. Indeed, much Caribbean sociology and history, from M. G. Smith through Kamau Brathwaite to recent work like Moore and Johnson's study of nineteenth-century Jamaica,[12] suggest the contrary. Nonetheless, it is useful to suggest that in recent decades the disintegration of a hegemonic order has served to underline disconnections and alienations.

However, in a moment in Jamaican history where order is in question, rules are notional, and violence is rife, where extremism and nihilism are prevalent, leading to innocent children being burnt to death in their homes, it is time to convene a conversation on the ethical foundations on which Jamaican society is constructed. In 1994 at an earlier phase of this slide, the Values and Attitudes Conference sought to bring delegates from across the island to discuss the state of morality in the country. Perhaps it was ahead of its time. The present contradictory moment is thus an opportunity to resuscitate a national and diasporic conversation around questions of morality and ethos and to use the appropriate Rastafarian word *livity*.

Among the outstanding questions that deserve to be mooted: What are the values that should guide our lives as we move into the first quarter of the twenty-first century? What is the relationship of Western individualism to the Jamaican and Caribbean personality? What approaches can be taken to address "hyper consumption"? What is the ethical foundation on which we construct resistance to the hierarchical narratives of color, race, class, and gender that persist at the center of our society? What is it to be human in Jamaica and the Caribbean today? There may be no absolute answers to any of these questions. And where tentative answers emerge, they might well be modified or discarded in the future. The answers, therefore, can only take the form of a conversation in which all have a seat and in which the conversation itself becomes the pole around which ethical considerations rotate. The Constituent Assembly of the Jamaican People at Home and Abroad would be the first step in initiating this conversation, which would then continue through the newspapers, talk shows, in living rooms, and on street corners as a normal part of national discourse in the future.

In Conclusion

Close listeners to this lengthy discussion may have noticed, as I draw to a close, that little time has been given to the cut and thrust of Jamaican politics, to the parties and their leaders. This has been entirely on purpose. In order to see the forest, it is necessary to climb above the trees. Yet, it is also true to say that, given the nature of Jamaican realpolitik, very few of these ideas might have any chance at all of becoming policy. I accept that conclusion, but counter with the assertion that it is the purpose of the academic, whatever the consequences, to speak the truth—as he or she sees it—to power. It is the task of the politician, I suggest, to refute its veracity, or, if there is agreement, to propose what is to be done. Otherwise, we remain ensconced in the forest, in a fog of obscurantism, convinced that the daily murmurs of the leaves signal business as usual, when all along the horizon a deadly fire is raging.

When prose fails, the only recourse left is to poetry. In his oft-quoted "Negus," Kamau Brathwaite asserts, lyrically:

> I
> Must be given words to refashion futures
> Like a healer's hand.[13]

If one takes Braithwaite's use of "words" liberally to also mean ideas, then this is a moment to pause, reflect on our condition, and search for the words and ideas to begin refashioning our future. We sit tonight on the beautiful Mona campus on this beautiful and bountiful island, as part of a people who, though small in numbers, have cast their indelible stamp on the world stage. We have human resources and ability far beyond our diminutive size; and when we envision ourselves as a vital component of a diverse but closely related region, this is even more decisively the case.

If we can only find the means to come together, find the words to refashion futures, and turn those words into concrete and mortar, we can begin to forge new ways of living and release the collective energy that lies within. Then, even with the caution that must accompany any gaze into the near future, we will be able to say that we have done our best to make a better life for our children and grandchildren. For even in an uncertain world, there is still room to launch a new season of adventure for this turtle island of Jamaica in the Caribbean pond, for its diaspora, and for the world beyond.

12. Caribbean Radical Traditions and the Turn in the Jamaican Moment (2006)

On Saturday February 25, 2006, Portia Simpson-Miller, Minister of Local Government, was elected by a narrow margin of some 237 votes to the post of president of the ruling People's National Party (PNP) of Jamaica. In front of a massive crowd of cheering supporters outside the PNP headquarters, dominated by the yellow t-shirts of her campaign team, Portia first read from the prophet Isaiah, then called for party unity and issued a message of hope: "I come to you with a promise of hope as we continue the transformation of the PNP and a promise of hope that all of us will unite and work for a better and brighter Jamaica."[1]

In some four to five weeks, when Prime Minister P. J. Patterson resigns, Simpson-Miller will become the first woman and the seventh person to lead Jamaica since independence in 1962. In the days following her victory, commentary in the newspapers and on the numerous talk shows that dominate the Jamaican airwaves, did not miss the significance of a woman coming to power, someone who was genuinely from the Jamaican grassroots and who—at least in the popular perception—had never severed her linkages with them. Most significant, though, were the powerful expectations that the victory seemed to have generated among her supporters and deep into the ranks of the opposition Jamaica Labor Party (JLP).

Elmore Briscoe, from working class community of Vineyard Town, felt that a woman needed the chance to rule the country: "I feel good for a woman. Mek a woman get a chance. I feel crime is going to reduce because she's a woman, she knows how to deal with things and she's down to earth."[2] Winnifred Stoddart, a 52-year-old party delegate and supporter of her main opponent Peter Phillips, recognized her significance: "They've allowed things to go too low with the workers of the party; they are helping people who can do without it; she's from the grassroots, she understands when somebody says they are hungry."[3]

It is evident that Latin American politics has made a decisive shift to the left. The startling presidential triumph of Evo Morales in Bolivia is only the latest in a series of electoral victories that has seen the rise and consolidation of left-wing candidates in Venezuela, Brazil, Argentina, Uruguay, and Chile.[4] This tendency is certainly not monolithic as Lula's PT, which, with its significant compromises with global capital, occupies an entirely different space from that of Chavez, with his aggressive use of Venezuelan oil revenues to loosen Latin and Caribbean reliance on traditional Western finance. Equally, Nestor Kirchner's attempts to chart a relatively autonomous path out of debt for Argentina is substantially different from the policies Michele Bachelet has inherited in Chile, where social democracy continues to embrace globalization with some albeit ambiguous success.

Similar tendencies have not so far been manifest in the Caribbean. Aside from the singular example of socialist Cuba and the stymied attempt at populist mobilization in Haiti under Aristide,[5] Caribbean governments since the collapse of the Grenada revolution in 1983 have largely avoided radical, transformational politics. From the Bahamas in the north, through Jamaica to Trinidad and Guyana in the south, there has been widespread adherence to the Washington Consensus and to neo-liberal policies of structural adjustment. As the Caribbean has become more firmly entrenched in the reformulated networks of global capital that has come to be termed globalization, there has been a shift from agricultural and mineral export emphases toward economies based on services, tourism, and the remittance of income from emigrants working in the North. Beyond the legal economy, an entire sub-economy of grey and illegal activities has mushroomed, including drugs transshipment, money laundering, extortion, and even kidnapping. The exact size of this sector is difficult to measure, though the Jamaican experience, such as the popular demonstrations that have followed the arrest of purported gang leaders, suggests that entire communities are dependent on the illegal economy for survival.

To assume, however, that the effects of globalization on the small states of the Caribbean has been uniformly negative would be a grave error. The smallest states in the region—and in particular, those still tied to their respective colonial powers—have, certainly on macro-economic indicators, prospered. Thus, for instance, the tourism and offshore banking economies of Cayman and the British Virgin Islands have grown exponentially in the last three decades, while many of their larger neighbors have languished with little growth. Trinidad and Tobago, in a period of rising prices for its oil and with the realization of its extensive natural gas reserves, has also experienced remarkable growth. Barbados, after a brief recession in the early nineties, has elaborated a social-partners arrangement that is in part accountable for the resumption of a path of robust growth that placed Barbados in 2004 ahead of all its neighbors and thirtieth in the world on the UNDP's human development index.[6]

The existence of a number of relative success stories within the region (as problematic as the notion of success may be) is certainly one reason why radical trends have vegetated in the past two decades, but there are also many other factors, among them:

• The collapse of the Grenadian revolution. When Prime Minister Maurice Bishop was killed by soldiers of his own People's Revolutionary Army in 1983, the Caribbean left suffered a mortal blow. The Grenadian collapse and subsequent U.S. invasion was not an instance of electoral defeat as in Nicaragua, or purely military defeat, in which the rump of the insurgency is able to regroup and engage again under different circumstances. In Grenada the instance of fellow revolutionaries killing the popular leader of the process vilified the notion of radical change and placed it outside the space of feasible options.

• The end of the Cold War had multiple effects in the region. The collapse of the Soviet Union and "really existing socialism" in Eastern Europe put an end to the flawed notion of "socialist orientation" as an alternative path of development for third world states. More specifically, the dramatic shrinkage of the Cuban economy as it entered the "special period" in the nineties sent the decisive signal that Cuban "basic needs" socialism was no longer on the agenda.[7]

• In Jamaica, the decisive turn of the PNP and of Michael Manley from a policy of resistance to one of engagement with global capital in the mid-eighties, closed the door on the search for alternative solutions, as the two dominant parties resumed a consensual pattern that had existed prior to Manley's original rise to power.[8]

• The massive migration of Caribbean citizens—primarily to the United States and Canada, but also, depending on colonial connections, to Britain, France, and Holland—had multiple consequences. The social and political tensions that would have arisen from the presence of large numbers of well-educated but unemployed young people were partially alleviated. Equally, to the extent that these migrants were able to get jobs in the North and send remittances home, this was able to address some of the immediate material problems of their families. However, as Prachi Mishra in a recent IMF study suggests, the share scale of migration has deprived the region of a significant proportion of its skilled workers. Between 1970 and 2000, the Caribbean as a whole lost 63 per cent of its tertiary-trained workforce to OECD countries. Individual cases are even more illustrative. Suriname lost 90 per cent of its tertiary workforce; Guyana lost 86 per cent and Jamaica lost 82 per cent.[9] Further, as Mishra concludes, remittances, seen by many commentators as an economic savior, have not compensated for the loss in productivity resulting from the mass exodus of well-trained citizens.[10] More critically, none of the statistics measures the loss of "social capital" in the sense of absent parents, teachers, community leaders, and role models, all the inevitable outcome of this mass exodus. On balance, migration has helped ease some social tensions, while laying the basis for longer-term alienation and dissatisfaction, as a generation of young people have become adults without the typical nurturing from community and with a narrow material nexus—the "Moneygram"—connecting them to family.

However, beyond the existence of some models of relative success and the absence of a vibrant politics of radical resistance, there is a wider, more textured picture. Trinidad and Tobago's economic buoyancy has been accompanied by social and ethnic tensions that are reflected in a crime rate that appears to be out of control. Guyana, on the South American continent, certainly the richest "Caribbean" country on the basis of its known resources, remains mired in a racial standoff between dominant Indian and African communities that has stalled any concerted policy of development. Crime and violence in Guyana, too, seem to have taken off on a steep trajectory with no clear end in sight. Further, the tendency toward the emergence of ruthless and violent drugs-related gangs is pan-Caribbean in its nature and mushrooms wherever the possibility of new, loosely monitored routes for the transshipment of cocaine might exist. The smallest territories are therefore often the most vulnerable, in a context where their security and wider institutional structures cannot withstand the power and resources wielded by wealthy drug lords. It is within this general context—of region-wide social alienation accompanied by increasing violence, encouraged by unemployment, and fed by the drugs trade—that the example of Jamaica is useful. In Jamaica, all of these problems are particularly well defined, yet the outline of a way forward might be emerging.

Jamaica, while far from the "failed state" described by some of its more pessimistic analysts,[11] in recent years has oscillated between periods of marginal growth to flat periods of no growth at all. It is evident that Jamaica fits into the pattern of many middle-income, non-oil-producing developing countries that respond to the impulses of the global economy, though with a broadly negative outlook for their prospects in the middle to long term.

The stasis within the Jamaican economy can be understood as part of a broader social and political moment, which this writer has elsewhere described as "hegemonic dissolution."[12] The old ruling bloc that defined Jamaica's social and political path in the pre- and immediately post-independence periods is moribund. Insurgent social forces from below are questioning the terms of the old hegemony across the gamut of symbolic and substantial spheres along the social terrain. For more than a decade, this contestation has manifested itself in culture wars surrounding the appropriateness of Jamaican "nation language," a new, assertive sense of blackness,[13] and in the quintessential space for popular expression, the dancehall and its music. Jamaican popular music in the post–Bob Marley era has moved from a period of the glorification of symbolic wealth and macho sexual conquest (slackness) to a more recent period of "consciousness" in which themes of unity, resistance, and rebellion have once more come to the fore.[14] Artistes like Bounty Killer, Sizzla, Anthony B, Capleton, and many more chant a message of renewed interest in the Rastafarian religion, but with a decidedly militant twist. Perhaps fittingly, one of the newer and most popular voices is Marley's son, Damian "Junior Gong" Marley. In his new album *Welcome to Jamrock*, he raises themes of uprising and revolution that are now part of the stock in trade of the contemporary deejays:

> Any day a revolution might erupt
> And the skys over Kingston lighting up
> For the new generation rising up[15]

While located within the sphere of cultural contestation, Marley's lyrics are only part of a wider social upheaval, which is increasingly taking more overtly confrontational forms. Three recent incidents, chosen for their locations across widely separated parts of the island, suggest the tensions in the social sphere and the depth of the emotions that have been unleashed.

Mandeville: Under the headline "Rage in Mandeville: Town loses its cool over beating of supermarket employee," the *Jamaica Observer* describes an incident on January 16 in which popular anger burst into spontaneous demonstrations after the alleged beating of an employee of SuperPlus supermarket:

> Jeremy Chen, the 34-year-old managing director of the SuperPlus Food
> Store at Park Crescent in Mandeville, and two of his managers were among
> five men denied bail when they appeared in court here yesterday, accused
> of assaulting and beating two young employees of the store. Normally
> sedate Mandeville was in an uproar for several hours as hundreds of people
> converged on the old courthouse at the centre of the town and also at the
> store. Police said the crowds were "noisy but orderly." . . . The arrests followed
> allegations that at about 7.30 pm on Monday, two young SuperPlus employ-
> ees Renardo Dawes, 20 and Michael Sinclair, 18 were accused of stealing.
> They were allegedly taken to Chen's home in Mandeville where the two men
> were allegedly tied up and beaten. A dog was allegedly set upon one of the
> men who was bitten. . . . A large crowd with some people bearing placards
> such as "we want justice" was outside the courthouse at yesterday morning's
> session. . . . Angry crowds then converged on SuperPlus stores, triggering

their closure. There was some suggestion yesterday that the police may have moved too hastily in taking the accused men to court before more thorough investigations. But senior policemen noted that not only did the law stipulate that arrested persons should be brought before the court as quickly as possible but that "in the immediate circumstance" yesterday, it was imperative to have quick action in order to maintain public order. "We are convinced that if we had not acted as we did, they (the protestors) would have burnt down Mandeville," one investigator told the Observer.[16]

Farm Town, St. Ann: Rural St. Ann is not normally associated with popular upheaval, but when a businessman was suspected of involvement in the death of a local resident and appeared to be escaping the net of justice, Farm Town erupted:

> Residents of this small and usually quiet rural district went on a rampage yesterday, burning a house, two motor cars and two businesses—a bar and a liquor store—owned by a man who was detained by the police and later released after being questioned about the death of a member of the community. The fuming residents, who were protesting yesterday for the third time within a week against the police's release of the man, vowed that they would continue their protests until the police reopen their investigations into the death of the member of the community. The saga started on February 1 with the shooting death of 31-year-old builder Ryan Whitehorn, whom the police say was gunned down by one of two men who accosted him along the Farm Town road that night. The police later held a businessman of the same community for questioning about the death of Whitehorn. However, the man's lawyer filed a writ in the St Ann's Bay Resident Magistrate's Court, forcing the police to release him. Upon hearing that the man was released the residents protested last week Thursday and again on Friday. The protest turned violent yesterday as rumors were spread throughout the community that the man was planning to leave the island. They set fire to the man's house, his liquor store and his bar, all located in the centre of the district. They also torched two motor vehicles belonging to him. However, the frightened businessman managed to flee the area during the disturbance.[17]

Spanish Town: The volatile city of Spanish Town, some fifteen miles west of Kingston, has gained notoriety as the battleground between two contesting gangs: "Clansman," reputedly sympathetic to the PNP, and "One Order" to the JLP. When the Clansman leader Donovan "Bulbie" Bennett was killed by the police in late 2005, there was widespread burning and the city had to be placed under curfew. The same thing happened on February 8, 2006, when Andrew "Bun Man" Hope, leader of One Order was gunned down by unknown assailants:

> The gang leader, the police said, was shot in the mid-afternoon by unknown assailants dressed in khaki clothes. Residents claimed, however, that a member of the police force was responsible for Hope's death and proceeded to block roads in several sections of the town in protest. Several armed men, believed to be members of Hope's gang, which operates mainly in Tawes Pen and Ellerslie Pen, and are scattered over other sections of the St Catherine capital, ran wildly through the town, firing shots, forcing several businesses to pull their shutters early and pedestrians to take cover. The gangsters also set fire to the town's old courthouse, which was used for sittings of the night court, as well as several cars parked in front of the building. Irate at the death of their "leader," residents shouted support for the torching of the courthouse. They also prevented firemen from putting out the blaze.[18]

The following features seem to be common to all three of these disparate examples:

• There is a popular perception, evidently fed by numerous concrete provocations, that there are two categories of law: one for those with power and influence and one for those without.
• There is a willingness to take popular action for what is conceived to be in the interest of justice. The notion of justice that is deployed demands that if the agents of the law are unable or unwilling to execute it, then it is within the right of the populace to execute the law on their own behalf.
• The form of this popular execution includes not only the apprehension of the alleged perpetrators, but also the elimination of their property and, if necessary, the property of other symbolic representatives of the alternate and unjust system of law.

The rapidity of the popular mobilizations, the similarity and severity of the actions taken, particularly in the two latter instances, all suggest the paper-thin acceptance of legitimacy and the depth of the disconnection. Using the earlier terminology, this might best be described as an advanced phase of hegemonic dissolution. The Jamaican state and the social bloc that operates within its circles, is still firmly in power, but the widespread evidence suggests that its hold is increasingly tenuous.

It is in this moment of advanced hegemonic dissolution that Simpson-Miller's ascendancy to a position of leadership has occurred. She has won a party election, buoyed by broad popular support, with a simple message bringing hope to the poor and calling for unity among the people of Jamaica. The problems she faces, however, are formidable. Within her own party she has few cabinet or senior technocratic supporters with the experience and ability to run the complex machinery of government. She will therefore have to rely on many persons who were lukewarm or openly hostile to her ascendancy to power only weeks ago. Within the PNP, the majority of leaders have long been won to the notion that even if it is possible to disagree with the war in Iraq and to protest the expulsion of Aristide from his own country, there is little room to maneuver around the macro-economic certitudes of the Washington Consensus. She will therefore need the sort of technical talent coupled with political skill that can forge a policy sensitive to job creation and poverty alleviation, conscious of the constraints of global capital and yet willing to negotiate and bargain with it.

Her support is undoubtedly strongest among the Jamaican poor, but whereas Jamaican working people have shown the ability to mount impressive, spontaneous community mobilizations around local concerns as in the three instances cited, there is little evidence of deep, layered community-based organization, building from the local level to address national and global issues. The political basis does not as yet exist for a Bolivian-type movement, like Evo Morales's Movimiento al Socialismo (MAS),[19] building on a history of popular militancy and organization around indigenous, trade union, and national issues. In addition, Simpson-Miller, despite her expressed love for the people and sometimes fiery rhetoric on their behalf, is not an Evo Morales with his long history of community-based agitation around indigenous, national, and global issues. Yet, in the particular conditions of Jamaica and the Anglophone Caribbean, where politics more often than not flows through the conventional channels of the dominant nationalist parties, Portia's election remains powerfully symbolic.

PNP delegates, riding on a national wave of hostility to business as usual, have elected a president whom the poor and the dispossessed perceive to be their own. If she chooses to deny her mandate and operate within the tight confines of business as usual, her widespread popularity will ebb and Jamaica will continue along its rocky path of high interest rates, widening income gaps, and low growth. If she chooses, however, to resist such a path, she may help to initiate a different kind of politics.

This would inevitably have to be a politics of consultation and inclusion. Elsewhere I have suggested that a Constituent Assembly of the Jamaican People at Home and Abroad[20] might be the pathway to discuss and ratify a new national consensus. Such a broad agreement would reexamine the present macroeconomic framework in order to push it in a direction more favorable to growth and employment. It would begin a dialogue of meaningful constitutional reform that would move in the direction of a deeper, more consultative democracy. It would reach out in unprecedented ways to incorporate the diaspora more tightly into the national and international political economy of Jamaica. And it would explore the deepening of regional integration arrangements, particularly at the level of skilled and semi-skilled workers, where the possibilities for employment creation are most evident.

Such a trajectory, while not the most likely outcome in the remarkably difficult constraints of the present moment, is nonetheless made possible by the presence of a powerful and palpable desire for a change of direction among the majority of the Jamaican people. If taken, it would have profound consequences for not only Jamaica but also the wider Caribbean, in the direction of a deeper democracy, greater accountability, and a new approach as to how the local might negotiate with the global in the twenty-first century.

13. The Dudus Events in Jamaica and the Future of Caribbean Politics (2011)

I am particularly happy to be able to be speaking at an event in honor of Pat Emmanuel. He was my first lecturer in politics at UWI St. Augustine, a quiet, somewhat reserved, but obviously very bright person. He was among a remarkable group of people including Lloyd Best, Roy Thomas, and Eric St. Cyr in economics; Susan Craig in sociology. Euric Bobb, Richard Jacobs, and Emmanuel himself in politics; and Bill Riviere and James Millette in history.

My generation marked its passage through university by the number of demonstrations and strikes that we were involved in. One of the most outstanding protests was our march and petition of the 1973 conference that signaled the start of Caricom at Chaguaramas on the northwestern peninsula of Trinidad. Bill Riviere and Pat Emmanuel had just been given their marching papers to leave Trinidad and Tobago by the Eric Williams government, purportedly for being involved in subversive activities but in reality, I suspect, for their intellectual sympathies with the popular Black Power movement of 1970. We students marched to the gate of the conference with our petition, which argued in substance that it was hypocritical for leaders to be celebrating a new phase of deeper Caribbean unity through Caricom while Trinidad, the host country, was declaring as personas non grata two young and highly qualified Caribbean sons. Our letter, of course, didn't change the Trinidad government's decision. Both Emmanuel and Riviere had to leave, disrupting their tender academic careers. Pat eventually ended up in Barbados, where he became a respected teacher and researcher, and the rest is history.

> It was the best of times, it was the worst of times, it was the age of wisdom, it was the age of foolishness, it was the epoch of belief, it was the epoch of incredulity, it was the season of Light, it was the season of Darkness, it was the spring of hope, it was the winter of despair, we had everything before us, we had nothing before us, we were all going direct to Heaven, we were all going direct the other way.[1]

Dickens's famous quotation from *A Tale of Two Cities*, reflecting on the French Revolution, has been used almost to distraction to reference the fraught, contradictory atmosphere that accompanies social revolution or moments of extreme social instability and uncertainty. It is an appropriate descriptor for the sense of tentativeness, of interminably postponed birth, and of anomie that is pervasive in contemporary Jamaica.

I offer one caveat at the beginning. Though my talk is entitled "The Dudus Events and the Future of Caribbean Politics," I am not here going to delve into the inner workings of Bajan, Trinidadian, Grenadian politics, or any other Caribbean sphere aside from that of Jamaica. This is a Jamaican presentation and the conjuncture is peculiar to her. Yet it would be foolish to conclude that these issues are not relevant to the future of the entire Caribbean region, particularly its Anglophone components. Jamaica is important not only because it is the largest Anglophone territory and therefore a central target for regional trade and investment, but because culturally, it is the dominant player in the region. Jamaican culture, as manifest through reggae, dancehall, language, attitude and style, has come to occupy (sometimes to the chagrin of educators, commentators, and politicians) an almost hegemonic position among the youth throughout the entire region. To the extent therefore, that Jamaican culture is reflective of a deep, impacted social schism and crisis in that island, then that crisis and its popular manifestation has been generalized as the lingua franca of youth and the dispossessed from Cuba and the Bahamas due south to Suriname and points beyond.

This Jamaican cultural hegemony is further cemented by the growth and consolidation of an increasingly integrated Caribbean diaspora. In cities like Brooklyn, Toronto, and Fort Lauderdale, as a generation before in London and Birmingham, West Indian or Caribbean integration is far advanced; and while significant elements of other Caribbean cultures are very present, it would not, I think, be entirely unfair to say that the young, diasporic Caribbean population speaks with a Jamaican accent. Thus, an unresolved social crisis in Jamaica, spiraling out of control, will have a profound and as yet uncalculated effect on the entire region, both at home and abroad.

The Dudus Events

On Labour Day, May 23, 2010, the combined armed forces of Jamaica, all three battalions of the Jamaica Defence Force, and the Jamaica Constabulary Force, in an unprecedented show of military strength, entered the dense, high-rise community of Tivoli Gardens, central and traditionally most loyal component of Prime Minister Bruce Golding's Western Kingston constituency. Breaching the heavily fortified community through a series of strategic holes blown out of concrete walls to the south, the military took the dozens of armed gunmen by surprise, engaging them in a series of sharp skirmishes which lasted the bet-ter part of two days. When peace was eventually restored, some seventy-three purported combatants along with one soldier was dead, hundreds of young men were detained, and—in a country used to the constant reportage of urban violence and police confrontations with gunmen—ordinary Jamaicans never-theless paused in shock at the sheer scale of the violence and carnage.[2]

George Lamming, in his profoundly prescient novel *Season of Adventure*[3] that covers the history of the imaginary island of San Cristobal from indepen-dence to the collapse of the first republic and the formation of the second, is a rich analogical source for the contemporary moment in Jamaica. The Tivoli invasion, I suggest, parallels in one respect the collapse of Lamming's first re-public, in that the socio-political arrangements that have provided a degree of cohesion since independence have collapsed. Here, however, the analogy ends, as the political structures—the formal state structures along with the two-par-ty arrangement—remain intact. This is the peculiarly hybrid nature of the pres-ent moment: a system that is no longer vibrant and functional exists alongside a superstructure that remains in place, thus, the relevance of the other analogy that I have mentioned, of a dangerously postponed birth.

Five Phases in Jamaican Politics

In order to arrive safely at this conclusion, however, let us retrace a little history familiar to any casual student of postcolonial Jamaican politics. The Jamaican two-party political system, while certainly not unique in the Commonwealth Caribbean, is among its most durable.[4]

It has provided for the recurrent if not regular transition from one party to the other over six decades. In a relatively poor and sharply hierarchical society, however, this has been accomplished through a particularly vicious system of machine or "clientelist"[5] politics, characterized by the winning party's distri-bution of scarce benefits in a biased manner to its supporters. From the very beginning, with survival being the ultimate stake for many, the system had the potential for sharp contestation and violence. This at first took the form of symbolic clashes between groups of supporters—often trade union–based—but it would be an error of history to conclude that violence was not embedded in the system from its early days.[6]

The second phase in its evolution was the emergence of distinct urban en-claves in which support for one party was or became overwhelming and which was used ultimately as a means of securing political control over a particular constituency. While there are debates as to the origins of violence, there is little contestation that the bulldozing of the Back o Wall slum and the displacement[7]

of its People's National Party (PNP) supporters, followed by the building of
Tivoli Gardens with its almost complete support for the Jamaica Labour Party
(JLP), signaled the beginning of "garrison politics,"[8] to use the term popular-
ized by Carl Stone. Henceforth, Tivoli would be a political and military bas-
tion under Edward Seaga's leadership. The PNP quickly moved to build its own
garrison communities and, with its wider popular and geographic support in
urban Kingston, soon would outstrip the JLP in the number of similarly designated communities. None, it is generally accepted, ever approached Tivoli in
terms of sheer organization and paramilitary capability.

The third phase occurred in the 1970s. With the partial consolidation in and
around Michael Manley's PNP of a movement to remove the final vestiges of
colonialism and deeply entrenched inequality from Jamaican social and political life, the stakes were raised. Contestation was now no longer between two
parties with reasonably similar programs, operating largely within the narrow
boundaries of parliamentary elections. Manley's project, while initially mild in
its policies, enraged important sections among the traditional elites, who were
determined from the early days of the regime to remove him from power. In a
classic process of escalation, the PNP's platform evolved from relatively mild
policies such as its proposal of a national youth service to become, in response
to growing opposition and rising popular expectations, the rhetorically com-
bative "democratic socialism."[9] The JLP for its part, moved to the right both in
its rhetoric and international associations, finding common cause in particular
with conservative elements in the U.S. Republican party. And after 1973, the
PNP grew closer to Fidel Castro, strengthened the country's already established
links with the Non-Aligned Movement, and built new contacts with what can
loosely be described as the international anti-imperialist movement, including
the establishment of economic and political ties with the Soviet Union.[10] Cold
war hostilities further exacerbated the already deep wounds in the body politic
as blood feuds—some accumulated over generations—morphed into ideological and philosophical divisions.

The rise of Manley's government also provided a fecund space for the
growth and proliferation of a rich and widely acknowledged popular cultural
movement. Bob Marley was only the brightest star in a firmament that included Peter Tosh, Dennis Brown, Burning Spear, Bunny Wailer, and the recently
departed Gregory Isaacs. It is the cultural movement[11] that has proved far more
enduring than the radicalized politics of the era; and yet analysts of contemporary Jamaican politics have failed, until very recently, to give culture its true
weight in the explicandum of the present impasse. This shall be the substance
of the last part of this presentation.

The defeat of Manley and the PNP, following the IMF-induced structural adjustment policies and economic contraction of 1977–80 and the bloody election of the latter year,[12] led to the fourth and penultimate phase of this process. The various political gangs that had amalgamated into the armed militias of the two parties in the war years 1975–80 were now no longer required, as the battle had been resolved with decisive victory for the JLP, free enterprise, and the West. Highly trained and combat-experienced veterans of the inner-city conflict on both sides of the political divide very quickly became freelancers. No longer at the behest of the parties, they sought to use their newly honed skills to advance their independent purposes, and did so effectively through the formation of various Posse and Yardie[13] gangs that operated effectively throughout the United States and the United Kingdom. It is this phase, too, in which the traditional power relations of Jamaican politics were first put to the test. The success in drug dealing and other illicit activities led to a novel reversal of fortunes, in which the heads of the gangs returned to Jamaica flush with cash. This was occurring at the same moment that the Jamaican state, under various IMF structural adjustment programs, was "downsizing" and unable, therefore, to provide the scarce benefits and largesse that had been the currency of dominance and control in the earlier period.

The result was that in this long interregnum that lasts from 1980 until 2010—some thirty years—the balance of power gradually shifted from the politicians—the traditional patrons of the clientelist system—to the dons, their former henchmen but now increasingly wealthy and autonomous associates.[14] The dons still required the politicians to provide them with legitimate government contracts and political cover to conduct their activities, but more critically, the politicians could no longer survive without the dons, not only for their military support at election time but, in the context of a parlous economy, for their cash. This is the period of the maturation of the dons, the features of which Anthony Harriott has succinctly described, including, inter alia, the emergence of legitimate businesses; geographic monopolies as administered territories; the growth of criminal firms as monopolies; the successful creation of social support in their host communities; immunity from local law enforcement; and the reverse co-optation of elements in the political parties (i.e., the opposite of the co-optation of communities into the parties in the sixties and seventies, now the gangs co-opt politicians to serve them in the legal sphere).[15]

This description is undoubtedly the one that prevailed as the prelude to the Dudus events of 2010. After years of the careful collection of evidence against Christopher "Dudus" Coke, the don of the notorious Tivoli Gardens "Shower Posse," the U.S. authorities, using the mutual extradition treaty with the Jamaican government, filed the appropriate papers for his extradition.[16] The process was revealing as it provided remarkable proof of the substance in Harriott's argument that, in essence, the balance of forces between the politician and the don has shifted significantly, if not decisively in favor of the latter. It took some nine months and the violent events in Tivoli Gardens from the initial request to his eventual capture and actual extradition to the United States to stand trial. The Jamaican government from the very beginning sought to delay the extradition, then claimed that the U.S. evidence was illegally obtained, while simultaneously seeking to hire the reputable American lobbying firm Manatt, Phelps and Phillips to intervene in order to "resolve" the situation. The inevitable questions would have to be, resolve what situation and in favor of whom? In recent years, numerous persons have been extradited to the United States under the extant treaty without the requirement of any government intervention to facilitate a resolution.

There are of course, many more turns to that particular screw that cannot be elaborated here, except to suggest that the prevarication, generally obstructive tactics, obfuscation, and lying of the Golding administration suggests more than anything else the depth of the impasse of credibility and legitimacy that is consolidating in Jamaica. The other side of the equation was, of course, the gathering strength of the don. Coke used the long wait provided by the government's maneuvering to gather his forces, prepare them politically, and turn Tivoli into what he thought was an impregnable fortress. Most stunningly, in May, two days after Golding recanted, admitted dissembling, and signaled that he would sign the note for Coke's extradition, a large force of women dressed in white emerged from Tivoli Gardens in support of Dudus, baring placards and chanting slogans proclaiming that he was "next to God" and that they would die for him.[17] A few days later, emboldened by this show of overwhelming support within the enclave and importantly, solidarity in the form of paramilitary support from surrounding communities, many of traditionally opposing political persuasion, the Tivoli machine seemed to go on the offensive, attacking and burning police stations and, crucially, ambushing and killing three policemen in the volatile eastern Kingston community of Mountain View. The burning of the stations and the death of the police officers led to a pivotal moment, as many awoke to the imminent threat to the very existence of the state. This provided the political foundation for the unprecedentedly fierce attack on Tivoli Gardens with its alarmingly high death toll.

Beyond Hegemonic Dissolution

The collapse of the Tivoli Gardens stronghold may signal the end of a long phase of maturation of the criminal system that developed out of the garrison politics of the sixties and seventies, or it may simply turn out to be a temporary setback. It is too early to arrive at a conclusive judgment, but the evidence is beginning to accumulate. Immediately after the Tivoli incursion and in the following months up until the present,[18] murder and major crime rates in Kingston and St. Andrew and throughout the island have been remarkably lower. Numerous gang leaders and associates have been arrested and, alongside those combatants who died in the violence of May or in subsequent encounters with the armed forces, real advances have been made against criminal gangs. Some minor initiatives have been taken, such as the decision by elements in the private sector to rebuild the economically vital Coronation Market in Western Kingston that had been partially destroyed in the battle, along with new initiatives to construct housing for citizens in depressed urban communities and a host of interventions of larger or smaller size from non-governmental organizations. These and the more determined stance of the present police and military leadership to stamp out crime are all contributing to the momentary ebb in violence, but in the end they are at best temporary palliatives that fail to address the deeper, fundamental contradictions in Jamaican society.[19]

Some fifteen years ago, in an analysis I still think provides useful insights, I suggested that Jamaica was in a moment of hegemonic dissolution: "The economic crisis, the collapse of the political project, the growing psychological independence of the subordinate classes, and the shelving of social leadership by the middle classes are the conditions under which a moment of hegemonic dissolution has emerged."[20] Using Gramscian categories, I understood hegemony to mean the effective control and direction of Jamaican society and concluded that "The social bloc in charge of Jamaican society is no longer ruling over a people convinced of its social superiority and its inherent right to 'run things.'"[21]

I think this analysis still has saliency in present-day Jamaica.[22] How else can we explain the performance of an economy with a vibrant, English-speaking population, more than reasonable outlay of resources for its admittedly small size, and perfect placing in the center of major trade routes from North to South America and Asia to the Americas that is unable to show any significant economic growth over the past three decades? How else can we explain the murder rate, even in its moment of decline among the highest in the world? How else can we explain the flood of migrants—some 85 per cent[23] of the professional classes, by some estimates—who have voted with their feet by seeking a better life elsewhere? Some roadblock, some arterial clogging is stifling Jamaica. The country's problems, I submit, are not primarily located in wrongheaded economic policies, though if the truth be told, there have been many; nor is it to be explained in the absence of human initiative; nor, importantly, is it to be primarily identified in the nature of the world capitalist system. If it were entirely the result of external factors, then how would we account for the contrary experiences of Barbados, or Mauritius, even further afield, Singapore, all with far less resources, both human and material and therefore more peripheral by most definitions, yet all achieving remarkable incidences of growth, human development, as well as resilience to shocks over the past five decades? The answer, I submit, is to be located in a period of stasis, identified by the failure of any significant social force to put a stamp on the society and haul other elements into an alliance to move the country forward. This is what I refer to as hegemonic dissolution. Yet, it is also important, in recognizing the significance of a moment of impasse, to also note that no social phenomenon or moment is ever motionless. This particular conjuncture is merely a passing crossroads in the onward flow of social traffic. We therefore need to focus on some of the changes that have accumulated over the past fifteen years and particularly in the most recent period.

On the positive side, coalescing before and since the events of May 2010, there are new and important initiatives that have been taken both through and around the government to address corruption The Independent Commission of Investigations into Police Offences, or INDECOM,[24] is one that allows for a degree of public control and oversight. Another is the Office of the Contractor General (OCG), embodied in the crusading presence of Glen Christie,[25] who has brought to his position a previously unimaginable sense of fairness, fearlessness, and integrity. Alongside Christie, a new cadre of apparently fearless officers have emerged in the public sector[26] who seem to be dedicated to rooting out corruption. Stealing a march on the ruling JLP, the PNP has appointed an Integrity Commission[27] of non-partisan individuals to vet its potential electoral candidates as fit and proper and has opened its accounts to the public. These initiatives have perhaps received less attention than they might in the general atmosphere in which the credibility of politicians and the policy initiatives of governments of whatever stripe are deeply discounted.[28]

But in other critical spheres of socio-political life, the results are at best dismal. In the new situation (which admittedly is in its very early phases), very little has been done to address the structural underpinnings of social inequality and concomitant hopelessness for the future that pervades the lives of most inner-city dwellers and the poor in general. Beyond the traditional road repair and building programs which are deeply implicated in the old patronage system and the occasional soundings about new industrial zones close to Kingston and in Clarendon, there is no new and bold thinking coming from either the government or opposition as to how to dramatically create jobs, increase wealth, and promote a virtuous cycle of prosperity. The present government, punch-drunk in the admittedly pusillanimous environment of the world recession and caught up with the dreadful routine of trying to balance savaged budgets, seems to have lost focus, if it ever existed, of the bigger picture. But neither is a clear image of possibilities, despite occasional releases about a new "progressive agenda"[29] emerging with any urgency from the opposition PNP.

More critically, there is no sense of the important cultural and psychological dimensions of the present moment and the implications therein for the derailing of any process of national development, which can only occur if there is a prior attempt to forge a modicum of consensus and unity. Obika Gray, in a penetrating and important paper "Culture and Development in Jamaica,"[30] written months after the Tivoli tragedy, has argued that postcolonial governments in Jamaica and the Caribbean have emphasized economic policy and political management to the detriment of any attempt to manage the sphere of moral culture and values. The result has been a grave mistake, because culture is at the heart of development, as it is "the ideological battleground for struggles concerning both the distribution of goods and the allocation of values."[31] The failure to engage effectively with the sphere of culture and values has led, Gray argues, to the proliferation of a subaltern culture of conflicting values, some of which are undoubtedly positive and others of which are profoundly negative from the perspective of generating a new project of national cohesion that might engender positive paths of human development in Jamaica and across the region.

The Crisis of Popular Culture

I want to develop Gray's important insights through two interventions in the Jamaican media. The first is from Gleaner columnist and well-known Baptist minister Devon Dick, entitled "The Spirituality of Mavado." David "Mavado" Brooks had recently been named a "person of interest" by the police along with competing deejay artiste Adidja "Vybz Kartel" Palmer. Dick, in his article, engages with Mavado's lyrics, which seem to vacillate between a pious Christianity, as in the recording "Messiah" where he sings "Me a bwoy, believe inna prayer," and glorification of violence, as in "Touch de Road," where he chants "Gunshot bun dem skin like the song me sing, when me done with him not even drankcrow want him."[32] Dick asks a number of penetrating questions about the nature of Jamaican culture and the ethical character of Old Testament morality, but seems somewhat baffled in the conclusion when he laments: "Apparently, in the spirituality of Mavado and others, there is no dissonance between songs of inspiration and songs that incite violence."[33]

The second intervention surrounds the media flurry that erupted after the shooting of Cedric "Doggy" Murray in August 2010. Wanted for numerous vicious murders, Murray was the notorious leader of the St. James–based Stone Crusher Gang. His diary, recovered after his death, revealed a quite literate and deeply conflicted human being. Murray had apparently been one of Coke's close associates, shooting his AK-47 at police in the Tivoli battle until, in his words, his "finger was numb." Yet, at the same time, Doggie revealed an apparently deep spirituality, to quote his diary: "I am a real gangster all out, but I love the Lord with a passion. Why I do the things I do? SIN I can do all things through Christ who strengthens me; that means I can repent and change but yet my faith is weak. My life is a book a puzzle."[34] In one of the best of a series of articles seeking to put meaning to Doggie's diary, Don Robotham argues: "A particular type of religiosity seems to be becoming an essential part of the psychological makeup and ideological armoury of the more intelligent Jamaican criminal."[35] Robotham concludes:

> Fire and brimstone Old Testament heroes such as Gideon provide inspiration capable of mobilising other youth and sustaining them through the many trials of their battles with "Babylon" and "Medianites." Given the glaring historical injustices in Jamaican Society and our innumerable social and racial divisions, this is a heady brew with a truly explosive social potential which could make the events in Tivoli in May look like a picnic.[36]

Hegemonic dissolution, if the phrase still has relevance, in its advanced phases is not just the rebellious distancing of subaltern classes from the Anglophilic, Christian, and creole notions of the traditional Jamaican middle classes, but the creation of substantially new cultural and philosophical spaces, which incorporate, among others, the following elements.

1. The assertion of post-emancipation notions of rights and justice.
2. The utilization of Old Testament concepts of righteous violence, incorporated into an embracing of gun culture as an avenue to power and wealth.
3. A Manichean notion of absolute right and wrong, captured most popularly in the omnipresent homophobia of the dancehall, but applied across the gamut of social relationships.
4. The subordination of democratic forms of governance to the imperative of the powerful and overarching chieftain, best exemplified in Doggie's acknowledged fealty to the "bigger don" Dudus.
5. A moral relativism, based on the notion that the entire society is corrupt and therefore that poor people getting their share via corrupt, illegal, and violent means is justifiable.
6. A deep hostility to Babylon, the police, and the higher-ups in society.

7. A clear accommodation to neo-liberal consumerism, most evident in the "bling" culture and the hyperconsumerism expressed in the lyrics and style of many in the dancehall.

If a new Jamaican consensus is to be built on the imminent collapse of the old, it will require not simply a condemnation of these new and often disturbing quasi-philosophical narratives, but a critical engagement with them. There are elements here, including moral relativism, neo-fascist authoritarianism, and the glorification of violence that may prove incompatible with any attempt to forge a collective national enterprise; but others, such as the appeal to consistency in applying rights and justice, themes of universality, and a persistent contempt for old hierarchies, are inevitable if a deeper and more inclusive democracy is ever to be placed on the agenda.

A Way Forward?

I present my proposal as to a possible way forward out of this impasse as a series of theses.

1. The critical and definitive feature of contemporary Jamaica for the entire period of the first postcolonial half-century is the deep social divide, with its outwardly inclusive edifice but deeply hierarchical and exclusionary daily reality.
2. The new feature of the past three decades is the failure—recognized by the entire society—of the middle and upper classes to manage and organize a functioning and effective state with a vibrant and buoyant economy.
3. The way forward must inevitably address security and forensic questions as it grapples to bring a modicum of peace to the society, but these will inevitably fail if there is no attempt to frontally address the central question of the social divide: the deeply flawed moral economy and the persistent political features of patronage and hierarchy that have accompanied them in the post-independence era.

I shall not address the forensic and security measures in my conclusion; I leave that to others like Anthony Harriott, who is far more versed on matters of community policing, social intervention in garrison communities, neighborhood watches, and the like.[37] Rather, I wish to concentrate on some of the key matters related to the social divide.

Missing, as earlier suggested, from the entire national debate is any serious, novel discussion on how to dramatically change deeply entrenched patterns of poverty in a short time period. Short of a social revolution in which the entire society is turned bottom up and which would be unlikely to survive in the hermetic international atmosphere of contemporary global capital domination, there is one avenue that might lead to a quick and rapid recalibration of wealth from the bottom—an urban and rural land reform program. Jamaica stands at a peculiar moment where the government possesses significant arable lands—primarily old cane lands which are only partially engaged in production; indeed, the government of Jamaica is, somewhat ironically from an historical perspective, the single largest landowner. Significant tracts of urban and suburban idle land also are owned by the government. A bold and determined program of land reform—carried out in a genuinely bipartisan manner and with oversight from untainted institutions such the office of the Contractor General, bolstered by the increasingly vigilant media and a reinvigorated body of public opinion—might simultaneously increase agricultural production, empower an entire renovated stratum of urban and rural small landowners, boost significantly national demand, and release hidden equity that would filter through the economy and give it a new unprecedented entrepreneurial energy and dynamism.[38] There are obvious dangers to such a policy, not least of which is the likelihood of it succumbing to the very patronage and corruption that is at the heart of the present moment. Yet, in a context where there are no clear alternatives, might it not be worthwhile to think through and weigh the pros and cons of such an approach via both formal technical discussions as well as a popular national conversation? Might not the conversation itself serve as a forum to not only debate this idea but propose feasible alternatives? Might it not also serve another function, to engender trust, open the avenues for non-partisan dialogue, and lay the foundation for greater consensus in the future?

The second proposal concerns the matter of rethinking the tattered constitutional arrangements, which are in need of major overhaul. The easy options have to do with checking and balancing the power of the executive and of other powerful institutions in the society, and there is indeed wide consensus on most of these.[39] The more difficult questions have to do with the deepening of democracy. The critical intellectual failure of the past two decades has been to abandon the matter of deepening democracy for the less difficult question as to how to check the power of the executive and entrenched bureaucracies. Elsewhere I have proposed the following as a possible agenda for constitutional and political reform.

1. A Constituent Assembly of the Jamaican People at Home and Abroad as a means of starting a genuine popular debate and arriving at a consensus on the main elements in new political and social arrangements. The assembly might be empowered to meet every decade to review the extent to which the agreed changes have become archaic and to include new generations in the act of writing their own constitution.

2. The utilization of the annual budget debate as a strategic measure and a specific event that can be open to public debate and that might establish a template for a new participatory approach to governance.

3. The abandonment of the member of parliament's office as the primary source of distributing benefits at the constituency level. In its place I suggest, following Stone,[40] the establishment of a constituency council composed of members of both parties and non-party representatives from the community.

4. The establishment of the principle of recall, with appropriate safeguards to prevent its frivolous and narrowly partisan use, to put an ultimate check between elections on MPs who fail to deliver.

5. The tabling of new laws related to party financing that would open the books to the public in order to undermine the ability of powerful financial interests to subvert democratic principles.

6. The devolution of greater power to local government, entrenched in law, to counter the overarching powers of the party, the center, and the city.[41]

Finally, to return to the matter of culture and philosophy: the hidden lynchpin in any movement away from the present crisis is the question of philosophical consensus, which is precisely not on the agenda in today's Jamaica. Any move toward a new consensus therefore cannot operate primarily at the level of structures, laws, and statutes, but must engage in a conversation around the worldviews that inform various options as we grapple for a way to forge a working and viable consensus. Such a conversation must place on the board not only basic ethical questions including universal norms of social living, which can no longer be taken for granted, but more troublesome matters, including the burgeoning of homophobia, gender inequality, and the resurgence of gendered violence. It would have as its overarching goal, almost two centuries after emancipation and fifty years since Anglo-Caribbean independence, the interrogation of the meaning of freedom, the rethinking of democracy, and the continuing salience of sovereignty[42] in the contemporary globalized world. It would have to do nothing less than attempt to lay the foundations for a new approach to social living as we move toward the middle of the twenty-first century.[43]

All crises, as difficult and debilitating as they might be, provide openings and opportunities. This thirty-year crisis, rising to a crescendo in the Labor Day Dudus events of May 2010, is no different: it provides the opportunity to begin rethinking the entire set of encrusted arrangements that have undergirded Jamaica's postcolonial journey. It is not, as I intimated at the beginning, a common proposal for any other jurisdiction of the Commonwealth Caribbean. I suggest, however, that if these or similar proposals are not addressed and efforts made to implement them through a project of national popular inclusion and engagement, then the situation will not improve in Jamaica and the consequences for the Caribbean as a whole will be profound. And Jamaica must not be allowed to fail, to quote once again your famous son George Lamming, because of a failure of the imagination.[44]

14. Jamaica on the Cusp of Fifty: Whither Nationalism and Sovereignty? (2013)

I say that the mission of my generation was to win self-government for Jamaica. To win political power, which is the final power for the black masses of this country from which I spring. I am proud to stand here today and say to you who fought with me, say it with gladness and pride, "Mission accomplished for my generation." And what is the mission of the generation, the generation that succeeds me now I quit my leadership? It is to be founded on the work of those who went before. It is to be made up by the use of your political power of tackling the job of reconstructing the social and economic society and life of Jamaica. This, then, is the hope of the future which can only be born of an understanding of the country today and what it thinks and what it feels.[1]

—Norman Washington Manley

On the evening of December 29, 2011, Portia Simpson-Miller led her People's National Party (PNP) to a decisive 42–21-seat victory over the incumbent Jamaica Labour Party (JLP),[2] setting a new precedent for Jamaica, as the JLP, only recently having anointed Andrew Holness to replace Bruce Golding as its leader and prime minister, turned out to be the first government in the country's modern political history to serve only one term in office. The election results took many by surprise. Most, including the majority of pollsters and political commentators,[3] holding conservatively to the traditional rhythms of Jamaican politics, felt that the electorate would give the JLP another chance and that the decision to replace the controversial and politically damaged Golding by the young (39 years old) and reasonably untainted Holness would lead to a narrow victory. No one foresaw a landslide, and while, in the keenly competitive waters of Jamaican politics, this translated into less than a sixty-thousand-vote and 6 percentile point advantage, it was nonetheless deeply demoralizing to the losers. Equally surprising was the low voter turnout, as only 52.7 per cent of the electorate felt compelled to vote for one of the two dominant political parties or any of the few and minuscule independents.[4] This latter trend, reflective of a secular decline in voting numbers since the watershed election of 1980,[5] was nonetheless precipitous, leading to another record, of the lowest voter turnout since universal adult suffrage elections began in 1944.

These two features—the fickleness of the electorate and its willingness to dump the incumbents after a little more than four years in office and a possible unhappiness with both parties evident in the low turnout—are indicative, I suggest, of a broader discontent with the state of politics, indeed of the political, in Jamaica. Ironically, this is consolidating at the same time that the electoral process in Jamaica is at a highpoint in terms of levels of organization, transparency of processes, and commitment to the system from the dominant parties—the latter most evident in the virtual absence of violence and evident mingling of opposing supporters, both in the lead-up to and during the 2011 election.[6] In the year, then, of Jamaica's fiftieth anniversary of independence, to be celebrated on August 6, 2012, it is both the best and the worst of times. In terms of the system and the social acceptance of its results, elections and the political process have never been more universally accepted and legitimate. Yet, in terms of the saliency of the electoral exercise as a means of forging genuinely alternative ways of social and political living, there is growing despondency.

The Dudus Events

The political occurrence most influential in determining the contours of the present conjuncture is, of course, what is commonly referred to as the "Dudus events" of May 2010.[7] On the day after Labour Day, May 24, 2010, the Jamaica Defence Force (JDF), supported by contingents from the police, via a flanking maneuver breached the carefully constructed barricades around the Western Kingston community of Tivoli Gardens, erected to protect from imminent arrest and extradition to the United States, Christopher "Dudus" Coke, self-proclaimed "president" and don of the community and erstwhile supporter of the governing JLP. The swift military action and the room-by-room search that followed led to the deaths of some seventy-three persons—an unprecedented number even in violence-prone Jamaica—providing fuel for a continuing controversy as to whether all or even most of the casualties had been combatants. What is uncontroversial is that the stonewalling of the U.S. extradition request by the Golding government, various degrees of obfuscation and dissimulation of the details to the parliament and public, and the attempt to use the reputable U.S. consulting firm Mannatt, Phelps and Phillips to lobby in favor of delaying or even rescinding the request, had emboldened Coke and his supporters, leading to the inevitable confrontation and tragic denouement.[8]

In the months that followed and until recently, rates of violent crime in the country fell dramatically. There were, for instance, 700 fewer murders between June 2010 and May 2011[9] compared with the previous year, encouraging claims by some members of the incumbent party that they should be returned at the polls, as it was under their watch that the intractable problem of violence had at last been brought under control. But of course, it had not been the government, which had resisted the extradition kicking and screaming all the way, but the insistence, not always behind the scenes, of the hegemonic power and the growing crescendo from civil society that established treaty and the rule of law should be followed that eventually forced the government's assent and precipitated the action that damaged the military apparatus of the Tivoli Gardens state within a state. Thus, it is not surprising that even as murders and other violent crimes subsided, so too did Golding's standings in the polls,[10] until the moment on September 25, 2011, when it became clear that he would not be reelected and he resigned in the ultimately futile hope that newer leadership would take the party to victory.

Questioning Sovereignty

At the heart of the extradition controversy and the debates that have raged in the following months, is the fraught notion of sovereignty. When it was brought to public attention that Peter Phillips, minister of national security under the earlier PNP regime, had signed memoranda of understanding facilitating the wiretapping of Coke and that this information had been shared with the United States, he was accused of acting against the national interest and chants of "CIA agent"[11]—even more ironic given the JLP's traditions of pro-American, right-of-center politics—were directed at him from the government benches of the House. Golding himself on more than one occasion alluded to and warned against outside interference in Jamaica's affairs, suggesting that his insistence on Coke's "rights"[12] was in the national interest. Even in the aftermath of the extradition and detention of Coke, rumors continue to swirl that other members and associates of the former government remain on a short list of persons likely to be served with extradition notices for various crimes.[13] Most bizarre of all was the matter of the U.S. surveillance plane, a Lockheed P-3 Orion that had been seen by many and was photographed circling the airspace above Kingston during the military action.[14] When asked in October 2011 whether the government knew about this, then Minister of Security Dwight Nelson at first denied that the plane even existed, only to be contradicted later by Prime Minister Holness, who suggested, confusingly, that it was a military matter and thus outside the purview of the minister of national security.[15]

The inflammatory accusations against Phillips; the inversion of traditional anti-imperialist positions, with the JLP seeking to claim the high, nationalist ground; the government's subsequent obfuscation on the actual relationship with the United States during the military action, all point to the need for a more careful, even forensic conversation on the status of sovereignty and its usefulness as a concept for small states in the early decades of the twenty-first century. On the one hand, the involvement of the United States, beginning with the initial drafting of the extradition treaties, through the request for Coke's extradition, to the military assistance, best manifested in the appearance of the P-3 Orion, suggests the continuing imbalance and consolidation of power in a region that, for more than a century has been considered an American lake. On the other hand, however, the clamor for Golding to abide by the extradition procedures and the refusal to buy into his "anti-imperialist" argument opposing Coke's extradition, suggest an unprecedented degree of tactical sophistication exercised by the Jamaican public, which, it might be argued, sought to use the U.S. war against drug lords to serve the "national" purpose of neutralizing a local security threat. Imbalance of power, then, if there is substance in this musing, may not always translate into impotence of action.

If, long before the collapse of the Soviet Union and the end of the Cold War, Gerard Chaliand could have described the romantic notion of "Third Worldism"—the idea that the independent states emerging out of the decolonization movements of the fifties and sixties could build new Utopias—as a myth,[16] then pessimistic perspectives have further consolidated in recent years. Thus, Samir Amin, one of the iconic anti-imperialist thinkers of the sixties, suggested in 2003 that the post-Bandung South can be divided into three distinct components. The first group, the "active periphery" of East Asian countries, is deeply involved in the processes of modern capitalism. The second group, consisting of India and many Latin American states, is also involved, but is far more vulnerable than the South East Asian countries. The third group, constituting much of Africa and smaller states (presumably including those in the Caribbean), is locked into "outmoded international divisions of labour"[17] and therefore extremely marginalized in the contemporary world. If, in Amin's assessment, even the dynamic peripheries remain vulnerable, there is little if any space left for the marginal countries beyond the provision of passive reserves (armies) of unemployed labor for the developed economies. Equally pessimistic in proposing the absence of any room for maneuver is Immanuel Wallerstein, who argues that, short of what he describes as "radical alterity" (Al Qaeda, Iran) or the failed policy of direct confrontation (Iraq), the only "weapon" that small, peripheral states have in their strategic armory is the somewhat ephemeral mass migration of persons from the South to the North, with the potential of these groups becoming a fifth column of support for the causes of the South in the center countries.[18]

Far more textured—perhaps out of disciplinary sensibility—in the appreciation of the continuing saliency of the state, though I fear, equally pessimistic in conclusion, are some of the positions from the international relations establishment. Thus Stephen Krasner, in his argument for sharing sovereignty, develops the proposition that conventional sovereignty has three elements: international/legal sovereignty, or the internationally recognized right to juridical independence; Westphalian/Vatellian sovereignty, or the right of each state to domestic authority structures; and domestic sovereignty, or the actual control of authority within a state's territorial boundaries.[19] Krasner's assertion, at first glance reasonable, is that the rules available to provide assistance for well-governed states are inappropriate for badly governed ones. Governance assistance and transitional administrative forms are inadequate, and "In the future, better domestic governance in badly governed, failed and occupied polities will require the transcendence of accepted rules, including the creation of shared sovereignty in specific areas. In some cases, decent governance may require some new form of trusteeship, almost certainly de facto rather than de jure."[20]

Aside from the evident hubris in the assumption of the common acceptance of a marker for "badly governed" and "failed" states, and the glib assertion that being "occupied" is a hazard facing developing countries, is the even more hubristic reassertion of the language of colonialism in the use of "trusteeship" as the descriptor for the proposed arrangement. I readily admit that Krasner has proposed exceptional conditions for his new arrangement, including instances of civil war and imminent starvation of the domestic population, all compellingly reasonable; yet I suggest that in the permanency implicit in his exhortation to rewrite norms of international sovereignty is the dangerous reaffirmation of archaic principles of imperial power and dominance rejected more than six decades ago. It is perhaps appropriate to reexamine those principles and the momentous struggles to de-center them in this moment of pause, before too rapidly marching down that hoary road.

What, however, if the onward march of capitalist globalization has so changed the world that the markers of power no longer pass mainly through the corridors of the state?[21] Susan Strange's argument, novel at first but now widely acknowledged, is that in the contemporary world, power has shifted upward from weak to strong states; sideways from states to the market; and that some power has "evaporated," in that it has diffused and no institution is exercising it.[22] A version of this argument is carefully elaborated by Barbadian political economist Hilbourne Watson, who argues that the "Techno-Paradigm Shift" is completely altering the traditional notions of nation, sovereignty, and citizenship:

Caribbean nation states have very little prospect of making it alone as separate entities in the coming century. National development strategies can offer little more than stillborn outcomes. Caribbean people understand that sovereignty offers them little beyond the symbolic. The Caribbean must grow beyond its internal limits if it is to grow at all. Since global integration is the wave of modern capitalism, the region's leaders must think of bold ways to transform the Caribbean into a globally linked region. However, it must find ways to identify the technologies, skills and commodities to drive such an option.[23]

Yet, in the interstices of Watson's paean in favor of the idea that capitalism has steamrolled the state, the nation, and all such archaic constructs is a clear and manifest call for an activist polity that will "grow," "think of bold ways," "find ways to identify," and "drive such an option." What are these if not the markers of a modified, yet still potent and activist state? And if, indeed, a new, activist state is required, what will be the purchase, the ground around which the significant majority will unite in this effort of common goals and a common future? Emerging from the *After Sovereignty*[24] debates, more philosophically grounded arguments address some of these questions frontally even as many arrive at somewhat unsatisfactory conclusions. New exegeses of Hobbes's *Leviathan*[25] utilizing Foucault's notions of "biopower"[26] as a qualitative extension of sovereign, state power, or Agamben's totalitarian readings of the contemporary state,[27] provide useful debating points for the scope and character of internal sovereignty in the post–Cold War context, but offer only limited bases for application to the precarious position of small states in the new world order.

More fertile points of departure might be located in historically grounded approaches that remind us of the foundations of contemporary sovereignty in the New World, deriving from an original action of imperialist usurpation. Thus, asking the rhetorical question "what is Canada?" Hogeveen replies:

> Put simply, the founding of euro-Canadian sovereignty amounts to a coup de force and a violence that obfuscated the previously founded authority of the Aboriginal peoples. The depths of Canadian sovereignty run little further than declarations such as "we are mighty and we say so"—is there any other kind? Canadian sovereignty, the founding of the nation, was authorized by itself, for itself and in itself: is justified in applying itself.[28]

This initial action is then followed up by "shifting horizons" of meaning, which serve to obscure the underlying though omnipresent "spectres of injustice" that accompany contemporary Canada. The only solution, Hogeveen asserts, with little direction as to how this might arise, would be to open the door to some formulation of restorative justice in the future.

Similarly, McVeigh and Pahuja,[29] focusing on the Third World's demands in the flush of the decolonization moment for Permanent Sovereignty over Natural Resources (PSNR), point to the uncertainties and instabilities associated with power and territorial space in the period after World War II. While appropriately identifying the international arena as inherently a "common space devoid of law," they propose that the creation of laws surrounding PSNR and other Third World demands is "mythopoetic," that is, "Jurisdictional ground is not given, it is poesis or created in the relation: the creation of a space of encounter."[30] Thus, while the weapons available to the strong (the Bretton Woods institutions, etc.) weigh heavily in their favor, they are not necessarily overwhelming or determinate. The international space, in other words, is a public space, is one of contestation, albeit not on a level ground for all participants.

McVeigh and Pahuja's suggestion of the porosity of the international space and the possibility of engagement without futility, coupled with Hogeveen's proposal of "justice" as a possible alternative project to that of a sovereignty based on usurpations, returns us to the possible foundations for a reconstructed, perhaps more modest notion of sovereignty for the Caribbean project. I suggest that Caribbean sovereignty has its own very reputable genealogy, tracing its way back to the Haitian revolution when, in the heat of the ultimate battles that would establish Haitian independence, Dessalines tore the white from the French tricolor and instead of the initials "RF" (Republique Francaise) transposed the words "Liberty or Death."[31] The approaches to a redefinition of Caribbean sovereignty, despite the subsequent meanderings of Haiti, might therefore need to be grounded in this symbolic space, i.e., an elaboration of more substantial notions of liberty than are to be found in the Western republican traditions, whether French or otherwise. The path for the future then, would seem to head in the direction of imagining[32] new national, or perhaps transnational projects that would seek to extend freedom and provide solid foundations for new modalities of living and producing.

Thus, we might take solace in the knowledge that, even if Susan Strange is right on the retreat of the power and room to maneuver of the contemporary state, she does not propose its negation as a player on the chessboard of globalization; and even if Hilbourne Watson is correct on the constrictions on statal agency inherent in densely integrated global supply chains, his conclusion, quoted above, is far removed from the helpless stasis evident in Amin's dismissal of "marginal peripheries" or the return to trusteeship explicit, if presented as the exceptional case, in Krasner's "shared sovereignty."

The somewhat simplistic, though I think important proposal that is being advanced here is that while it is possible to think about and identify genu-inely failed states, or imagine very small states that fall below the threshold to possess any meaningful agency, the notions of sovereignty and agency are to be considered points along a continuum more than absolute values. From such a stance, the challenge facing small, vulnerable states is how to elaborate a worthwhile "national" project and advance along this continuum, to accumu-late, as it were, greater sovereignty through a variety of strategies, in order to provide the widest range of policy options for the development and prosperity of the citizens who live within their boundaries.

Auditing Jamaica's Sovereignty

What, then, is the state of Jamaica's sovereignty? Using Krasner's framework, we can propose that international juridical sovereignty, though its saliency is and always has been debatable, is still very much in existence, as is West-phalian/Vatellian sovereignty, though the latter has historically been compro-mised. Domestic sovereignty on the other hand, has survived recent tests to its integrity and has, in the present moment, if the project of the nation is re-defined, the greatest potential for enhancement. If all three elements are to be seen as interlinked and thus mutually enforcing, then sovereignty, writ large, might be advanced (or retarded) by movement along one or more of these avenues.[33]

Jamaican international juridical sovereignty is written into law, the country's membership in the United Nations, and numerous other international and re-gional associations. It has never been formally compromised, and though real power has always resided in the Security Council, votes in the UN General As-sembly still matter. Voting and statehood are thus not entirely ephemeral and Jamaica has shown a remarkable ability, even within the confines of the post–Cold War, globalized world, to adopt independent positions. Substantial cases include the opposition to George W. Bush's invasion of Iraq and to the ouster of President Aristide from Haiti,[34] for both of which Jamaica (along with her sister Commonwealth Caribbean (Caricom) states) drew the ire of the United States but did not waiver.[35] The interesting lesson that might be drawn from a regional perspective is that regional unity matters in the face of a potentially hostile hegemon, but the numerous votes of the independent small states of the Caribbean are also important. Unity enhances sovereignty, but unification, which could reduce Caricom to one vote, might not necessarily achieve the same objective.

Westphalian/Vatellian sovereignty, or the right to non-interference, has been formally honored, though there is a substantial body of opinion that sug-

gests that the Manley regime of 1976–80 was destabilized by covert intervention[36] from the United States as well as by International Monetary Fund (IMF)
policies that served to undermine the credibility of the government.[37] More
recently, it has been proposed that international and bilateral binding trade
agreements, such as those advanced by the World Trade Organization (WTO)
and the European Partnership Agreement (EPA), severely restrict the policy
options available to small states, often forcing them to pursue trade regimes
that might prove inimical to the nurturing of productive domestic sectors.[38]
In the case of the EPA, despite widespread reservations from business and intellectual sectors, Commonwealth Caribbean countries waivered in the face
of determined pressure from the EU and accepted an agreement that is only
now being fully debated in the region. Yet, among African states notably, concerted resistance to the stock provisions of the EPA have led to negotiations
with greater options for flexibility and compromise than the Caribbean case
would suggest.[39] The approach toward greater agency and assertiveness would
seem therefore to be in the direction of maintaining unity at the regional level
while developing a common technical capacity to negotiate in favor of those
common positions that emerge. Recent experience with Caricom's Regional
Negotiating Machinery (RNM), now restructured as the Office of Trade Negotiations (OTN), suggests that both these requirements must be met.

The most complex dimension is that of domestic sovereignty. Despite a
healthy debate in the national media over the last decade, Jamaica is not a
failed state.[40] The country has been able to reduce poverty, improve infant
mortality rates,[41] maintain a credible if stressed system of health care, and provide a modicum of basic education for its population. There are caveats for
each of these assertions, particularly in the failure to educate far more citizens
to the tertiary level, but they are made as a counter to the "failed state" assertion. Economically, however, Jamaica's performance over the last two decades,
and more broadly over the fifty years since independence, has been poor, with
periods of low growth interspersed by periods of stagnation. The World Bank's
2011 Memorandum suggested that Jamaica ranked 180 out of 196 countries in
terms of rates of economic growth, with an average growth rate of only 1 per
cent over the past twenty years.[42] Among the outcomes has been a wholesale
exodus of human talent, with the World Bank estimating some 85 per cent of
the country's tertiary-trained population now residing outside of her boundaries.[43] Yet despite this reality, dominated by an overwhelming debt burden that
is projected to grow to 150 per cent of GDP by 2012,[44] the World Bank's conclusion is that growth can be "unlocked" if a few critical and painful measures
are addressed. The bank suggests that the key factor inhibiting the country's
growth is low productivity, eliciting a multi-pronged strategy including reduc-

ing crime, investing more in education, removing entrenched "perverse" tax incentives, and moving away from the "enclave development model."[45]

While there are substantial points to be debated in all of these proposals, there is a prior and overarching consideration contributing to economic stagnation that is associated with the breakdown of social consensus. Elsewhere, I have proposed that Jamaica is in a prolonged moment of hegemonic dissolution.[46] The social pact between the classes that took the country into independence came apart in the seventies, as the Michael Manley regime sought to rapidly advance outstanding demands for social equality and inclusion. It was never put back together again, and Jamaica has endured a long interregnum in which neo-liberal platitudes of the "magic of the market" and grassroots interpretations, such as the crude materialism of the "bling"[47] culture, proliferated. This profound social and political collapse came with important ethical/philosophical dimensions, as common-sense certitudes of right and wrong were jettisoned along with notions of the nation and a particular concept of the Jamaican national project, embodied in the 1962 independence slogan "Out of Many One People." A critical political dimension of this moment was the emergence of the don and the so-called "garrison communities" of the inner cities.[48] These semi-autonomous fiefdoms were both a reflection of ethical and philosophical dimensions of advanced hegemonic dissolution and an indication of the failure of the formal state to provide the social and security needs of a significant cross section of its urban citizens.

The 2010 Dudus events and the extradition of Coke severely undermined but have not entirely eroded the emergence of autonomous states within the state. What they have provided is a moment for pause, which has been further prolonged by the election of December 2010. Politics like nature abhors a vacuum, and this moment could either segue into a phase of regeneration of the garrisons and even more intense urban warfare and uncertainty; or it could lead to a set of national conversations that would lay the basis for new social arrangements, new ethico-philosophical foundations and an enhanced domestic sovereignty that would give Jamaica greater maneuverability in the world.

A Way Forward

I present my way forward as a series of theses:

1. The severe damage to the Dudus-led empire in 2010, the role of civil society in raising its collective voice against the apparent cohabitation between the government and the don, and the decisive victory of the PNP at the polls together provide a moment for rethinking not only Jamaican politics, but the nature of the Jamaican polity.

2. The fiftieth anniversary of independence is a most appropriate time to consider these matters and launch a conversation, a Constituent Assembly of the Jamaican People at Home and Abroad, that would look closely at constitutional matters, the economy, terms of social engagement, and the philosophical underpinnings of the society.[49]

3. The philosophical question needs special attention. It is a patently false assumption that there is a common set of precepts that unites Jamaica. The debate that emerged following the publication in 2010 of excerpts from the diary of a notorious gunman, Cedric "Doggy" Murray, leader of the Stone Crusher gang, is noteworthy.[50] Doggy's musings suggested a seamless intermingling of Old Testament religiosity with murder to avenge perceived social inequality, a view often voiced in different ways by many dancehall deejays. These and similar anti-establishment perspectives find fertile ground among the vast swathes of unemployed and underemployed youth in Kingston, Montego Bay, Spanish Town and other urban areas, suggesting the failure not only of the state but of an older generation to provide a meaningful and compelling ethical framework for the young.[51] Similarly, the 2010 LAPOP study Political Culture and Democracy in Jamaica found, in assessing support for the political system on a 100-point index, that "Jamaica's 48.6 points score places it close to the bottom of the chart,"[52] supporting the assertion of extreme alienation among the poor and dispossessed.

4. A new philosophical conversation would have to address questions of social equality; place on the agenda lingering matters such as pervasive but subtle forms of color discrimination that have led numerous persons to bleach their skins; confront the blatant homophobia that has grown in the past decade;[53] and give due respect in appropriate institutional ways to Patwa, the despised but irrepressible language of the majority which is simultaneously and ironically the gold-sealed signature of Jamaica to the rest of the world. It would have to consider an entirely new definition of the nation that is sensitive to the fact that half of all Jamaicans live elsewhere while still considering themselves integrally part of the nation. This "long distance nationalism,"[54] packed with cultural, political, social, and economic implications[55] and contradictions, is critical to understand in any conversation surrounding the renaissance of a vibrant Jamaican and Caribbean project.

5. Such a conversation would lead to a discussion of the necessary reforms in the political system that would learn from those successes that already exist, such as the Electoral Commission of Jamaica,[56] which has been successful in finding a way to bring together the dominant political parties and members of civil society in a common program that has largely ended corruption and violence in the electoral process. It would have to address matters associated with the deepening of democracy, such as phasing out the unelected Senate and introducing principles of recall for non-performing members of parliament.[57]

6. Similarly, the conversation, and its resolution in a renewed notion of community and a clear political direction for the future, would lay the foundation for a parallel economic discourse that would explain structural and fiscal limitations, propose democratic approaches to the balancing and sharing of sacrifices across social sectors, and suggest an economic path for the next fifty years.[58]

7. The politics of such a strategy has not been elaborated. The events surrounding the Dudus case has not yielded new and innovative forms of street action parallel to the popular mobilizations emerging from the "Arab Spring" of 2011 or even the recent marches and demonstrations against metropolitan France in the Caribbean DOMs.[59] Yet, in the Jamaican case, the density of calls to the numerous radio talk shows, voluminous Facebook messages and tweets, letters to the editor, and general crescendo of opinions served similar ends, the effect of which was evident in Golding's resignation and the subsequent electoral defeat of his party. It is sufficient to say that even broader and more persistent coalitions, utilizing both traditional and novel forms of popular mobilization involving as well as circumventing the traditional parties, will be required to force through the reforms proposed here.

8. The regional agenda is closely tied into this. Gilbert Roberts, Bishop and Payne, and many others have lamented the failure of Caribbean states to shed island sovereignty more rapidly in favor of a shared regional sovereignty that would enhance prospects for autonomy and development.[60] If the argument advanced here is substantial, then it is evident that in order for Jamaica to participate effectively in a shared arrangement of sovereignty at the regional level, it must resolve critical matters related to domestic sovereignty in the national space. While one agenda need not be stalled until the other is completed, it is fair to say that the national takes precedence over the regional and will bring it crashing to the ground, as in the past with Federation,[61] if it is not largely resolved before the latter.

Conclusion: Guerrilla Sovereignty

The flaw in most discussions on globalization and the demise of the state and sovereignty is the failure to properly account for the pesky persistence of states in the contemporary world. While it is true that there are states that reasonably qualify as failed and others that barely survive without aid and international assistance of various kinds, many more persist with varying levels of prosperity within the world system. And, as I have suggested, even as the balance of power between these small states and inordinately more powerful hegemons remains and even increases, this need not always translate into impotence and futility. If these are true, it would be neglectful, to say the least, to end the discussion at the point of recognition of the severe obstacles in the path of small, resource-poor states in the contemporary global order. Instead, what is required is the necessary discussion as to how to build the appropriate alliances within the state; consider the philosophical questions that might be appropriate in forging a common ethos, central to crafting a new, inclusive notion of the nation, cognizant of the importance of long-distance nationalism; advance for the widest discussion and popular approval a suite of achievable mid-term objectives; build the appropriate alliances with regional neighbors that face similar obstacles and share common objectives; and proceed to bob and weave through the underbrush of the globalized world, using a sort of guerrilla sovereignty[62] to seek, against the odds, to improve the social and economic lives of the majority within the national space of Jamaica and, beyond her, the people of a future, more meaningful, Caribbean alliance.

NOTES

Preface

1. Martin Carter, "Looking at Your Hands," *Martin Carter: Selected Poems*, George-town, Guyana: Demerara, 1989, 11.

2. Among the main venues for these conversations, exchanges, and debates have been the *CLR James Journal*, now the official journal of the Caribbean Philosophical Association (CPA) and edited by Paget Henry; *Small Axe*, edited by David Scott; and *Social and Economic Studies*, edited by Annie Paul. Among the main sites for these encounters have been the Caribbean Reasonings series of conferences to honor lead-ing Caribbean thinkers and held by the Center for Caribbean Thought (CCT) at UWI Mona from 2001–2010; the annual conferences of the Caribbean Studies Association and numerous other encounters in the Caribbean, the United States, the United King-dom, and South Africa. Among the leading collaborators and protagonists have been my colleagues in the CCT Anthony Bogues and Rupert Lewis, as well as Hilbourne Watson, David Scott, Charles Mills, Lewis Gordon, Cecelia Green, Paget Henry, Nor-man Girvan, Rhoda Reddock, Carolyn Cooper, Linden Lewis, Kari Levitt, Anton Al-lahar, Percy Hintzen, Horace Campbell, Obika Gray, Patsy Lewis, Anthony Harriott, Deborah Thomas, Pat Mohammed, Pedro Noguera, Alissa Trotz, Folke Lindahl, Alex Dupuy, Gina Ulysse, Carole Boyce Davies, the late Barry Chevannes, Holger Henke, Bill Schwarz, Christine Cummings, Kate Quinn, the late Manning Marable, Sonjah Stan-ley-Niaah, Clinton Hutton, Jay Mandle, Tennyson Joseph, Aaron Kamugisha, Jermaine McCalpin, Maziki Thame, among many others who have been in the forefront of the debate around Caribbean intellectual thought, social movements, and radical politics.

3. Chief Economist Olivier Blanchard, writing, though not officially from the IMF, admitted that contrary to their predictions, IMF austerity measures in Greece and oth-er European countries had been a significant drag on growth. See Howard Schneider, "An Amazing Mea Culpa from the IMF's Chief Economist on Austerity," *Washington Post*, January 3, 2013.

4. See Norman Girvan, "Are Caribbean Countries facing Existential Threats?" www.normangirvan.info/girvan-existential-threats/.

5. See Paget Henry, *Caliban's Reason: Introducing Afro-Caribbean Philosophy*, New York and London: Routledge, 2000.

6. See Brian Meeks and Folke Lindahl, *New Caribbean Thought: A Reader*, Kingston: University of the West Indies Press, 2001.

7. See Anton Allahar, *Caribbean Charisma: Reflections on Leadership, Legitimacy*

and Populist Politics, Kingston: Ian Randle, and Boulder and London: Lynne Rienner, 2001.

8. See Brian Meeks, *Envisioning Caribbean Futures: Jamaican Perspectives*, Kingston: University of the West Indies Press, 2007.

9. Originally published in Linden Lewis, *Caribbean Sovereignty: Development and Democracy in an Age of Globalization*, New York and London: Routledge, 2013.

10. There is, however, hope in a younger generation of Caribbean social scientists and theorists, who seem to be both sensitive to major philosophical debates and willing to engage in empirical explorations of the Caribbean region's tenuous place in the global political economy. See for instance, Tennyson Joseph, *Decolonization in St. Lucia: Politics and Global Neoliberalism, 1945–2010*, Jackson: University Press of Mississippi, 2011; and Aaron Kamugisha's two edited volumes, *Caribbean Political Thought: The Colonial State to Caribbean Internationalisms* and *Caribbean Political Thought: Theories of the Post-Colonial State*, Kingston and Miami: Ian Randle, 2013.

Chapter 1

I use "frontline" in three senses: as the central field of engagement in a battle; the lead group of singers in a chorus; and a gathering place on Red Hills road in Kingston, where cutting-edge reggae artistes displayed their talents in the early nineties.

1. Beyond his sterling work as dean of the faculty of social sciences at Mona, Barry's post-WPJ interventions in Jamaican life were legendary. Among the most outstanding were his work on the government of Jamaica's "Ganja Commission," which argued that marijuana should be decriminalized; his role in developing a vibrant peace initiative against violence in the country; and, not least of all, his critical anthropological work on Rastafari. Chevannes died in November 2010.

2. I accept Chevannes's notion of worldview as a "substrate" of underlying ideas that influence and guide other more immediate practices and actions. See Barrington Chevannes, "The Jamaican Worldview and Africa: Spirit as Power," Monthly Graduate Seminar Paper, Department of Sociology and Social Work, UWI, Mona, April 1994.

3. Mervyn Alleyne, *Africa: Roots of Jamaican Culture*, Chicago: Research Associates School Times Publications, 1996, 150.

4. Paget Henry, *Caliban's Reason: Introducing Afro-Caribbean Philosophy*, London and New York: Routledge, 2000, 59.

5. See, for instance, Maurice Patterson, *Big Sky, Little Bullet: A Docu-Novel*, Grenada: Maurice Patterson, 1992; and Horace Campbell, *Rasta and Resistance: From Marcus Garvey to Walter Rodney*, New Jersey: Africa World Press, 1988.

6. See, *Programme: Workers Party of Jamaica*, Kingston, 1978, 106–10.

7. See Brian Meeks, "The Development of the 1970 Revolution in Trinidad and Tobago," M.Sc. thesis, UWI Mona, 1978.

8. See Brian Meeks, "NUFF at the Cusp of an Idea: Grassroots Guerrillas and the Politics of the Seventies in Trinidad and Tobago," in *Narratives of Resistance: Jamaica, Trinidad, the Caribbean*, Barbados, Jamaica, Trinidad and Tobago: University of the West Indies Press, 2000, 48–74.

9. See, for instance, Gordon Lewis's otherwise excellent study, *Grenada: The Jewel Despoiled*, Baltimore and London: Johns Hopkins University Press, 1987.

10. Horace Campbell's study on Rastafari is a notable exception. See Campbell 1988.

11. See Henry 2000, "Caribbean Marxism after the Neoliberal and Linguistic Turns," 221–46. Henry is referring to the extent to which postmodernist and postcolonial notions of deconstruction and signification have become influential among Caribbean intellectuals in recent times. Among other important interventions are Holger Henke's attempt to understand the "nature" of the Caribbean, "Towards an Ontology of Caribbean Existence"; exchange with Merle Jacob on the nature of Caribbean society, in *Social Epistemology* 11, no. 1 (January–March 1997): 39–58; Antonio Benitez Rojo, *The Repeating Island: The Caribbean and the Postmodern Perspective*, Durham and London: Duke University Press, 1996; and Tony Bogues's new work on "dread history," *Black Heretics, Black Prophets: Radical Political Intellectuals*, New York and London: Routledge, 2003.

12. Henry 2000, 213.

13. Ibid., 212–13.

14. See Brian Meeks, chapter 2 in this volume, "Reasoning with Caliban: A Critical Reading of Paget Henry's *Caliban's Reason: Introducing Afro-Caribbean Philosophy*."

15. For a sustained argument in support of this perspective, see Clinton Hutton and Nathaniel Samuel Murrell, "Rastas' Psychology of Blackness, Resistance and Somebodiness," in Nathaniel Murrell, William Spencer, and Adrian McFarlane (eds.), *Chanting Down Babylon: The Rastafari Reader*, Kingston: Ian Randle, 1998, 36–54.

16. David Scott, *Refashioning Futures: Criticism after Postcoloniality*, Princeton: Princeton University Press, 1999, 198–99.

17. Ibid., 213.

18. This approach is further elaborated in response to a more recent phase of Jamaican politics in David Scott, "The Permanence of Pluralism," in Paul Gilroy, Lawrence Grossberg, and Angela McRobbie (eds.), *Without Guarantees: In Honour of Stuart Hall*, London and New York: Verso, 2000, 282–301.

19. Ibid., 217.

20. Ibid., 199.

21. See, for instance, Wayne Sandiford, *On the Brink of Decline: Bananas in the Windward Islands*, St. George's, Grenada: Fedon, 2000.

22. See for instance, Barry Gills (ed.), *Globalization and the Politics of Resistance*, London and Basingstoke: Macmillan, 2000; and Amory Starr, *Naming the Enemy: Anti-Corporate Social Movements Confront Globalization*, London: Zed, 2000.

23. Rude Boy: 1960s predecessors to the contemporary heavily armed urban gangs with loose affiliations to the two major political parties. See Scott, 195.

24. Stuart Hall, "The Problem of Ideology: Marxism Without Guarantees," in David Morley and Kuan-Hsing Chen (eds.), *Stuart Hall: Critical Dialogues in Cultural Studies*, London: Routledge, 1996, 45.

25. Ibid., 41. The quote within the quote is from Antonio Gramsci, *Selections from the Prison Notebooks*, London: Lawrence and Wishart, 1971.

26. Ibid., 323-377.

27. Ibid., 325.

28. Ibid., 325.

29. See liner notes for *Reggae Greats: Pablo Moses*, Mango Records, 1984.

30. Ibid.

31. For the only attempt to gather his calypsos together, with some biographical treatment, see Zeno O. Constance (ed.), *Life is a Stage: The Complete Calypsoes of Brother Valentino, Anthony Emrold Phillip*, Port of Spain: Zeno Constance, 1996.

32. See Louis Regis, *The Political Calypso: True Opposition in Trinidad and Tobago, 1962–1987*, Barbados, Jamaica, Trinidad and Tobago: University of the West Indies Press, 1999, 86–90.

33. However, how we wish to describe "mainstream" might alter this conclusion. The liner notes on Moses, for instance, suggest his iconic status, if not his broad popularity; and at least one website has listed Valentino's "Life Is a Stage" as among the 100 best calypsos of the twentieth century; see www.djtonyttempo.com.

34. See Dick Hebdige, "Subculture: The Meaning of Style," in Ken Gelder and Sarah Thornton (eds.), *The Subcultures Reader*, London and New York: Routledge, 1997.

35. Both David Scott and Tony Bogues explore the nature and politics of dreadness. See Scott 2000 and Anthony Bogues, *Black Heretics, Black Prophets: Radical Political Intellectuals*, New York and London: Routledge, 2003.

36. This exact scene is utilized effectively in the cult movie classic *The Harder they Come*, when the hero attends the cinema for the first time in the city.

37. Gordon Rohlehr described an earlier slowing down, the transition from ska to rock steady, as an "almost conscious attempt to cool the country down." This is as good as any, though Rohlehr enigmatically leaves out the "by whom" and "for what." See Gordon Rohlehr, "Sounds and Pressure," *My Strangled City and Other Essays*, Port of Spain: Longman Trinidad, 1992, 89.

38. Literally, "without mercy," it refers to the early calypso tradition of singing against one's opponent in a verbal duel, the intention being to defeat the adversary by sheer superiority of rhetoric and allusion. See, for instance, Gordon Rohlehr, *Calypso and Society in Pre-Independence Trinidad*, Port of Spain: Gordon Rohlehr, 1990, 57–68.

39. Interestingly, biographies of the jazz giant Miles Davis and comments on the life

of the Jamaican trombonist Don Drummond point to an almost identical relationship between artiste and audience in both instances.

40. For earlier references to the respective references to Africa and black consciousness in calypso and reggae, see Carole Boyce Davies, "The Africa Theme in Trinidad Calypso," *Caribbean Quarterly* 31, no. 2 (June 1985): 67–86; and Erna Brodber, "Black Consciousness and Popular Music in Jamaica in the 1960s and 1970s," in Ibid., 53–66.

41. Valentino, "Third World," *Third World Messenger*, Port of Spain, 1978, in Constance 1996, 10–11.

42. See, for instance, Henry 2000.

43. See Scott 2000, 205.

44. Pablo Moses, "Revolutionary Dream," *Revolutionary Dream*, Shanachie 44016, 1992.

45. Pablo Moses, "We Should Be in Angola," Ibid.

46. Ibid., "Give I Fe I Name."

47. Valentino, "Third World."

48. Pablo Moses, "Blood Money," *Revolutionary Dream*.

49. Valentino, "Dis Place Nice," in Constance 1996, 16.

50. Alleyne 1996, 158.

51. Pablo Moses, "Grasshopper," *Revolutionary Dream*.

52. Valentino, "Every Brother Is Not a Brother," in Constance 1996, 18.

53. Pablo Moses, "Blood Money," *Revolutionary Dream*. "Donesa" is a typical midseventies Rastafarian play with words. Money is never enough, it is always finishing. Thus, it becomes "doney" and then evolves, through a more obscure process, into "donesa."

54. See "Social Living," *Reggae Greats: Burning Spear*, Mango Records, 1984.

55. The Congos, "Row Fisherman Row," The Congos, 1977, rereleased on *Congos*, Blood and Fire, BAFCD 009, 1996.

Chapter 2

1. See Wilson Harris, "History, Fable and Myth in the Caribbean and Guianas," in Andrew Bundy (ed.), *Wilson Harris: The Unfinished Genesis of the Imagination*, London and New York: Routledge, 1999, 152–66.

2. As invoked from Frantz Fanon, see Paget Henry, *Caliban's Reason: Introducing Afro-Caribbean Philosophy*, London and New York: Routledge, 2000, 276. Henceforth referred to as Henry.

3. See ibid., 276.

4. Ibid., 24.

5. Ibid., 24.

6. Ibid., 27.

7. Ibid., 89.

8. See ibid., 89.

9. See ibid., 124.

10. See ibid., 128.

11. Ibid., 136.

12. See, for two early examples that incorporate both institutional and ideological explanations, Gordon Lewis, *Grenada: The Jewel Despoiled*, Baltimore and London: Johns Hopkins University Press, 1987; and Manning Marable, *African and Caribbean Politics: From Kwame Nkrumah to Maurice Bishop*, London: Verso, 1987.

13. See Brian Meeks, *Caribbean Revolutions and Revolutionary Theory: An Assessment of Cuba, Nicaragua and Grenada*, London and Basingstoke: Warwick University/Macmillan Caribbean, 1993.

14. See Mervyn Alleyne, *Africa: Roots of Jamaican Culture*, Chicago: Research Associates School Times Publications, 1996, especially "The Modern Period," 149–66.

15. Henry 2000, 212–13.

16. For a perspective similar to mine, see Horace Campbell, *Rasta and Resistance: From Marcus Garvey to Walter Rodney*, New Jersey: Africa World Press, 1987.

17. See in particular, Barry Chevannes, *Rastafari: Roots and Ideology*, New York: Syracuse University Press and Jamaica, Barbados, Trinidad: University of the West Indies Press, 1995, especially "Repatriation," 248–53.

18. I say "men" intentionally, as one of the justifiable limitations to Rastafarian theology is that it is male-centered. On this ground there is room for significant critique, though Henry does not take it up. Its absence is perhaps a broader indicator of a failure to look at gender seriously in the process of mapping Afro-Caribbean philosophy. Henry is quite obviously sensitive to matters of gender, but they are not, on the whole, in the foreground of his analysis.

19. See Henry 2000, 271.

20. C. L. R. James, "Preface," *Beyond a Boundary*, London: Stanley Paul, 1963, 8.

Chapter 3

1. I thank Rupert Lewis, Charles Mills, Pedro Noguera, Percy Hintzen, Mikey Witter, and Patsy Lewis for thoughtful comments on earlier drafts of this paper.

2. For a pioneering study on the recent Caribbean left, see Perry Mars, *Ideology and Change: The Transformation of the Caribbean Left*, Detroit: Wayne State University Press and Mona: University of the West Indies Press, 1998. For a critical overview of the Jamaican left, see Rupert Lewis, "Learning to blow the Abeng: A critical look at anti-establishment movements of the 1960s and 1970s," *Small Axe* 1 (March 1997): 5–17. See also Brian Meeks, *Narratives of Resistance: Jamaica, Trinidad, the Caribbean*, Mona: University of the West Indies Press, 2000, especially "The Caribbean Left at Century's End," 155–73.

3. See Brian Meeks (ed.), "New Currents in Caribbean Thought," *Social and Economic Studies* 43, no. 3 (September 1994).

4. See Brian Meeks, "Re-Reading the Black Jacobins: James, the Dialectic and the Revolutionary Conjuncture," *Social and Economic Studies* 43, no. 3 (September 1994): 75–103. Republished in Brian Meeks, *Radical Caribbean: From Black Power to Abu Bakr*, Mona: University of the West Indies Press, 1996, 102–23. References used here are from the original article.

5. The Wellesley conference was important for more than academic reasons, as it brought together in the immediate aftermath of the collapse of Eastern European socialism all of James's "constituents," i.e., artists, individuals on the Caribbean left, African Americans, and "anti-statist" Marxists from the European and North American left. See, for the rich discussion, Selwyn Cudjoe and William Cain (eds.), *C. L. R. James: His Intellectual Legacies*, Amherst: University of Massachusetts Press, 1995.

6. See C. L. R. James, *The Black Jacobins: Toussaint L'Ouverture and the San Domingo Revolution*, New York: Vintage, 1989. Henceforth referred to as BJ.

7. Like so many before me, I am inspired by E. P. Thompson's approach to writing history from within the lived experiences of the (extra)ordinary people. See E. P. Thompson, *The Making of the English Working Class*, London: Penguin, 1980. Among his descendants, I think that Wright, Levine, and Sober have made significant headway in developing an approach of "historical trajectories" to avoid a mechanistic Marxist analysis. See Erik Olin Wright, Andrew Levine, and Elliott Sober, *Reconstructing Marxism: Essays on Explanation and the Theory of History*, London and New York: Verso, 1992.

8. See Hilbourne Watson, "Themes in Liberalism, Modernity, Marxism, Postmodernism and Beyond: An Interpretation and Critique of 'Re-Reading the Black Jacobins,'" in Brian Meeks and Folke Lindahl (eds.), *New Caribbean Thought: A Reader*, Mona: University of the West Indies Press, 2001, 355–94. Henceforth referred to as Watson. The article, first delivered at a seminar I co-hosted with Folke Lindahl at Michigan State University in 1997, was later published in our jointly edited volume *New Caribbean Thought: A Reader*, without a rejoinder.

9. Ibid., 355.

10. Ibid., 358.

11. Ibid., 363.

12. Ibid., 363. The assumption here seems to be that any invocation of the word individual leads, without divergences, to the worst forms of reckless, atomistic individualism. There is no acknowledgment of the fact that even within the liberal tradition there are powerful tendencies, from J. S. Mill through to John Rawls, that stress varying notions of accompanying positive rights, ending up in a somewhat different political space from, say, that of a Robert Nozick. Absence of generosity as to my intentions is therefore only matched by an overabundance of reductionism.

13. Ibid., 367.

14. Ibid., 370. This is particularly irritating, in light of the fact that I have repeatedly expressed my disagreement with Francis Fukuyama's glib pronouncements on the "end of history." For instance, in response to Abu Bakr's failed coup attempt in Trinidad in 1990, I wrote: " If Bakr's aborted insurrection of 1990 tells us anything, it is that below a line extending from Washington, through London and Paris and on via Berlin and Moscow to Tokyo, history is continuing at breakneck speed. Certainly, the traditional narrative of the Left has been exhausted; but so too has a traditional notion of Western democracy in its Third World export variation. However, in the absence of grand narratives, prophecy asserts itself." Brian Meeks, "The Imam, the Return of Napoleon and the End of History," in Meeks 1996, 83–100.

15. On the contrary, much of my work has strongly critiqued the limitations of narrowly representative electoral forms. Thus, in the conclusion of *Narratives of Resistance*, I propose a general strategy for a future Caribbean left: "Without addressing the first issue, that is, the struggle for democracy, the second, the struggle against the market is impossible. But without the second, the first becomes empty and meaningless. Without a concerted attempt to deepen democracy and include the powerless in a flanking movement, around traditional wealth and entrenched power, then any short-term project of social renewal will follow a familiar trajectory, spiralling to disaster." In Meeks 2000, 172.

16. Meeks 1994, 100.

17. Brian Meeks, "Preface," *Social and Economic Studies* 43, no. 3 (September 1994): 2.

18. Though perhaps more correctly, the genesis of these changes might be sought in the demoralization of the French intellectual left after the 1968 revolt and the subsequent rise of various postmodernist currents. For an eclectic conversation on Marxism and culture on the eve of the ending of the Cold War that addresses this and other historical junctures, see Cary Nelson and Lawrence Grossberg (eds.), *Marxism and the Interpretation of Culture*, Urbana and Chicago: University of Illinois Press, 1988.

19. Watson, 355.

20. Meeks, "Preface," 2.

21. I think that Hayek is strongest on the epistemological ground, where he argues that knowledge is dispersed and the "fatal error" of socialism is that it assumes that the state can know what people want and thereby plan for their needs. He argues—with striking historical evidence to support him—that this always ends in an inefficient allocation of resources, corruption, or repression, as human activity and needs always outstrip the capacity to know and plan. The answer, for those who remain opposed to the inherent inequities of the market, must lay in a different kind of state, run not by a central planning institute, but by unprecedented means of popular consultation and involvement. For one such argument, see Theodore Burczak, "Subjectivism and Demo-

cratic Forms: A Response to Hayek's Critique of Socialism," in Antonio Callari, Stephen Cullenberg, and Carole Biewener (eds.), *Marxism in the Postmodern Age: Confronting the New World Order*, New York and London: Guilford Press, 1995, 169–77.

22. BJ, 49, in Meeks 1994, 99.

23. Alex Dupuy's intervention is a lucid elaboration of the hard, class thesis. He proposes that in order to understand the respective behaviors of Toussaint, Dessalines, etc., we need to see their distinct and separate interests as representatives of an emergent class of black property owners. I think this is a useful but partial explanation. Sylvia Wynter, in focusing on the sweep of James's life, comes to a different conclusion. She argues that despite James's outward adaptation of a similar approach, his understanding of race, of cultural and other forms of domination, and their respective resistances leads to a far more nuanced conclusion as to how modernity is constructed and how it must be challenged. See Alex Dupuy, "Toussaint L'Ouverture and the Haitian Revolution: A Reassessment of C. L. R. James's Interpretation," in Cudjoe and Cain 1995, 106–17; and Sylvia Wynter, "Beyond the Categories of the Master Conception: The Counter Doctrine of the Jamesian Poesis," in Paget Henry and Paul Buhle (eds.), *C. L. R. James's Caribbean*, London and Basingstoke: Macmillan Caribbean, 1992, 63–91.

24. BJ, 96.

25. Not least of all in Haiti itself. In response to the revisionist literature, which suggests that blacks were no better off than they had been under slavery, Blackburn convincingly argues: "While the Caribbean slave populations invariably had a negative growth rate, with deaths outnumbering births by a considerable margin, Haiti's population recovered and grew. Though the Haitian peasants were poor, they did not spend six days a week working for someone else; they built themselves simple but attractive dwellings and developed a rich folklore. Haitian women were not at the mercy of overseers and planters." Robin Blackburn, "The Black Jacobins and New World Slavery," in Cudjoe and Cain 1995, 96.

26. Meeks 1994, 101.

27. This is in reference to President Bush's statement from Congress and addressed to the nations of the world in the aftermath of the September 11, 2001, bombings in New York and Washington, D.C.

28. Watson, 364.

29. Ibid., 367.

30. Ibid., 375. I have tremendous problems with this narrow formulation of Toussaint's social location, as intimated in my earlier comment on Dupuy's analysis as only partial. It fails to appreciate the extent to which there is a folding over of Toussaint's class-based interests with race and embryonic national issues that made it possible for him to be the outstanding leader he was.

31. Watson, 370. The WPJ is the Workers Party of Jamaica.

32. This position is developed in greater depth in Brian Meeks, *Caribbean Revo-*

lutions and Revolutionary Theory: An Assessment of Cuba, Nicaragua and Grenada, London and Basingstoke: Warwick University Caribbean Studies/Macmillan, 1993.

33. For a discussion on the course of the WPJ, see David Scott, "The Dialectic of Defeat: An Interview with Rupert Lewis," *Small Axe* 10 (September 2001): 85–177.

34. Watson, 370.

35. People's National Party, "Principles and Objectives," Kingston, February 1979, 14.

36. Ibid., 14.

37. See Michael Manley, *Jamaica: Struggle in the Periphery*, London: Writers and Readers, 1982.

38. Meeks 1994, note 57, 96. This argument is supported in Carolyn Fick, *The Making of Haiti: The St. Domingue Revolution from Below*, Knoxville: University of Tennessee Press, 1990. She argues that "voodoo" in St. Domingue became a broad synthesis of the beliefs of the various African nations, creating the basis for a common cultural resistance (57) and providing the organizational setting as well as ideological underpinnings for Mackandal's failed revolt of the 1750s (59–63) and for Boukman Dutty's initiation of the revolution in 1791 (93).

39. Watson, 380.

40. It is precisely such a hegemony, despite the existence of persons from numerous other tribes, which Fick suggests existed, with the Dahomey being the dominant group. See ibid., 58.

41. See Mervyn Alleyne, *Africa: Roots of Jamaican Culture*, Chicago: Research Associates, 1989, 74.

42. Watson, 380.

43. The Haitian Declaration of Independence, 1804, in Charles Arthur and Michael Dash (eds.), *Libete: A Haiti Anthology*, Kingston: Ian Randle, 1999, 44.

44. Meeks 1994, 100. For an interesting exploration of roads not taken in history, see Robert Cowley (ed.), *What If? The World's Foremost Military Historians Imagine What Might Have Been*, New York: G. P. Putnam's Sons, 1999.

45. Watson, 386.

46. Watson, 387.

47. See C. L. R. James, "The Black Jacobins," in Anna Grimshaw (ed.). *The C. L. R. James Reader*, Oxford (UK) and Cambridge (USA): Blackwell, 1993, 110.

48. Watson, 384.

49. To this extent, I think Stuart Hall expresses such a perspective accurately, when he says:

I accept the critique of the vulgar theory of Marxism in terms of reductionism. But I don't go so far as to say that, therefore, there are simply disparate, fragmented discursive chains, one after another, endlessly slipping past one another. I'm trying to *think* that relationship in a way that brings them back together, but *not* as a simple unity or identity. . . . Marxism's temporal perspective suggests that the connections between the people, say, and the slogans that mobilize them are given in their class position or place in the mode of production. . . . From my perspective, it is only when you get the right people to speak the right language at the right time, to have the right identifications, that you can mobilize them behind a set of concrete slogans. So the class/ideology identity Marxism assumes in the beginning is, for me, the end result, the product of politics. . . . That is what gives political practice a necessary openness.

Stuart Hall, Discussion, in "The Toad in the Garden: Thatcherism among the Theorists," in Ibid., 60.

50. E. P. Thompson, *The Poverty of Theory and Other Essays*, New York and London: Monthly Review Press, 1978, 186–87.

Chapter 4

1. *Daily Gleaner*, March 17, 1997. One of the important historical footnotes concerns the arrival at the funeral of Manley's close friend and erstwhile ally of the seventies, Cuban leader Fidel Castro. The response from the crowd, more than that for any other leader, local or foreign, was overwhelming. According to the *Daily Gleaner*: "'Companero Fidel' and 'Quiero Castro' were repeated at regular intervals and one American journalist remarked 'this is absolutely amazing,' at which point a Jamaican man shouted to him: 'Please sir, no propaganda; please write what you have seen here today when you get back to America.'" *Daily Gleaner*, March 17, 1997.

2. John Reed, *I Saw the New World Born: An Anthology*, Moscow: Progress Publishers, 1976, 121–22.

3. The issues, personalities, and tenuousness of this tense moment are all captured dramatically in Norman Girvan's article "'Not For Sale': Three Episodes in the Life of Democratic Socialism," delivered at the PNP Sixtieth Anniversary Symposium, September 17, 1998.

4. For an early and still very useful assessment of the PNP government's tortuous engagement with the IMF, see Norman Girvan, Richard Bernal, and Wesley Hughes, "The IMF and the Third World: The Case of Jamaica," *Development Dialogue* 2 (1980): 113–55.

5. See Michael Manley, *Jamaica: Struggle in the Periphery*, 1982.

6. Indeed, the shooting death of Minister Roy McGann was an earlier and equally definitive moment. There was outrage and spontaneous mobilization in the urban PNP communities. Civil war could easily have erupted had Manley not firmly come down against any act of retaliation. I thank Tony Harriott for a comment leading to this note. Far more research is obviously required on this critical period.

7. As a young TV producer at the Jamaica Broadcasting Corporation, I witnessed

this firsthand. We were all listening to the PNP general secretary in a surreal daze when it suddenly dawned on us that he was speaking on the studio monitor, but was not on the air.

8. For all the above, see Carl Stone, *The Political Opinions of the Jamaican People*, Kingston: Blackett, 1982.

9. *Daily Gleaner*, March 17, 1997.

10. In the Stone Organization poll of December 2000, when asked which prime minister had done the most to improve the lot of the people, 54 per cent said Manley, 16 per cent said Edward Seaga. Current Prime Minister P. J. Patterson was third with 4.5 per cent of the vote. *Weekend Observer*, December 1, 2000.

11. See Max Weber, *Max Weber: Economy and Society Vol. 2: An Outline of Interpretive Sociology*, Berkeley: University of California Press, 1978, 1111–12.

12. Ibid., 1113–14.

13. Ibid., 1117.

14. Ibid., 1113.

15. Ibid.

16. Robert Tucker, "The Theory of Charismatic Leadership," in Dankwart Rustow (ed.), *Philosophers and Kings: Studies in Leadership*, New York: George Braziller, 1970.

17. Ibid., 78.

18. Ibid., 81.

19. Ibid., 85.

20. George Danns, "Leadership, Legitimacy and the West Indian Experience," 27.

21. Ibid., 29.

22. Ibid., 41.

23. Manley's biography and rise to power are captured through a number of sources. Among the more accessible are Darrel Levi, *Michael Manley: The Making of a Leader*, London: Andre Deutsch, 1989; Rachel Manley, *Drumblair: Memories of a Jamaican Childhood*, Kingston: Ian Randle, 1996; Rachel Manley, *Slipstream: A Daughter Remembers*, Kingston: Ian Randle, 2000; and Brian Meeks, *Narratives of Resistance: Jamaica, Trinidad, the Caribbean*, Mona: University of the West Indies Press, 2000.

24. For a sensitive comparison of the two brothers' characters, see Rachel Manley, *Drumblair*, 87–92.

25. Levi 1989, 7.

26. Ibid., 8.

27. Ibid., 9.

28. Ibid.

29. Seaga's parents were Jamaican, though of Syrian descent, and thus recent "jus' come" migrants to Jamaica. In addition, he suffered from the fact that he was born in the United States and was thus doubly inauthentic.

30. For details see *Struggle in the Periphery*, in particular the appendix "Destabilisation Diary," 223–37.

31. I thank Jan deCosmo for her photograph from which this excerpt was taken.

32. *Slipstream*, 76.

33. Ibid., 89.

34. Ibid., 51.

35. This chagrin is certainly one of the central themes in *Slipstream*. See especially the sequence in which he takes his daughter out of boarding school to lunch and then pays more attention to the attractive lady on the nearby table. See *Slipstream*, 96.

36. *Slipstream*, 129–30.

37. Ibid., 132.

38. Ibid., 131.

39. See Rupert Lewis, *Walter Rodney's Intellectual and Political Thought*, Detroit: Wayne University Press, 1998.

40. See Olive Senior, *The Message is Change: A Perspective on the 1972 General Elections*, Kingston: Kingston Publishers, 1972.

41. Even at the nadir of PNP popularity in 1979, when Carl Stone asked whether more social justice would help Jamaica's progress, a large 86 per cent agreed. See Carl Stone 1982, 31.

42. See the debate between Manley and Kari Levitt—perhaps his final political controversy—as to the timing of middle-class disenchantment with the PNP. Kari Levitt and Michael Manley, "The Michael Manley/Kari Levitt Exchange," *Small Axe* 1 (1997): 81–115.

43. Manley's ability to connect with the crowd at the level of style and panache, speaks to a sensitive grasp of the nuances of Afro-Jamaican culture. This, however, would seem to be contradicted by his social profile, which should have distanced him from the people. A careful analysis of how the middle class is acculturated into the popular culture and at the same time alienated from it is required to explain this. I thank Rupert Lewis for his comments at the Caribbean Studies Association Conference in St. Lucia (May 2000), which led to this footnote. See, for a discussion of the role of "panache" in Jamaican culture Mervyn Alleyne, *Africa: Roots of Jamaican Culture*, 1996, 164.

44. Michael Manley, "Address to the 38th Annual Conference of the People's National Party, September 19, 1976," in *Not for Sale: By Michael Manley and Jamaicans with a relevant supplement by C. L. R. James*, n.d.

45. Though Manley himself disputes that it was a capitulation. It is difficult however, not to conclude that this was the case, from the subsequent history of Jamaica's free market policies that have opened the country for business, though with little sign of growth nor of long-term development. See Levitt 1997.

46. I thank Louis Lindsay, sometime advisor to Michael Manley and my colleague in

the Department of Government at Mona, for reminding me of this important dimension of Manley's character.

47. Antonio Gramsci, *The Modern Prince and Other Writings*, New York: International, 1970, 174.

Chapter 5

This essay was written in 1998 as part of a symposium celebrating the Fiftieth Anniversary of the University of the West Indies. See Marlene Hamilton (ed.), *The University of the West Indies: Celebrating the Past, Charting the Future: Proceedings of the Fiftieth Anniversary Symposium*, Mona, July 22, 1998.

1. Trevor Munroe was then a young Rhodes Scholar, whose career in the Caribbean left had only just begun. He later became president of the University and Allied Workers Union (UAWU)—a position he held for many years—and general secretary of the now-defunct Workers Party of Jamaica (WPJ). Munroe has since served as a Senator in the Jamaican parliament and, following retirement as a Professor in Government at the Mona campus of the UWI, has been executive director of the NGO National Integrity Action.

2. The quantity of literature on the seminal Black Power "revolution" in Trinidad and Tobago has increased in recent years. See, in particular, Selwyn Ryan and Taimoon Stewart (eds.), *The Black Power Revolution 1970: A Retrospective*, St. Augustine: Institute of Social and Economic Research, 1995.

3. I am indebted to Harry Goulbourne's earlier attempt to generate a conversation on the role of the UWI in Caribbean intellectual formation, which has helped inform some of the ideas expressed here. See Harry Goulbourne, "The Institutional Contribution of the University of the West Indies to the Intellectual Life of the Anglophone Caribbean," in Alistair Hennessy (ed.), *Intellectuals in the Twentieth Century Caribbean: Volume 1. Spectre of the New Class: The Commonwealth Caribbean*, London and Basingstoke: Macmillan, Warwick University Caribbean Series, 1992, 21–49.

4. Denis Benn's analytic chronology of West Indian nationalist thought is among the more important of the relatively sparse literature on this phase of Caribbean intellectual history. See Denis Benn, *The Growth and Development of Political ideas in the Caribbean: 1774-1983*, Mona: Institute of Social and Economic Research, 1987.

5. For two new and significant attempts to trace the organizational and theoretical trajectory of the Caribbean left, see Perry Mars, *Ideology and Change: The Transformation of the Caribbean Left*, Detroit: Wayne State University Press and Kingston: University of the West Indies Press, 1998; and Rupert Lewis, *Walter Rodney's Intellectual and Political Thought*, Kingston: University of the West Indies Press, 1998.

6. See, especially, Lewis 1998, chapter 5, "Walter Rodney and the Cultural Politics of Rastafari and Rude Boy," 85–123.

7. Some of my preliminary comments on the damaging features of Caribbean Marxism in the seventies are to be found in Brian Meeks, "NUFF at the Cusp of an Idea: Grassroots Guerrillas, Issues in Methodology and the Politics of the Seventies in Trinidad and Tobago," presented at the 22nd annual Caribbean Studies Association Conference, Barranquilla, May 1997. See also Rupert Lewis, "Learning to Blow the Abeng: A Critical Look at Anti-Establishment Movements of the 1960s and 1970s," *Small Axe* 1 (March 1997): 5–17; Charles Mills, "Marxism and Caribbean Development: A Contribution to Rethinking," in Judith Wedderburn (ed.), *Rethinking Development*, Mona: Consortium Graduate School of the Social Sciences, 1991; and Mars 1998, especially chapter 4, "The Left Agenda," 62–85.

8. The Working People's Alliance (WPA) provided some of the most trenchant and useful criticisms of Caribbean Marxism-Leninism from within the left, and its 1986 "Draft Programme for the Democratic Republic" (mimeo, Georgetown, 1986), remains an important statement on the attempt to imagine a radical and democratic agenda beyond the constraints of vanguardist politics.

9. For an analysis of Grenada's early post-invasion situation, see James Ferguson, *Grenada: Revolution in Reverse*, London: Latin American Bureau, 1990.

10. Nothing more clearly illustrates the dire situation of Jamaica than the popular nationwide roadblock protest of April 1999. On the first full working day following the announcement of increases in the price of gasoline and other items by the Minister of Finance in his annual budget, a dense network of burning roadblocks were set up throughout the island. The demands—emanating primarily, though not only from the poorest sections of the population—were both for a rollback in the price increases and for the removal of the government. Jamaica for most of the nineties, has sustained an unemployment rate in excess of 15 per cent, while the growth rate of its GDP—negative in both 1996 and 1997—has not exceeded 1.4 per cent since 1993. And, while between 1989–94 Jamaica has recorded some 32 per cent of its population below the poverty line, her neighbors have fared significantly better. The comparable figure for Trinidad and Tobago is 21 per cent; Antigua, 12 per cent: St. Lucia, 25 per cent; and the Dominican Republic, 21 per cent. For these, see UNDP, *Human Development Report, 1998*, New York and Oxford: Oxford University Press, 1998, 146; for the Jamaican statistics, *Economic and Social Survey: Jamaica, 1997*, Kingston: PIOJ, 1998.

11. For a reading sensitive to the deterioration of social cohesion and "good governance" in Trinidad, Guyana, and the wider Caribbean, see Selwyn Ryan, *Democratic Governance in the Anglophone Caribbean: Threats to Sustainability*, St. Augustine: Institute of Social and Economic Research, 1997.

12. See Patsy Lewis, "Beyond Bananas: Globalization, Size and Viability in the Windward Islands," presented at the seminar "Coming in from the Cold: Small States Responses to Globalization," Department of Government, UWI Mona, January 1999.

13. The phrase, regretfully, is not mine, but borrowed from Edward Said's 1993 Reith

Lectures. See Edward Said, *Representations of the Intellectual: The 1993 Reith Lectures*, London: Vintage, 1994, 64.

14. For a critical and insightful reading of the economic crisis in East Asia, which argues, in essence, that it is an instance of Wall Street and the IMF reasserting their hegemony over an attempt at regional capital autonomy, see Robert Wade and Frank Veneroso, "The Asian Crisis: The High Debt Model vs. the Wall Street-Treasury-IMF Complex," *New Left Review* 228 (March/April 1998): 3–24.

15. I try to make sense of the politics of driving in Jamaica and its role as both reflection and accelerator of a deteriorating social order in "Careening on the Edge of the Abyss: Driving, Hegemony and the Rule of Law in Jamaica," presented at the 24th Annual Caribbean Studies Association Conference, Antigua, May 1998.

16. For this, I use as illustration my own Department of Government at UWI, Mona. Throughout the 1980s, with one or two notable exceptions, one man—the late professor Carl Stone—was responsible for most of the books produced from within the department. He published some three substantial volumes and an edited collection in that decade. In the nineties, by contrast, some twelve volumes have so far appeared from seven members of the department. The extent to which this quantitative increase represents new and potentially fruitful philosophical thrusts is beyond the scope of this brief paper and a basis for future discussion.

17. Ann Hudson has written a timely paper that seeks to suggest a future trajectory for university education in the Caribbean. It refers, in part, to some of the ideas raised here. See Ann Hickling-Hudson, "Caribbean Universities and Future Scenarios," presented to the 26th Annual Conference of Australian and New Zealand Comparative and International Education Society, Auckland, New Zealand, December 1998.

Chapter 6

1. Dennis Brown, "Revolution," from the album *Revolution*, Yvonne's LP YS4, 1985.

2. See Peniel E. Joseph, *Waiting 'Til the Midnight Hour: A Narrative History of Black Power in America*, New York: Owl, 2006, xvii.

3. For a crisp description of the New World Group, which functioned throughout the Caribbean and the diaspora in the sixties and early seventies, see Norman Girvan, "The New World Group: a Historical Perspective," in Brian Meeks and Norman Girvan (eds.), *The Thought of New World: The Quest for Decolonisation*, Kingston and Miami: Caribbean Reasonings Series, Ian Randle, 2010, 3–29.

4. See Kate Quinn (ed.), *Black Power in the Caribbean*, Gainesville: University Press of Florida, 2013, in which this essay in modified form is the conclusion.

5. Immanuel Wallerstein, Terrence Hopkins, and Giovanni Arrighi, *Antisystemic Movements*, London: Verso, 1989.

6. See Rupert Lewis, "Walter Rodney and the Cultural Politics of Rastafari and Rude

Boy," *Walter Rodney's Intellectual and Political Thought*, Kingston: University of the West Indies Press and Detroit: Wayne State University Press, 1998, 47–84.

7. See Selwyn Ryan and Taimoon Stewart (eds.), *The Black Power Revolution 1970: A Retrospective*, St. Augustine: Institute of Social and Economic Research, 1995.

8. See, for instance, Evelyne Huber Stephens and John D. Stephens, *Democratic Socialism in Jamaica: The Political Movement and Social Transformation in Dependent Capitalism*, Basingstoke and London: Macmillan, 1986.

9. See Anthony Bogues, *Black Heretics, Black Prophets: Radical Political Intellectuals*, New York and London: Routledge, 2003, 189; and Lewis 1998 op. cit., 91.

10. See Norman Girvan, "After Rodney: The Politics of Student Protest in Jamaica," *New World Quarterly* 4, no. 3 (1968): 59–68.

11. Rupert Lewis eloquently speaks to the variety of publications that were emerging in this period in his *Small Axe* interview. See David Scott, "The Dialectic of Defeat: An Interview with Rupert Lewis," *Small Axe* 10 (September 2001): 85–177.

12. See Bogues 2003, chapter 7, "The Redemptive Poetics of Bob Marley," 187–208.

13. Bob Marley and the Wailers "Fire, Fire," Wail n Soul m, 45rpm, ca. 1969.

14. See Olive Senior, *The Message Is Change: A Perspective on the 1972 General Elections*, Kingston: Kingston Publishers, 1972.

15. William Powell, *The Anarchist's Cookbook*, New York: L. Stuart, 1971.

16. See David Millette, "Guerrilla War in Trinidad 1970–1974," in Ryan and Stewart 1995, 625–60; and Brian Meeks, "Nuff at the Cusp of an Idea: Grassroots Guerrillas and the Politics of the Seventies in Trinidad and Tobago," in *Narratives of Resistance: Jamaica, Trinidad, the Caribbean*, Kingston: University of the West Indies Press, 2000, 48–74.

17. *National Joint Action Committee, Conventional Politics or Revolution?*, Port of Spain: NJAC Publications, 1971.

18. See John LaGuerre, "The Indian Response to Black Power: a Continuing Dilemma," in Ryan and Stewart 1995, 273–308.

19. For a discussion of Trinidadian politics in the period of the rise of the United Labour Front, see Selwyn Ryan, *Revolution and Reaction: Parties and Politics in Trinidad and Tobago 1970–1981*, St. Augustine: Institute of Social and Economic Research, 1989.

20. For a reading of this period closer to my own, see Michael Manley, *Jamaica: Struggle in the Periphery*, London: Writers and Readers, 1982. For an opposing perspective, see Edward Seaga, *My Life and Leadership Vol. 1: Clash of Ideologies*, Oxford: Macmillan, 2010.

21. See Ann Hickling-Hudson, "Grenada: Education and Revolution," in Rupert Lewis (ed.), *Caribbean Political Activism: Essays in Honour of Richard Hart*, Kingston and Miami: Caribbean Reasonings Series, Ian Randle, 2012, 227–53.

22. See, for instance, Brian Meeks, "Social Formation and People's Revolution: A Grenadian Study," diss., University of the West Indies Mona, Kingston, 1988; and Ber-

nard Coard, *Grenada: Village and Workers, Women, Farmers and Youth Assemblies during the Grenada Revolution*, London: Caribbean Labour Solidarity and the NJM, Karia Press, 1989.

23. This is evident in the post-invasion, post-mortem conference hosted in part by the U.S. Naval Postgraduate School, which arrives at similar conclusions. See Jiri Valenta and Herbert Ellison (eds.), *Soviet/Cuban Strategy in the Third World after Grenada: Toward Prevention of Future Grenadas*, Washington: Wilson Center, 1984.

24. See, most notably, former deputy prime minister of the PRG Bernard Coard's interview for the *Journal of Eastern Caribbean Studies*, in which he admits that many people were detained unnecessarily. See Wendy Grenade, "Retrospect: A View from Richmond Hill Prison: An Interview with Bernard Coard," *Journal of Eastern Caribbean Studies* 35, nos. 3 and 4 (September–December 2010): 108–39.

25. See, for a partial selection, *The Grenada Documents: An Overview and Selection*, Washington: Departments of State and Defense, 1984.

26. See Brian Meeks, "Grenada, Once Again: Revisiting the 1983 Crisis and Collapse of the Grenadian Revolution," in Rupert Lewis (ed.), *Caribbean Political Activism: Essays in Honour of Richard Hart*, Kingston and Miami: Caribbean Reasonings Series, Ian Randle, 2012, 199–226; and chapter 9 in this volume.

27. See Joseph 2007, especially 132–275.

28. See Victoria Pasley, "Gender, Race, and Class in Urban Trinidad: Representations in the Construction and Maintenance of the Gender Order 1950–1980," diss., University of Houston, May 1999.

29. See Acton Camejo, "Racial Discrimination in Employment in the Private Sector in Trinidad and Tobago: A Study of the Business Elite and the Social Structure," *Social and Economic Studies* 20, no. 3 (September 1971).

30. See Rex Nettleford, "African Redemption: The Rastafari and Wider Society," in *Mirror Mirror: Identity, Race and Protest in Jamaica*, Kingston: Kingston Publishers, 1998 (First published 1970), 41–111.

31. See Associated Press, "Skin Bleaching a Growing Problem in Jamaica," *Jamaica Observer*, April 11, 2011.

32. See Norman Girvan, Richard Bernal, and Wesley Hughes, "The IMF and the Third World: The Case of Jamaica," *Development Dialogue* 2 (1980): 113–55.

Chapter 7
1. Lloyd Best, "Whither New World?," *New World Quarterly* vol. iv, no. 1 (dead season 1967): 5.

2. Ivor Oxaal, *Race and Revolutionary Consciousness: An Existential Report on the 1970 Black Power Revolt in Trinidad*, Cambridge (US) and London: Schenkman, 1971.

3. Ibid., 85.

4. Ibid.

5. Ibid., 86.

6. Winston Suite, "The Arrogance of NJAC," in Selwyn Ryan and Taimoon Stewart (eds.), *The Black Power Revolution 1970: A Retrospective*, St. Augustine: Institute of Social and Economic Research, 356.

7. See Paget Henry, *Caliban's Reason: Introducing Afro-Caribbean Philosophy*, London and New York: Routledge, 2000; and chapter 2 in this volume.

8. Suite 1995, 356–57.

9. Lloyd Best, "On the Current National Crisis," *Tapia Special Supplement no. 1* (pre-April 1970), in Oxaal 1971, 68.

10. Ibid.

11. Ibid., 69–70.

12. Garth White, "New World: Two Views," *New World Quarterly* 3, no. 4 (cropover 1967): 57–59.

13. Ibid., 60.

14. Best 1967, 3.

15. Ibid., 5–6.

16. Lloyd Best, "Independent Thought and Caribbean Freedom," *New World Quarterly* 3, no. 4 (cropover 1967): 24.

17. Ibid., 28.

18. Ibid., 29.

19. Ibid., 32–33.

20. Antonio Gramsci, "Political Struggle and Military War," *Selections from the Prison Notebooks*, London: Lawrence and Wishart and New York: International Publishers, 1992, 229–39.

21. One answer to this question is scathingly posited by Trinidadian historian James Millette, who argues that Best's absence from the political frontline can be attributed to his tendency to destroy, or "mash up" organizations he is associated with. In a letter written to conference convenor Selwyn Ryan and summarized in one of the plenaries, Millette asserts that Best destroyed the Trinidadian chapter of New World and contributed to Tapia's marginalization from Trinidadian politics. Millette's explicit conclusion is that the proof of Best's theoretical pudding is in its eating and that is evident in the demise or marginalization of all organizations that he has been associated with. See James Millette, "Letter to Selwyn Ryan, Re: Testimonial Conference in Honour of Lloyd Best," Oberlin College, Ohio, September 16, 2002.

22. The Centre for Caribbean Thought was established at the University of the West Indies, Mona, in 2001 as an interdisciplinary institution to recognize, foster, and develop the many streams of Caribbean thought. Its first function, following the launching, was a seminar entitled "Towards an Encyclopaedia of Caribbean Thought." In May 2002 its second major activity honored Jamaican scholar Sylvia Wynter, in a seminar entitled: "After Man, Towards the Human: The Thought of Sylvia Wynter."

23. A particularly relevant instance of this is to be found in Best's afterword to George Lamming's edited collection *Enterprise of the Indies*. Here he searches for a Caribbean essence in its popular culture and finds in carnival a metaphor for Caribbean creativity: "Carnival is not only total theatre combining mas, pan, calypso and limbo, as metaphor. It is the central and legitimating rite of the culture. We have only to fathom it to make mas with the possible." Lloyd Best, "Afterword," in George Lamming (ed.), *Enterprise of the Indies*, Port of Spain: Trinidad and Tobago Institute of the Indies, 1999, 297.

24. See, for instance, my argument in Brian Meeks, "Reinventing the Jamaican Political System," chapter 10 in this volume, originally published in *Souls* 3, no. 4 (Fall 2001 Special Issue, "Reinventing Jamaica: A Conversation about the Renewal of a Diasporic Society"): 9–21. It is also of interest to note Best's enticing but unfortunately undeveloped argument as to the difference between the "populist obsession" of the Mona contingent, grounded in the sharp class distinctions of Jamaican society and the absence of this in Trinidad, where the relative openness of the society places few barriers between the academics and "we the people." See Lloyd Best, "Whither New World?" 3.

Chapter 8

This chapter was first presented as the inaugural lecture in the Cuba Lecture Series, Brown University, September 2007.

1. Brian Meeks, "Cuba One," in Edward Brathwaite, *New Poets from Jamaica*, Kingston: Savacou, 1979, 58–59.

2. See Richard Hart, *The End of Empire: Transition to Independence in Jamaica and Other Caribbean Region Colonies*, Kingston: Arawak, 2006, 335.

3. See Francisco Morales Padrón, *Spanish Jamaica*, Kingston: Ian Randle, 2003.

4. See Olive Senior, *The Encyclopedia of Jamaican Heritage*, Kingston: Twin Guinep, 2003, 295–96.

5. See ibid., 488.

6. See Anthony Bogues and Brian Meeks, "A Caribbean Life: An Interview with Lloyd Best," in Brian Meeks and Norman Girvan (eds.), *The Thought of New World: The Quest for Decolonisation*, Kingston and Miami: Ian Randle, 2010, 307.

7. See for instance, *Ska-Mania: The Sound of the Soil*, Carlos Malcolm & His Afro-Jamaican Rhythms, Up-Beat, 1962.

8. *Daily Gleaner*, April 7, 1960.

9. For differing perspectives on Henry's movement, see Anthony Bogues, *Black Heretics, Black Prophets: Radical Political Intellectuals*, London: Routledge, 2003, 153–85; Brian Meeks, *Narratives of Resistance: Jamaica, Trinidad, the Caribbean*, Kingston: University of the West Indies Press, 2000, 25–47; and Barrington Chevannes, "The Re-

pairer of the Breach: Reverend Claudius Henry and Jamaican Society," in Frances Henry (ed.), *Ethnicity in the Americas*, The Hague: Mouton, 1976, 263–89.

10. See the Skatalites, *Foundation Ska*, Studio One, originally released 1964–65, re-released 1997.

11. Michael Thelwell, *The Harder They Come*, New York: Grove Press, 1980, 377.

12. Born in Port of Spain, Trinidad, Corina Achong was the first female Island Scholarship winner from that country. She met her future husband Charlie Meeks at McGill University in Montreal and later moved back to Jamaica with him, where she worked for the rest of her life between the government information system and private sector public relations. Following her tenure as Manley's assistant she was appointed director of the Agency for Public Information (API), resigning from that post after the PNP defeat in the 1980 general election.

13. See Associated Press, "Cuba Enjoys Warm Ties with Caribbean Nations," August 9, 2006, www.msn.com; and Robert Huish and John M. Kirk, "Cuban Medical Internationalism and the Development of the Latin American School of Medicine," *Latin American Perspectives* 34 (2007): 77.

14. Michael Manley, *Jamaica: Struggle in the Periphery*, London: Writers and Readers, 1982, 111.

15. Ibid., 112–13.

16. See Ibid., especially 97–115.

17. See Kevin O'Brien Chang and Wayne Chen, *Reggae Routes*, Philadelphia: Temple University Press, 1998, 53.

18. See Carl Stone, *The Political Opinions of the Jamaican People (1976–1981)*, Kingston: Blackett, 1982, 49.

19. Ibid., 49.

20. *Gleaner*, March 17, 1997.

21. Oxford Dictionaries Online defines *facety* as "rude, arrogant, excessively bold." This in part captures a Jamaican adjective that also needs to be connected to a history of sharp social, racial, and color disparities and the use of "facetyness" as a means of reclaiming a modicum of self-respect and as a hidden text of resistance. See oxford dictionaries.com/definition/facety.

22. See David Scott, *Refashioning Futures: Criticism after Postcoloniality*, Princeton: Princeton University Press, 1999, 208–20.

23. See Michel Foucault, *The Care of the Self: The History of Sexuality Volume Three*, London: Penguin, 1984.

24. This is the cleverly tweaked Jamaican interpretation of "masses" to denote not just numbers, but heft and weight.

Chapter 9

This chapter is dedicated to Richard Hart in honor of his indomitable spirit and lifelong struggle on behalf of the working people of the Caribbean at home and abroad, and for being one of the few voices to mine below the surface in seeking to understand the reasons for the fall of the Grenada revolution.

1. Under the leadership of Professor Alissa Trotz of the University of Toronto's Caribbean Studies Programme, a remarkable series of events were hosted in October 2008, among them: an audiovisual presentation by Shalini Puri entitled "Operation Urgent Memory: The Grenada Revolution and the US Invasion Twenty Five Years Later"; a lecture by Brian Meeks on "Pan-Caribbean Futures 25 Years after Grenada"; and two cultural presentations reflecting on the Grenada revolution, one at the University of Toronto and the other at the Jamaican Canadian Association building, featuring writers Merle Collins, Jacob Ross, and Dionne Brand, among others.

2. See Rupert Roopnarine, "Resonances of Revolution: Grenada, Suriname, Guyana," presented at the colloquium "Remembering the Future: The Legacies of Radical Politics in the Caribbean," Center for Latin American and Caribbean Studies, Pittsburgh University, April 3–4, 2009.

3. "Thirty Years Later: The Regional Legacy of the Grenada Revolution," Caribbean Studies Association xxxiv Annual Conference, Kingston, June 1–5, 2009, 50.

4. See Wendy C. Grenade, *Beyond the Legal Chapter: An Opportunity for Rebirth*, email courtesy the author.

5. See Patsy Lewis, "Grenadian Reflections," *Stabroek News*, www.stabroeknews .com, September 14, 2009.

6. Randal Robinson, "Forgiveness Day?" *Stabroek News*, www.stabroeknews.com, September 14, 2009.

7. See Jorge Heine, "The Return of Bernard Coard," *Jamaica Gleaner Online*, glean er-ja.com.

8. Ibid.

9. Ibid.

10. Roopnarine 2009, 14.

11. Brian Meeks, *Caribbean Revolutions and Revolutionary Theory: An Assessment of Cuba, Nicaragua and Grenada*, London and Basingstoke: Warwick University Series, Macmillan, 1992, 172.

12. Ibid., 155.

13. See Fidel Castro (interview with Jeffrey M. Elliott and Mervyn Dymally), *Nothing Can Stop the Course of History*, New York, London, and Sydney: Pathfinder, 1986.

14. See Maurice Bishop, "Maurice Bishop Speaks to U.S. Working People, June 5, 1983," in *Maurice Bishop Speaks: The Grenada Revolution 1979–1983*, New York: Pathfinder, 1983, 287–312.

15. I owe many thanks to the late Jamaican prime minister Michael Manley, who in his very generous speech at the launch of my 1992 book on Cuba, Nicaragua, and Grenada made the mild critique that as a "participant" he would have wished for more of my personal narrative in the historical record. This paper attempts in part to redress that earlier failure. See Meeks 1992.

16. Robert "Bobby" Clarke, "Statement on Grenada by Robert 'Bobby' Clarke" (email document), October 14, 2009.

17. See Castro 1986.

18. See Meeks 1992, 169–70.

19. See Meeks 1992, interview with George Louison, 170.

20. Clarke 2009, 4.

21. Ibid., 4.

22. Ibid., 4.

23. For somewhat different approaches to this period, see Perry Mars, *Ideology and Change: The Transformation of the Caribbean Left*, Detroit: Wayne State University Press and Barbados, Jamaica, Trinidad and Tobago: University of the West Indies Press, 1998; and Brian Meeks, *Radical Caribbean: From Black Power to Abu Bakr*, Mona: University of the West Indies Press, 1996.

24. The WLL was the pre-party organization that became the Workers Party of Jamaica (WPJ) in 1978.

25. See *The Grenada Documents: An Overview and Selection*, Washington: Departments of State and Defense, 1984; and Paul Seabury and Walter A. McDougall (eds.), *The Grenada Papers: The Inside Story of the Grenadian Revolution and the Making of a Totalitarian State—As Told in Captured Documents*, San Francisco: Institute for Contemporary Studies, 1984.

26. See Brian Meeks, "Social Formation and People's Revolution: A Grenadian Study," diss., University of the West Indies, 1988.

27. See ibid., which seeks to understand long-term instability as a peculiar feature of the Grenadian "social formation."

28. I borrow this turn of phrase from George Lamming's reflections on the 1983 crisis. See George Lamming, "The Plantation Mongrel," in Richard Drayton and Andaiye (eds.), *Conversations: Essays, Addresses and Interviews 1953–1990*, London: Karia Press, 1992, 248.

29. This was expressed most vividly in the infamous "Line of March of the Party" speech delivered by Bishop himself. See Maurice Bishop, "Line of March of the Party," in *Grenada Documents* 1984.

30. See Meeks 1988, especially chapter 3, "The Revolutionary Situation."

31. See Meeks 1992 for a more detailed discussion of the transformation to a vanguard party and some of the resulting political effects.

32. See Meeks 1988, 485–86.

33. For an accounting of the relationship, see John Walton Cottman, *The Gorrion Tree: Cuba and the Grenada Revolution*, New York: Peter Lang, 1993.

34. See for a discussion Frederic Pryor, *Revolutionary Grenada: A Study in Political Economy*, New York: Praeger, 1986, 63–64.

35. Dov Zakheim, "The Grenada Operation and Superpower Relations: A Perspective from the Pentagon," in Jiri Valenta and Herbert J. Ellison (eds.), *Soviet/Cuban Strategy in the Third World After Grenada: Toward Prevention of Future Grenadas: A Conference Report*, Washington: Kennan Institute for Advanced Russian Studies and the Wilson Center, 1984, 21.

36. "Minutes of Extraordinary Meeting of the Central Committee, NJM, 12-15 October 1983," in *Grenada Documents* 1984, 105-1.

37. See Meeks 1992, 177–78.

38. Ibid., 173.

39. See "TAWU Balance of Forces Assessment, August 19 1983" in Meeks 1988, 460.

40. The primary text, in the absence of easily available histories of Grenada, was the EPICA task force book in celebration of the revolution. See EPICA Task Force, Cathy Sunshine (ed.), *Grenada: The Peaceful Revolution*, Washington: EPICA, 1982.

41. See Meeks 1988, 462–63.

42. "Minutes of Emergency Meeting of Central Committee, NJM, 26 August, 1983," *Grenada Documents* 1984, 111-1.

43. See Gordon Lewis, *Grenada: The Jewel Despoiled*, Baltimore: Johns Hopkins University Press, 1987.

44. See Meeks 1988, 473.

45. Ibid., 485.

46. Ibid., 488.

47. Richard Hart, *The Grenada Revolution: Setting the Record Straight*, United Kingdom: Socialist History Society (SHS) Occasional Paper No. 20, 2005, 39.

48. Meeks 1988, 493

49. Meeks 1992, 176.

50. See John "Chalky" Ventour, *October 1983: The Missing Link*, self-published, 1999; and Bernard Coard, *Summary Analysis of the October 1983 Catastrophe in Grenada*, self-published, 2002.

51. Maurice Paterson's self-published book is still the best source as to the real extent of Grenadian involvement in defending their small island despite the political catastrophe that had occurred in the days before the invasion. It belies the myth of a Cuban resistance and asserts unquestionably the agency of Grenadians acting in defense on their soil. See Maurice Patterson, *Big Sky, Little Bullet: A Docu-Novel*, St. George's: Maurice Paterson, 1992.

52. See for instance, Hart 2005, 40–42; Lewis 1983, 53–55.

53. See Coard 2002, 68.

54. Ibid., 6.

Chapter 10

1. *Sunday Gleaner*, January 21, 2001.

2. Ibid. A crude calculation suggests that if there are 50,000 connections and each leads, say, to a household of 5 people, then there are roughly 250,000 people or 5 per cent of the entire population that is illegally connected to the electricity network.

3. Ibid.

4. Ibid.

5. Ibid.

6. The paper was first published under the title "The Political Movement in Jamaica . . ." in *Race and Reason* vol. 3 (1996–97): 39–47. It was later republished as a chapter in Brian Meeks, *Radical Caribbean: From Black Power to Abu Bakr*, Mona: University of the West Indies Press, 1996; and more recently in Manning Marable (ed.), *Dispatches from the Ebony Tower: Intellectuals Confront the African American Experience*, New York: Columbia University Press, 52–74. References are to the version in the UWI edition.

7. Meeks 1996, 134.

8. Ibid., 137.

9. William Shakespeare, *As You Like It*, II vii (139).

10. For a critical reading of these events, see the Introduction to my *Narratives of Resistance: Jamaica, Trinidad, the Caribbean*, Mona: University of the West Indies Press, 2000.

11. For an insightful analysis of the social situation in the inner city and the root causes of violence, see Horace Levy, Barry Chevannes, et al., *They Cry Respect: Urban Violence and Poverty in Jamaica*, Mona: Centre for Population, Community and Social Change, University of the West Indies, 1996.

12. While police killings per year have declined from an average of some 200 in the 1980s to 130 in the 1990s, the numbers are still unacceptably high, as are the numerous reported cases of summary justice, though, as Harriott suggests, very few of these cases were ruled as unjustifiable and the offenders charged with murder. See Anthony Harriott, *Police and Crime Control in Jamaica: Problems of Reforming Ex-colonial Constabularies*, Mona: University of the West Indies Press, 2000, 82.

13. *Gleaner*, March 20, 2001.

14. See Carl Stone, "Survey of Public Opinion on the Jamaican Justice System" (unpublished report), Kingston: U.S. Agency for International Development, 1991, 30; and Anthony Harriott, "Race, Class and the Political Behaviour of the Jamaican Security forces," diss., University of the West Indies, Mona, 324.

15. See Trevor Munroe, *Renewing Democracy into the Millennium: The Jamaican Experience in Perspective*, Mona: University of the West Indies Press, 1999, 127.

16. In 1997, after a half-decade of a freewheeling financial bubble, the banking sector experienced a severe crash. Many smaller banks folded, leaving depositors high and dry. When the momentum threatened to engulf the entire economy, the minister of

finance intervened purportedly to rescue the small investors with a sector-wide bailout. The cost of this and the subsequent "restructuring" exercise has even more severely encumbered the government and, by implication, the taxpayers in debt. See, for instance, "Davies Explains Restructuring," *Sunday Gleaner*, April 26, 1998.

17. However, it should be noted that, in the face of the loss of the NE St. Ann seat, there seems to be an early attempt to regroup the PNP around the slogan of "deepening democracy." The governor general's "Throne Speech" opening the 2001–2002 financial year in parliament emphasized, for instance, the need to deepen democracy at the local and community levels. See "A Vision for Prosperity," *Gleaner*, April 3, 2001.

18. Jamaica's GDP grew at a rate of 0.1 per cent for the period 1990–98. This put it behind all Caribbean territories except Haiti, which experienced negative growth and whose own performance in the previous decade, while relatively anemic, was an average of 2.0 per cent. See World Bank, *World Development Report 1999–2000, Entering the 21st Century*, New York: Oxford University Press, 2000, 250.

19. *Human Development Report 2000*, New York: United Nations Development Program, Oxford University Press, 2000, 34.

20. For a discussion of the convoluted and sorry history of urban transport in Jamaica, in which I laud the minister's efforts but argue for an as yet untried popular approach to the management of public transport, see my *Narratives of Resistance: Jamaica, Trinidad, the Caribbean*, Mona: University of the West Indies Press, 2000.

21. *1999 Survey of Living Conditions*, Kingston: Planning Institute of Jamaica, table 7.22, 40.

22. In a three-way race on March 8, 2001, the JLP candidate, Shahine Robinson, defeated the PNP's Carrol Jackson by a margin of 509 votes on first count. The significance of this is profound, as the NE St. Ann seat was one of the ruling party's safest rural seats. In the last general election in 1997, the PNP romped home in this seat by a margin of some 2,000 votes. If such a remarkable swing were to be repeated islandwide, the ruling party would be lucky to retain a handful of seats in the next election. See *Jamaica Gleaner*, March 9, 2001, www.jamaica-gleaner.com.

23. This is the name of a popular electronic service for the quick remittance of foreign exchange to family and dependents.

24. The *Palm Beach Post*, closely involved in the unofficial recount of the decisive Florida ballots, has suggested that if the infamous "butterfly" ballot alone had been less confusing, Democratic candidate Al Gore would have gained some 6,600 votes, or more than ten times what he needed to win the election. See "Overvotes Cost Gore the Election," *Palm Beach Post*, March 19, 2001, www.gobpi.com/partners/pbpost/news/election2000.html.

25. President Bush's early backtracking on a variety of environmental and budgetary issues set off the alarm bells of many commentators, who see a return to the profligacy of "Reaganomics" and, more ominously, the inflated military spending of the Cold War. Such an approach is likely to exacerbate the underlying weaknesses in the U.S. econo-

my. See, for instance, Paul Krugman, "The Money Pit," *New York Times*, March 18, 2001; and Maureen Dowd, "The Asbestos President," *New York Times*, April 1, 2001.

26. See "Stocks Fall in Early Trading as Wary Investors Sell Again," *New York Times* online, www.nytimes.com, March 14, 2001.

27. Fareed Zakaria, "Show Us the Money," *Newsweek*, March 26, 2001.

28. Ibid.

29. The IMF itself seemed to be supportive of the view that this bear market was more a correction than a crash. In an early comment, a senior official, speaking on condition of anonymity, felt that while U.S. growth would fall to 1.7 per cent this year, it would recover next year and register a healthy 3.0 per cent growth. See *Financial Gleaner*, March 16, 2001.

30. See *OECD National Accounts Statistics*; *IMF International Financial Statistics*.

31. Harry Shutt, *The Trouble with Capitalism: An Enquiry into the Causes of Global Economic Failure*, London and New York: Zed Books, 1998, 39.

32. Ibid., 130–31.

33. See Kari Levitt, "Fifth Sir Arthur Lewis Memorial Lecture," Eastern Caribbean Central Bank, St. Lucia, November 22, 2000, 13.

34. Ibid., 13–14.

35. See, for instance, Michael Manley, *Up the Down Escalator: Development and the International Economy: A Jamaican Case Study*, Washington: Howard University Press, 1987; and Michael Manley, *The Poverty of Nations*, London: Pluto Press, 1991.

36. The front-page headline of *Newsweek* in the first few days of the stock market decline is as indicative as any. It stated: "Are You Scared Yet? The Sinking US Economy. Will It Take the Rest of the World Down with It?" *Newsweek*, March 26, 2001.

37. Levitt 2000, 21.

Chapter 11

1. George Lamming, *Season of Adventure*, London: Allison and Busby, 1979, 332.

2. Lorna Goodison, "My Island Like a Swimming Turtle," *Travelling Mercies*, Kingston: Ian Randle, 2001, 85.

3. Prachi Mishra, "Emigration and Brain Drain: Evidence from the Caribbean," in Paul Cashin et al. (eds.), *Eastern Caribbean Currency Union: Selected Issues*, Washington: International Monetary Fund, 2005, 102.

4. See Brian Meeks, "The Political Moment in Jamaica: The Dimensions of Hegemonic Dissolution," in Brian Meeks, *Radical Caribbean: From Black Power to Abu Bakr*, Kingston: University of the West Indies Press, 1996, 124–43.

5. Ibid., 130.

6. See Carl Stone, *Democracy and Clientelism in Jamaica*, New Brunswick and London: Transaction, 1983.

7. Moneygram is the brand name of a money transfer agency, now used idiomatically.

8. This was the name of an initiative led by then PNP Minister of National Security Peter Phillips, aimed at identifying and arresting leading drugs and criminal gang leaders. It is generally considered to have had some success and, with the help of seconded British police officers, to have moved beyond typical partisan-driven approaches to investigation and interdiction. See Vernon Davidson, "Operation Kingfish," *Jamaica Observer*, October 20, 2004; and Jamaica Information Service, "Operation Kingfish Netting Big," December 13, 2004, www.jis.gov.jm.

9. These and other proposals are elaborated in Brian Meeks, *Envisioning Caribbean Futures: Jamaican Perspectives*, Kingston: University of the West Indies Press, 2007.

10. See ibid., 119–26, and, for a perspective on which I am in part reliant, Tony Weis, "(Re-) Making the Case for Land Reform in Jamaica," *Social and Economic Studies* 53, no. 1 (2004): 35–72.

11. See Havelock Brewster, "Identity, Space and the West Indian Union," in Kenneth Hall and Denis Benn, *Contending with Destiny: The Caribbean in the Twenty-First Century*, Kingston: Ian Randle, 2000, 37–44.

12. See Brian Moore and Michele Johnson, *Neither Led nor Driven: Contesting British Cultural Imperialism in Jamaica, 1865–1920*, Kingston: University of the West Indies Press, 2004.

13. Edward Kamau Brathwaite, "Negus," *Third World Poems*, Essex: Longman, Harlow, 1983, 42.

Chapter 12

1. *Sunday Observer*, February 26, 2006, 3.

2. *Gleaner*, Monday, February 27, 2006, A3.

3. Ibid., A9.

4. See Mark Weisbrot, "Latin America Shifts Left," *ZNet*, www.zmag.org, February 13, 2006.

5. See Alex Dupuy, *Haiti in the New World Order: The Limits of the Democratic Revolution*, Boulder: Westview Press, 1997.

6. United Nations Development Program, *Human Development Report*, New York: United Nations Development Program, 2005, 219.

7. However, as Susan Eckstein has suggested, the actual pragmatic response to the sudden termination of Soviet aid saved Cuba from destruction and laid the basis for economic recovery in the following years. See Susan Eckstein, "From Communist Solidarity to Communist Solitary," in Aviva Chomsky et. al. (eds.), *The Cuba Reader: History, Culture, Politics*, Durham and London: Duke University Press, 2003, 607–22.

8. For a critical discussion of this turning moment in Jamaica's and the Caribbean's recent history, see Kari Levitt and Michael Manley, "The Michael Manley/Kari Levitt Exchange," *Small Axe* 1 (1997): 81–115.

9. Prachi Mishra, "Emigration and Brain Drain: Evidence from the Caribbean," in

Paul Cashin et al. (eds.), *Eastern Caribbean Currency Union: Selected Issues*, Washington: International Monetary Fund, 2005, 110.

10. Ibid., 94.

11. See, for instance, William Clarke, "The Disappointment of the Promise," *Sunday Gleaner*, May 22, 2005.

12. See Brian Meeks, "The Political Moment in Jamaica: The Dimensions of Hegemonic Dissolution," in Manning Marable (ed.), *Dispatches from the Ebony Tower*, New York: Columbia University Press, 2000, 32–52.

13. See Deborah Thomas, *Modern Blackness: Nationalism, Globalization, and the Politics of Culture in Jamaica*, Durham and London: Duke University Press, 2004.

14. See, for instance, Carolyn Cooper, *Sound Clash: Jamaican Dancehall Culture at Large*, Basingstoke: Palgrave Macmillan, 2004; and Norman Stolzoff, *Wake the Town and Tell the People: Dancehall Culture in Jamaica*, Durham and London: Duke University Press, 2000.

15. Damian "Junior Gong" Marley, "Confrontation," *Welcome to Jamrock*, Tuff Gong/Universal Records, 80005416-02, 2005.

16. *Jamaica Observer*, Friday January 20, 2006.

17. *Jamaica Observer*, Tuesday, February 14, 2006.

18. *Jamaica Observer*, Thursday, February 9, 2006.

19. See, for instance, Heinz Dieterich (interview), "Evo Morales, Communitarian Socialism, and the Regional Power Block," *ZNet*, www.zmag.org, January 9, 2006.

20. See Brian Meeks, "Reinventing the Jamaican Political System," chapter 10 in this volume, originally published in *Souls: A Critical Journal of Black Politics, Culture, and Society* 3 no. 4 (Fall 2001): 9–21.

Chapter 13

This chapter was first delivered as the Annual Patrick Emmanuel Lecture at the University of the West Indies, Cave Hill, Barbados, on November 25, 2010.

1. Charles Dickens, *A Tale of Two Cities*, Oxford and New York: Oxford World Classics, 1988, 7.

2. For one of the earliest and most insightful analyses, see Rupert Lewis, "Notes on the West Kingston Crisis and Party Politics," delivered at States of Freedom, Freedom of States symposium, UWI/Duke University, UWI Mona campus, June 16–18, 2010. See also Horace Levy, "May 2010," typescript, June 2011, which argues that the events of 2010 suggest the capability of civil society to affect deep change in Jamaica. For a somewhat sympathetic but sketchy account of the "Dudus events," see K. C. Samuels, *Dudus, 1992–2010: His Rise, His Reign, His Demise*, Jamaica: Pageturner, 2011.

3. George Lamming, *Season of Adventure*, London: Alison and Busby, 1979 (first published 1960).

4. For an elaboration of this argument, see Brian Meeks, *Radical Caribbean: From*

Black Power to Abu Bakr, Barbados, Jamaica, Trinidad and Tobago: University of the West Indies Press, 1996, 127.

5. See Carl Stone, *Democracy and Clientelism in Jamaica,* New Brunswick and London: Transaction, 1983.

6. See Obika Gray, *Radicalism and Social Change in Jamaica, 1962–1972,* Knoxville: University of Tennessee Press, 1991; Obika Gray, *Demeaned but Empowered: The Social Power of the Urban Poor in Jamaica,* Kingston: University of the West Indies Press, 2004; and Amanda Sives, *Elections, Violence, and the Democratic Process in Jamaica, 1944–2007,* Kingston and Miami: Ian Randle, 2010.

7. See Gray 1991, 73–82.

8. See Carl Stone, *Class, State, and Democracy in Jamaica,* New York: Praeger, 1986; and Mark Figueroa and Amanda Sives, "Garrison Politics and Criminality in Jamaica: Does the 1997 Election Represent a Turning Point?" in Anthony Harriott (ed.), *Understanding Crime in Jamaica: New Challenges for Public Policy,* Kingston: University of the West Indies Press, 2003, 63–88.

9. See Kari Polanyi Levitt, *Jamaica: Lessons from the Manley Years,* Maroon Pamphlet No. 1, Morant Bay, Jamaica: Maroon, 1984.

10. See Holger Henke, *Between Self-Determination and Dependency: Jamaica's Foreign Relations, 1972–1989,* Kingston: University of the West Indies Press, 2000.

11. See, for instance, Brian Meeks, "The Frontline: Valentino, Pablo Moses, and Caribbean Organic Philosophy in the Seventies," chapter 1 in this volume, first published in Holger Henke (ed.), *Modern Political Culture in the Caribbean,* Kingston: University of the West Indies Press, 2003, 276–301; and Anthony Bogues, "Get Up Stand Up: The Redemptive Poetics of Bob Marley," in *Black Heretics, Black Prophets: Radical Political Intellectuals,* New York and London: Routledge, 2003, 187–205.

12. See Michael Kaufman, *Jamaica under Manley: Dilemmas of Socialism and Democracy,* London: Zed, 1985; and Evelyne Huber Stephens and John D. Stephens, *Democratic Socialism in Jamaica: The Political Movement and Social Transformation in Dependent Capitalism,* London and Basingstoke: Macmillan, 1986.

13. See Laurie Gunst, *Born Fi Dead: A Journey Through the Jamaican Posse Underworld,* New York: Henry Holt, 1995.

14. See Anthony Harriott, *Organized Crime and Politics in Jamaica: Breaking the Nexus,* Mona: Canoe Press, 2008, 16–17.

15. See ibid.

16. The nature of the extradition treaty and the attempt by the prime minister and other members of his administration to lobby the State Department, presumably in favor of dropping or modifying the extradition demand, have been the subject of a 2011 commission of enquiry, which, unprecedentedly was broadcast widely across the country. Despite conceding that there had been "errors of judgment," most notably on the

part of the prime minister, the tepid conclusions of the commission led to no condemnations or indictments. At the time of writing public opinion was still divided, though leaning toward dismissal of the findings as captured in the comments of the general secretary of the Jamaica Baptist Union Karl Johnson: "I get the impression that the commissioners are wanting us to believe that the whole series of events was just a whole comedy of errors. . . . This country was almost brought to her knees, 73 people minimum died and they are wanting us to believe that the whole thing was simply a comedy of error? Something is wrong." *Gleaner*, Thursday June 16, 2011.

17. See Samuels 2011, 214–15.

18. This talk was given in November 2010 and revised for publication in June 2011. The trend of declining murders continues. The murder rate for October 2010 showed a 43 per cent decline over the same month in 2009 (Gleaner, November 26, 2010). Between June 2010 and May 2011 there were 700 fewer murders than the previous year. The police also claimed that since the beginning of 2011 they have dismantled 50 per cent of the fifty-seven gangs they had targeted. See Petre Williams-Raynor, "Iron Fists Can't Curb Crime," *Sunday Gleaner*, June 19, 2011.

19. This approach was echoed to some extent by Police Commissioner Owen Ellington, who in June 2011 argued that ". . . it cannot be an endless fight within the battle space between the police and the gangs, so there has to be another phase of strategy." This, he suggested, should include the physical upgrading of communities and greater use of community policing. The commissioner, however, stops short of addressing more fundamental policies of social reform that might alleviate entrenched inequality and poverty. See ibid.

20. Meeks 1996, 131.

21. Ibid.

22. As it is indeed apparently applicable elsewhere in the world. Achille Mbembe's insightful analysis of African politics fifty years after independence comes to remarkably similar conclusions when he describes features of the contemporary African political landscape as including "the absence of a concept of democracy that would constitute a real alternative to the predatory model that thrives everywhere . . . the reversal/withdrawal of any radical vision of social revolution on the continent . . . the cystification of entire pockets of society and the irrepressible desire, among hundreds of millions, to live anywhere except home [and] the emergence of a culture of racketeering." See Achille Mbembe, "Fifty Years of African Decolonisation," *Chimurenga Online*, www .Chimurenga.co.za.

23. Docquier and Marfouk found that 85.1 per cent of Jamaicans with a college education were resident outside of the country between 1990 and 2000. Frederic Docquier and Abdselam Marfouk, *International Migration by Educational Attainment (1990–2000)*, Release 1.1, Washington: World Bank, Tables A1-1 and A1-2.

24. See, for instance, "Wanted: Bright Investigators to Fill INDECOM Posts," *Gleaner*, December 28, 2010.

25. See Corbin Lyday, Margaret O'Donnell, and Trevor Munroe, *Corruption Assessment for Jamaica*, Washington: U.S. Agency for International Development, September 11, 2008, 16.

26. Among the leading of these is Danville Walker, who left his position as chief electoral officer to be commissioner of customs. See ibid., 17.

27. See "PNP Unveils Integrity Commission," *Jamaica Observer*, September 1, 2010.

28. Powell and Lewis's 2009 study of political culture in Jamaica found that there is declining interest in the party as an avenue for social change and for political parties in general. See Lawrence Powell and Balford Lewis, *Political Culture of Democracy in Jamaica, 2008: The Impact of Governance*, Washington: U.S. Agency for International Development, Latin American Public Opinion Project, 2009, 171–90.

29. There is to date no final, comprehensive statement from the PNP on its planned rethink of policy and theoretical orientation that is to be captured in the "Progressive Agenda." For an attempt to identify where the process of elaborating it has reached, see Winston Davidson, "The Progressive Agenda Explained," *Sunday Gleaner*, October 3, 2010.

30. Obika Gray, "Culture and Development in Jamaica," typescript, 2010.

31. Ibid., 23.

32. See Mavado, "Messiah" and "Touch de Road," in Devon Dick, "The 'Spirtuality' of Mavado," *Gleaner*, November 18, 2010.

33. Ibid.

34. Quoted in Don Robotham, "From Natty to Doggie," *Gleaner*, September 12, 2010.

35. Ibid.

36. Ibid.

37. See, for instance, Anthony Harriott, "The Emergence and Evolution of Organized Crime in Jamaica: New Challenges to Law Enforcement and Society" (draft given to author, 2010).

38. I develop these ideas in greater detail in Brian Meeks, *Envisioning Caribbean Futures: Jamaican Perspectives*, Kingston: University of the West Indies Press, 2007.

39. See Trevor Munroe, *Renewing Democracy into the Millennium: The Jamaican Experience in Perspective*, Kingston: University of the West Indies Press, 1999. And for comparative discussions of constitutional reform initiatives in the Anglophone Caribbean generally, see Selwyn Ryan, *Winner Takes All: The Westminster Experience in the Caribbean*, St. Augustine: Institute of Social and Economic Research, 1999.

40. See Carl Stone, "Report of a Committee Appointed to Advise the Jamaican Government on the Performance, Accountability and Responsibilities of Elected Parliamentarians," typescript, Kingston, 1991.

41. See Meeks 2007.

42. See, for instance, Norman Girvan, "Existential Threats in the Caribbean: Democratising Politics, Regionalising Governance," C. L. R. James Memorial Lecture, Trinidad and Tobago, May 12, 2011, www.normangirvan.info.

43. To stimulate such a conversation is in large measure the goal of the Sir Arthur Lewis Institute for Social and Economic Studies (SALISES) in its research project to examine fifty years of independence and look toward the next fifty years, entitled "Fifty-Fifty: Critical Reflections in a Time of Uncertainty." See thesalises5050project.blogspot .com/.

44. See George Lamming, "The Plantation Mongrel," in Richard Drayton and Andaiye (eds.), *Conversations: Essays, Addresses, and Interviews, 1953–1990*, London: Karia Press, 1990, 248.

Chapter 14

1. Norman Washington Manley, "Mission Accomplished: The Wheel Has Come Full Circle," in Rex Nettleford (ed.), *Manley and the New Jamaica: Selected Speeches and Writings, 1938–1968*, Longman Caribbean, 1971, 368–84. I use Manley's famous quote because of the clarity (and also, in retrospect, the naiveté) of his exposition of the nationalist project, but also because it captures a missing element in the contemporary discourse—of the need to reconfigure and nurture the public space, captured in his call for an understanding of what the country "thinks and feels."

2. See "It's Portia! PNP Delivers Crushing 41–22 Seat Defeat to JLP," *Daily Observer*, Friday December 30, 2011. The initial seat count shifted by one seat from 41–22 to 42–21 in favor of the PNP when, on the basis of recounts, the former JLP minister of industry Christopher Tufton narrowly lost his South West St. Elizabeth seat to the PNP candidate.

3. See Arthur Hall, "Ignoring the Polls," *Sunday Gleaner*, January 1, 2012.

4. See jamaica-elections.com/general/2011/results/index.php.

5. The 1980 elections, contested under what has often been described as near–civil war conditions, witnessed the highest turnout in the country's modern electoral history, with some 86 per cent of registered voters actually voting. See Carl Stone, *Politics versus Economics: the 1989 Elections in Jamaica*, Kingston: Heinemann Caribbean, 1989, 168.

6. See "The Maturing of the Political Process" (editorial), *Daily Observer*, December 30, 2011.

7. See, for instance, Rupert Lewis, "Notes on the West Kingston Crisis and Party Politics," delivered at the "States of Freedom, Freedom of States" conference, UWI Mona, June 16–18, 2010; and Brian Meeks, "The Dudus Events in Jamaica and the Future of Caribbean Politics," *Social and Economic Studies* 60, nos. 3–4 (September/December 2011): 183–202.

8. The subsequent enquiry and report on what came to be known as the Manatt/Du-

dus events mildly scolded the prime minister for acting "inappropriately." It was sharply critiqued by the PNP as a whitewash. See "Report of the Commission of Enquiry into the Extradition Request for Christopher Coke," www.jis.gov.jm/pdf/Manatt-Final-Report-1.pdf.

9. "Iron Fists Can't Curb Crime," *Sunday Gleaner*, June 19, 2011.

10. A poll conducted in April 2011 found that 57 per cent felt that Golding had no credibility in the Manatt/Dudus affair. Of these, 49 per cent felt that he should resign and only 38 per cent felt that he should remain in office. See "Golding's Credibility Falls Further—Poll," *Jamaica Observer*, May 3, 2011, www.jamaicaobserver.com/news/Golding-s-credibility-falls-further.

11. See Ian Boyne, "Downtown Bangarang," *Sunday Gleaner*, February 20, 2011.

12. See "Golding Defends Dudus Delay," go-jamaica.com/news/read_article.php?id=17315.

13. See "Prominent Jamaican Politician Indicted by US Grand Jury? Extradition Soon?" Caricom News Network, October 12, 2011, caricomnewsnetwork.com.

14. See Mattathias Schwartz, "A Massacre in Jamaica," *New Yorker*, December 12, 2011, 62–71.

15. See Edmond Campbell, "PM Admits Jamaica Gave Go-ahead for US Spy Plane," go-jamaica.com/news/read_article.php?id=33752.

16. Gerard Chaliand, *Revolution in the Third World*, Brighton: Harvester Press, 1977.

17. Samir Amin, *Obsolescent Capitalism: Contemporary Politics and Global Disorder*, London and New York: Zed, 2003, 18.

18. Immanuel Wallerstein, *The Decline of American Power*, New York and London: New Press, 2003. Similarly, see Hardt and Negri, who go a step further in their well-ventilated manifesto *Empire*, in welcoming what they describe as the globalized, capitalist "Empire" as an advance in human progress, much in the same way that capitalism, despite its exploitative essence, is an advance over feudalism. Thus, anyone who refuses empire is in effect engaged in dangerously reactionary nostalgia: ". . . we insist on asserting that the construction of Empire is a step forward in order to do away with any nostalgia for the power structures that preceded it and refuse any political strategy that involves returning to that old arrangement, such as trying to resurrect the nation-state to protect against global capital." They are, however, entirely silent on the experience of a generation of colonial revolutionaries, including people like George Padmore and Aime Cesaire, supporters of earlier "internationals" but who soon discovered that despite the formal recognition of equality, old hierarchies of race and nation continued to assert themselves. Michael Hardt and Antonio Negri, *Empire*, Cambridge, MA, and London: Harvard University Press, 2000, 43.

19. Stephen D. Krasner, "Sharing Sovereignty: New Institutions for Collapsed and Failing States," *International Security* 29 no. 2 (2004): 85–120.

20. Ibid., 85.

21. This question has arisen with renewed vigor in the context of the world recession of 2008 and its subsequent damaging effects on the southern tier of states in the European Union. Thus, the unelected European Commission in Brussels is given the right to recommend sanctions against the elected Greek government, potentially leading to havoc in Greece without any political responsibility, and therefore, according to "Charlemagne," creating a dangerous "democratic deficit": "Citizens are thus left feeling impotent. Their governments are eviscerated at home, yet voters lack the means to throw the bums out of Brussels. This is dangerous. Bringing debt under control and, more importantly, promoting reforms to boost growth, will take years of sacrifice and suffering. It can be sustained only with a strong national mandate. Without that, both governments and the EU will eventually be discredited." Charlemagne, "Angela the Lawgiver," *Economist*, February 4–10, 2012, 58.

22. See Susan Strange, *The Retreat of the State: The Diffusion of Power in the World Economy*, Cambridge: Cambridge University Press, 1996.

23. Hilbourne Watson, "Global Power Shift and the Techno-paradigm Shift: The End of Geography, World Market Blocs and the Caribbean," in Maribel Aponte Garcia and Carmen Gautier Mayoral (eds.), *Post-integration Development in the Caribbean*, Rio Piedras: Social Science Research Centre, University of Puerto Rico, 1995, 78.

24. See Charles Barbour and George Pavlich (eds.), *After Sovereignty: On the Question of Political Beginnings*, Abingdon and New York: Routledge, 2010.

25. See Thomas Hobbes, *Leviathan*, London: J. M. Dent and New York: E. P. Dutton, 1957.

26. See Michel Foucault, "Society Must Be Defended," *Lectures at the College de France, 1975–76*, New York: Picador, 2003.

27. See, for instance, George Pavlich, "On the Subject of Sovereigns," in Barbour and Pavlich 2010, 22–36.

28. Bryan Hogeveen, "After Sovereignty: Spectres of Colonialism," in Barbour and Pavlich 2010, 117.

29. See Shaun McVeigh and Sundhya Pahuja, "Rival Jurisdictions: The Promise and Loss of Sovereignty," in Barbour and Pavlich 2010, 97–114.

30. Ibid., 98.

31. See C. L. R. James, *The Black Jacobins: Toussaint L'Ouverture and the San Domingo Revolution*, New York: Vintage, 1963, 365.

32. See Benedict Anderson, *Imagined Communities: Reflections on the Origin and Spread of Nationalism*, London and New York: Verso, 1991. By consciously invoking Dessalines's famous gesture, though in full recognition of its primarily mythical and symbolic character (but with its profound historical and philosophical significance, particularly for the Caribbean), I am suggesting that it might be the best foundation on which a renewed democratic, national, regional, and transnational politics might coalesce.

33. See Krasner 2004, 87.

34. See Ricky Singh, "Caricom Firm Against War," March 27, 2003, madimc.org; and Ricky Singh, "Caricom/Haiti Relations Again on Tenterhooks," *Jamaica Observer*, July 11, 2004, www.jamaicaobserver.com.

35. There is of course, a prior history of resistance to U.S. Cold War policy, including the 1974 recognition of Cuba by the independent Anglophone Caribbean states and a continuing open policy to that state that has consistently annoyed the United States. See Frank O. Mora and Jeanne A. K. Hey, *Latin American and Caribbean Foreign Policy*, Oxford: Rowman and Littlefield, 2003, 120–41.

36. See Michael Manley, *Jamaica: Struggle in the Periphery*, London: Writers and Readers, 1982.

37. See ibid.

38. See Norman Girvan, "Implications of the Economic Partnership Agreement (EPA) for the CSME," *Social and Economic Studies* 58, no. 2 (June 2009): 91–127; and Jessica Byron and Patsy Lewis, *Formulating Sustainable Development Benchmarks for an EU-Cariforum EPA: Caribbean Perspectives*, report prepared for ICTSD and APRO-DEV, 2007.

39. Admittedly, there is a perspective within the region and internationally that concedes defeat, that the notion of sovereignty is dead, if it ever had real meaning for small states. For instance, in the wake of the NATO-led "no-fly" initiative over Libya which morphed into the overthrow of Muammar Gadhafi, including his capture and brutal execution against all international norms, the *Jamaica Observer* proclaimed: "Since the implosion of the Soviet Union, the globe consists of the West and the rest of the World . . . and a government/leader who defies the West will be punished sooner or later." This perspective, however, fails to appreciate the special window of opportunity provided by the "Arab Spring," the temporary favorable international alignment that emerged, and the sizable internal anti-Gadhafi coalition, all, ultimately, facilitating Western intervention. These together suggest that while Westphalian sovereignty may be under its severest test, it is not to be entirely discounted. See "Lessons from the demise of Gadhafi" (editorial), *Jamaica Observer*, November 3, 2011.

40. See, for instance, Mark Wignall, "Failed State Status on the Horizon," *Jamaica Observer*, February 7, 2012; and Earl M. Bartley, "Jamaica: Failed or Failing State?" *Jamaica Gleaner*, January 26, 2003.

41. See *Economic and Social Survey Jamaica 2010*, Kingston: Planning Institute of Jamaica, 2010.

42. See *Jamaica: Unlocking Growth*, Country Economic Memorandum, Washington: World Bank, May 26, 2011.

43. See F. Docquier and A. Marfouk, *International Migration by Educational Attainment (1990–2000)*, Washington: World Bank, Tables A1-1 and A1-2.

44. See World Bank 2011.

45. Ibid.

46. See Brian Meeks, "The Political Moment in Jamaica: The Dimensions of Hegemonic Dissolution," *Radical Caribbean: From Black Power to Abu Bakr*, Kingston: University of the West Indies Press, 1996, 124–43.

47. For a somewhat more optimistic reading on the significance of the bling culture of overt, demonstrative materialism in contemporary Jamaican popular culture, see Deborah Thomas, *Modern Blackness: Nationalism, Globalization, and the Politics of Culture in Jamaica*, Durham and London: Duke University Press, 2004.

48. See Anthony Harriott, "The Crisis of Public Safety in Jamaica and the Prospects for Change," *Souls: A Critical Journal of Black Politics, Culture and Society* 3, no. 4 (Fall 2001): 56–65.

49. The Sir Arthur Lewis Institute of Social and Economic Studies at UWI has already launched its own critical look at fifty years of independence in the Commonwealth Caribbean, "Fifty-Fifty: Critical Reflections in a Time of Uncertainty," with a series of scholarly and public discussions around key sectors, policies, and individuals associated with the project of national development in Jamaica and across the region. See thesalises5050project.blogspot.com/.

50. See Meeks 2011, 196–98.

51. See, for instance, Obika Gray, "Culture and Development in Jamaica," typescript, leant to the author, 2010.

52. Lawrence Powell and Balford Lewis, *The Political Culture of Democracy in Jamaica 2010: Democratic Consolidation in the Americas in Hard Times*, Nashville: Vanderbilt University Press, 2011, 117.

53. For various perspectives on sexualities, homophobia, and beauty in Jamaica and the Caribbean, see Karen Carpenter and Anneka Marshall (eds.), "Sexualities in the Caribbean," *Social and Economic Studies* 60, no. 1 (March 2011).

54. See Nina Glick Schiller and Georges Eugene Fouron, *Georges Woke Up Laughing: Long-Distance Nationalism and the Search for Home*, Durham and London: Duke University Press, 2001.

55. Not the least of which is that, in recent years, remittances from overseas Jamaicans have become the leading foreign-exchange earner, in many years exceeding tourism, bauxite/alumina, and agriculture. See *Economic and Social Survey Jamaica, 2010*, Kingston: Planning Institute of Jamaica, 2010, ii. Jay Mandle has argued for a more aggressive approach to wooing skilled immigrants and in making these "argonauts" the vanguard of a new diaspora-based investment strategy. See Jay Mandle, "The Role of Migration in Caribbean Integration and Development," *Social and Economic Studies* 60, nos. 3–4 (September/December 2011): 3–20.

56. See Arnold Bertram and Trevor Munroe, *Adult Suffrage and Political Administrations in Jamaica, 1944–2002*, Kingston and Miami: Ian Randle, 2006.

57. See Brian Meeks, *Envisioning Caribbean Futures: Jamaican Perspectives*, Kingston: University of the West Indies Press, 2007, 131–44.

58. The recent *Growth Inducement Strategy* from the Planning Institute of Jamaica is a tentative start in the right direction, with divergence from IMF orthodoxy in its proposals for stimulating demand and priming the productive sector. It falls short, however, in failing to advance a comprehensive strategy in the direction of forging a new inclusive social contract. See *A Growth Inducement Strategy for Jamaica in the Short and Medium Term*, Kingston: Planning Institute of Jamaica, 2011.

59. See, for instance, Yarimar Bonilla, "Guadeloupe Is Ours: The Prefigurative Politics of the Mass Strike in the French Antilles," *Interventions: International Journal of Postcolonial Studies* 12, no. 1 (2010): 125–37.

60. See Terri-Ann Gilbert Roberts, "The Dynamics of Regional Governance: The Caribbean Community (Caricom) Experience in a Context of Sovereignty Paradox," diss., Department of Politics, Sheffield University, July 2010; and Matthew Louis Bishop and Anthony Payne, "Caribbean Regional Governance and the Sovereignty/Statehood Problem," The Centre for International Governance Innovation, Paper no. 8, February 2010.

61. While perspectives naturally vary on the reasons for the collapse of the West Indies Federation (1958–61), underlying causalities lay in Jamaica's physical and historical distance from the other territories in the eastern Caribbean, the failure to bridge this gap with appropriate social and economic measures, and the gaping social and political divisions within Jamaica herself. See John Mordecai, *The West Indies: The Federal Negotiations*, London: George Allen and Unwin, 1968, especially the epilogue by W. Arthur Lewis, 455–62. And on his assessment of the social divisions as critical to understanding the Jamaican economy, see W. Arthur Lewis, "Jamaica's Economic Problems: A Series of Seven Articles," in Patrick Emmanuel (ed.), Sir *William Arthur Lewis: Collected Papers, 1941–1988, Vol. 2*, Cave Hill, Barbados: Institute of Social and Economic Research, 1994, 1438–70.

62. I use the phrase "guerrilla sovereignty" provocatively, though I hope appropriately, to conjure up the imbalance of power that is explicit in the present conjuncture, but also the necessity of finding modalities of resistance that might hit and run, gather forces where appropriate for specific advances, yet not seek to confront power in a hopelessly suicidal manner. Such an approach, of course, has, in a sense, always been the tactic of the weak and vulnerable. I am simply restating it forcefully in the context in which the demise of the state and the negation of agency is being trumpeted even as there are inevitable and indeed imminent battles to be fought that demand the recognition and the utilization of an agency that, for better or worse, remains the state.

BIBLIOGRAPHY

Alleyne, Mervyn. *Africa: Roots of Jamaican Culture*. Chicago, Philadelphia, and Trinidad: Research Associates School Times Publications, 1996.

Amin, Samir. *Obsolescent Capitalism: Contemporary Politics and Global Disorder*. London and New York: Zed, 2003.

———. *Spectres of Capitalism: A Critique of Current Intellectual Fashions*. New York: Monthly Review Press, 1998.

Anderson, Benedict. *Imagined Communities: Reflections on the Origin and Spread of Nationalism*. London and New York: Verso, 1991.

Arthur, Charles, and Michael Dash (eds.). *Libete: A Haiti Anthology*. Kingston: Ian Randle, 1999.

Balakrishnan, Gopal (ed.). *Debating Empire*. London and New York: Verso, 2003.

Barber, Benjamin. *Jihad vs. McWorld: How the Planet Is Both Falling Apart and Coming Together and What This Means for Democracy*. New York: Times Books, 1995.

Barbour, Charles, and George Pavlich (eds.). *After Sovereignty: On the Question of Political Beginnings*. Abingdon and New York: Routledge, 2010.

Barriteau, Eudine (ed.). *Confronting Power, Theorizing Gender: Interdisciplinary Perspectives in the Caribbean*. Kingston: University of the West Indies Press, 2003.

Bartley, Earl M. "Jamaica: Failed or Failing State?" *Jamaica Gleaner*, January 26, 2003.

Benitez Rojo, Antonio. *The Repeating Island: The Caribbean and the Postmodern Perspective*. Durham and London: Duke University Press, 1996.

Bertram, Arnold, and Trevor Munroe. *Adult Suffrage and Political Administrations in Jamaica, 1944–2002*. Kingston and Miami: Ian Randle, 2006.

Best, Lloyd. "Afterword." In George Lamming (ed.), *Enterprise of the Indies*. Port of Spain: Trinidad and Tobago Institute of the Indies, 1999, 294–97.

———. "Independent Thought and Caribbean Freedom." *New World Quarterly* 3, no. 4 (cropover, 1967): 13–34.

———. "Whither New World?" *New World Quarterly* 4, no. 1 (dead season, 1967): 1–6.

Bishop, Matthew Louis, and Anthony Payne. *Caribbean Regional Governance and the Sovereignty/Statehood Problem*. Centre for International Governance Innovation, Paper no. 8, February 2010.

Bishop, Maurice. "Line of March of the Party." In *Grenada Documents: an Overview and Selection*. Washington: Departments of State and Defense, 1984.

———. "Maurice Bishop Speaks to U.S. Working People, June 5, 1983." In *Maurice Bishop Speaks: The Grenada Revolution 1979–1983*. New York: Pathfinder Press, 1983, 287–312.

Blackburn, Robin. "The Black Jacobins and New World Slavery." In Selwyn Cudjoe and William Cain (eds.), *C. L. R. James: His Intellectual Legacies*. Amherst: University of Massachusetts Press, 1995, 96.

Bogues, Anthony. *Black Heretics, Black Prophets: Radical Political Intellectuals*. New York and London: Routledge, 2003.

Bogues, Anthony, and Brian Meeks. "A Caribbean Life: An Interview with Lloyd Best." In Brian Meeks and Norman Girvan (eds.), *The Thought of New World: The Quest for Decolonisation*. Kingston and Miami: Ian Randle, 2010.

Bonilla, Yarimar. "Guadeloupe Is Ours: The Prefigurative Politics of the Mass Strike in the French Antilles." *Interventions: International Journal of Postcolonial Studies* 12, no. 1 (2010): 125–37.

Bounty Killa. "Fed Up." VP Records, 1996.

Bourdieu, Pierre. "A Reasoned Utopia and Economic Fatalism." *New Left Review* 227 (January/February 1998): 125–30.

Boyce Davies, Carole. "The Africa Theme in Trinidad Calypso." *Caribbean Quarterly* 31, no. 2 (June 1985): 67–86.

Boyne, Ian. "Downtown Bangarang." *Sunday Gleaner*, February 20, 2011.

Brenner, Robert. *The Boom and the Bubble: The US in the World Economy*. London and New York: Verso, 2002.

Brewster, Havelock. "Identity, Space and the West Indian Union." In Kenneth Hall and Denis Benn (eds.), *Contending with Destiny: The Caribbean in the Twenty First Century*. Kingston: Ian Randle, 2000, 37–44.

Brewster, Havelock, and C. Y. Thomas. *The Dynamics of West Indian Economic Integration*. Mona: Institute of Social and Economic Research, UWI, 1967.

Brodber, Erna. "Black Consciousness and Popular Music in Jamaica in the 1960s and 1970s." *Caribbean Quarterly* 31, no. 2 (1985): 53–66.

Brown, Dennis. "Revolution." *Revolution*, Yvonne's, LP YS4, 1985.

———. "What About the Half." *Dennis Brown: Money in My Pocket: Anthology 1970–1995*. Trojan Records USA, 2002.

Burczak, Theodore. "Subjectivism and Democratic Forms: A Response to Hayek's Critique of Socialism." In Antonio Callari, Stephen Cullenberg, and Carole Biewener (eds.), *Marxism in the Postmodern Age: Confronting the New World Order*. New York and London: Guilford Press, 1995, 169–77.

Burning Spear. *Reggae Greats: Burning Spear*. Mango Records, 422-806 204-2, 1984.

Byron, Jessica, and Patsy Lewis. *Formulating Sustainable Development Benchmarks for an EU-Cariforum EPA: Caribbean Perspectives*. Report prepared for ICTSD and APRODEV, 2007.

Campbell, Edmond. "PM Admits Jamaica Gave Go-ahead for US Spy Plane." go-jamai ca.com/news/read_article.php?id=33752.

Campbell, Horace. *Rasta and Resistance: From Marcus Garvey to Walter Rodney*. New Jersey: Africa World Press, 1987.

Carlos Malcolm & His Afro-Jamaican Rhythms. *Ska-Mania: The Sound of the Soil.* Up-Beat, 1962.

Carnegie, Charles. *Postnationalism Prefigured: Caribbean Borderlands.* New Jersey and London: Rutgers University Press, 2002.

Carpenter, Karen, and Anneka Marshall (eds.). "Sexualities in the Caribbean." *Social and Economic Studies* 60 no. 1 (March 2011).

Carter, Martin. *Selected Poems: Martin Carter.* Georgetown, Guyana: Demerara, 1989.

Castro, Fidel. Interview with Jeffrey M. Elliott and Mervyn Dymally. *Nothing Can Stop the Course of History.* New York, London, and Sydney: Pathfinder, 1986.

Chaliand, Gerard. *Revolution in the Third World.* Brighton: Harvester Press, 1977.

Charlemagne. "Angela the Lawgiver." *Economist,* February 4–10, 2012, 58.

Chevannes, Barrington. "The Repairer of the Breach: Reverend Claudius Henry and Jamaican Society." In Frances Henry (ed.), *Ethnicity in the Americas.* The Hague: Mouton, 1976, 263–89.

Chevannes, Barry. "The Jamaican Worldview and Africa: Spirit as Power." Monthly Graduate Seminar Paper. Mona: Department of Sociology and Social Work, UWI, 1994.

———. *Rastafari: Roots and Ideology.* New York: Syracuse University Press and Jamaica, Barbados, Trinidad: University of the West Indies Press, 1995.

Clarke, Robert. "Statement on Grenada by Robert 'Bobby' Clarke." Email document. October 14, 2009.

Coard, Bernard. *Grenada: Village and Workers, Women, Farmers, and Youth Assemblies During the Grenada Revolution.* Caribbean Labour Solidarity and the NJM. London: Karia Press, London, 1989.

———. *Summary Analysis of the October 1983 Catastrophe in Grenada.* Self-published, 2002.

The Congos. "Row Fisherman Row." 1977, rereleased on *Congos,* Blood and Fire, BAFCD 009, 1996.

Constance, Zeno (ed.). *Life Is a Stage: The Complete Calypsoes of Brother Valentino, Anthony Emrold Phillip.* Port of Spain: Zeno Constance, 1996.

Cottman, John Walton. *The Gorrion Tree: Cuba and the Grenada Revolution.* New York: Peter Lang, 1993.

Cowley, Robert (ed.). *What If? The World's Foremost Military Historians Imagine What Might Have Been.* New York: Putnam, 1999.

"Cuba Enjoys Warm Ties with Caribbean Nations." Associated Press, August 9, 2006.

Cudjoe, Selwyn, and William Cain (eds.). *C. L. R. James: His Intellectual Legacies.* Amherst: University of Massachusetts Press, 1995.

Danns, George. "Leadership, Legitimacy, and the West Indian Experience, a Rethematization of Max Weber's typology of Domination," Institute of Development Studies, University of Guyana, Working Paper Series No. 1, 1978c.

Dick, Devon. "The 'Spirtuality' of Mavado." *Gleaner*, November 18, 2010.

Dickens, Charles. *A Tale of Two Cities*. Oxford and New York: Oxford World Classics, 1988.

Docquier, Frederic, and Abdselam Marfouk. *International Migration by Educational Attainment (1990–2000)*. Release 1.1. Washington: World Bank, 2004.

Dowd, Maureen. "The Asbestos President." *New York Times*, April 2001.

Dunn, Hopeton, and Leith Dunn. "Tourism and Popular Perceptions: Mapping Jamaican Attitudes." *Social and Economic Studies* 51, no. 1 (March 2002): 25–45.

Dupuy, Alex. "Toussaint L'Ouverture and the Haitian Revolution: A Reassessment of C. L. R. James's Interpretation." In Cudjoe and Cain 1995, 106–17.

Estrin, Saul. "Workers Cooperatives: Their Merits and Limitations." In Julian LeGrand and Saul Estrin, *Market Socialism*. Oxford: Clarendon Press, 1989, 185–92.

Ferguson, James. *Grenada: Revolution in Reverse*. London: Latin American Bureau, 1990.

Fick, Carolyn. *The Making of Haiti: The St. Domingue Revolution from Below*. Knoxville: University of Tennessee Press, 1990.

Figueroa, Mark, and Amanda Sives. "Garrison Politics and Criminality in Jamaica: Does the 1997 Election Represent a Turning Point?" In Anthony Harriott (ed.), *Understanding Crime in Jamaica: New Challenges for Public Policy*. Kingston: University of the West Indies Press, 2003, 63–88.

Foucault, Michel. "Society must be Defended." *Lectures at the College de France, 1975-76*. First edition. New York: Picador, 2003.

———. *The Care of the Self: The History of Sexuality Volume Three*. London: Penguin, 1984.

Gilbert Roberts, Terri-Ann. "The Dynamics of Regional Governance: The Caribbean Community (Caricom) Experience in a Context of Sovereignty Paradox." Diss., Department of Politics, Sheffield University, July 2010.

Gills, Barry (ed.). *Globalization and the Politics of Resistance*. London and Basingstoke: Macmillan, 2000.

Girvan, Norman. "After Rodney: The Politics of Student Protest in Jamaica." *New World Quarterly* 4, no. 3 (1968).

———. "Existential Threats in the Caribbean: Democratising Politics, Regionalising Governance." Trinidad and Tobago: C. L. R. James Memorial Lecture, May 12, 2011. www.normangirvan.info.

———. "Implications of the Economic Partnership Agreement (EPA) for the CSME." *Social and Economic Studies* 58, no. 2 (June 2009): 91–127.

———. "The New World Group: A Historical Perspective." In Brian Meeks and Norman Girvan (eds.), *The Thought of New World: The Quest for Decolonisation*. Caribbean Reasonings Series. Kingston and Miami: Ian Randle, 2010, 3–29.

———. "'Not for Sale': Three Episodes in the Life of Democratic Socialism." Paper delivered at the PNP Sixtieth Anniversary Symposium, Kingston, Jamaica, September 17, 1998.

Girvan, Norman, Richard Bernal, and Wesley Hughes. "The IMF and the Third World: The Case of Jamaica." *Development Dialogue* 2 (1980).

Glick Schiller, Nina, and Georges Eugene Fouron. *Georges Woke Up Laughing: Long-Distance Nationalism and the Search for Home*. Durham and London: Duke University Press, 2001.

Gordon, Lewis. *Existentia Africana: Understanding Africana Existential Thought*. New York and London: Routledge, 2000.

Gramsci, Antonio. *The Modern Prince and Other Writings*. New York: International Publishers, 1970.

———. "Political Struggle and Military War." *Selections from the Prison Notebooks*. London: Lawrence and Wishart and New York: International Publishers, 1992, 229–39.

Gray, Obika. "Culture and Development in Jamaica." Typescript, 2010.

———. *Demeaned but Empowered: The Social Power of the Urban Poor in Jamaica*. Kingston: University of the West Indies Press, 2004.

———. *Radicalism and Social Change in Jamaica, 1962–1972*. Knoxville: University of Tennessee Press, 1991.

The Grenada Documents: An Overview and Selection. Washington: Departments of State and Defense, 1984.

Grenade, Wendy. "Beyond the Legal Chapter: An Opportunity for Rebirth." Email courtesy the author. 2009.

———. "Retrospect: A View from Richmond Hill Prison: An Interview with Bernard Coard." *Journal of Eastern Caribbean Studies* 35, nos. 3–4 (September–December 2010) 108–39.

Gunst, Laurie. *Born fi Dead: A Journey Through the Jamaican Posse Underworld*. New York: Henry Holt, 1995.

Hall, Arthur. "Ignoring the Polls." *Sunday Gleaner*, January 1, 2012.

Hall, Stuart. "The Problem of Ideology: Marxism without Guarantees." In David Morley and Kuan-Hsing Chen (eds.), *Stuart Hall: Critical Dialogues in Cultural Studies*. London: Routledge, 1996, 45.

———. "The Toad in the Garden: Thatcherism among the Theorists." In Cary Nelson and Lawrence Grossberg (eds.), *Marxism and the Interpretation of Culture*. Urbana: University of Illinois Press, 1988.

Hardt, Michael, and Antonio Negri. *Empire*. Cambridge, MA, and London: Harvard University Press, 2000.

Harriott, Anthony. "The Crisis of Public Safety in Jamaica and the Prospects for Change." *Souls: A Critical Journal of Black Politics, Culture, and Society* 3, no. 4 (Fall 2001): 56–65.

———. *Organized Crime and Politics in Jamaica: Breaking the Nexus.* Mona: Canoe Press, 2008.

———. *Police and Crime Control in Jamaica: Problems of Reforming Ex-Colonial Constabularies.* Mona: University of the West Indies Press, 2000.

———. "Race, Class and the Political Behaviour of the Jamaican Security Forces." Diss., University of the West Indies, Mona, Jamaica, 1994.

Harris, Wilson. "History, Fable and Myth in the Caribbean and Guianas." In Andrew Bundy (ed.), *Wilson Harris: The Unfinished Genesis of the Imagination.* London and New York: Routledge, 1999, 152–66.

Hart, Richard. *The End of Empire: Transition to Independence in Jamaica and Other Caribbean Region Colonies.* Kingston: Arawak, 2006.

———. "The Grenada Revolution: Setting the Record Straight." Occasional Paper No. 20. United Kingdom: Socialist History Society (SHS), 2005.

Hayek, Friederich von. *The Constitution of Liberty.* London: Routledge, 1990.

Hebdige, Dick. "Subculture: The Meaning of Style." In Ken Gelder and Sarah Thornton (eds.), *The Subcultures Reader.* London and New York: Routledge, 1997.

Heine, Jorge. "The Return of Bernard Coard." *Jamaica Gleaner Online*, September 20, 2009. http://gleaner-ja.com.

Henke, Holger. *Between Self-Determination and Dependency: Jamaica's Foreign Relations 1972–1989.* Kingston: University of the West Indies Press, 2000.

———. "Towards an Ontology of Caribbean Existence." *Social Epistemology* 11, no. 1 (January–March 1997): 39–58.

Henry, Paget. *Caliban's Reason: Introducing Afro-Caribbean Philosophy.* London and New York: Routledge, 2000.

———. "Caribbean Marxism: After the Neoliberal and Linguistic Turns." In Brian Meeks and Folke Lindahl (eds.), *New Caribbean Thought: A Reader.* Kingston: University of the West Indies Press, 2001, 325–54.

Hickling-Hudson, Ann. "Caribbean Universities and Future Scenarios." Paper presented to the 26th Annual Conference of Australian and New Zealand Comparative and International Education Society, Auckland, December 1998.

———. "Grenada: Education and Revolution." In Rupert Lewis (ed.), *Caribbean Political Activism: Essays in Honour of Richard Hart.* Kingston and Miami: Ian Randle Caribbean Reasonings Series, 2012, 227–53.

Hintzen, Percy. "Diaspora, Globalization and the Politics of Identity." In Brian Meeks (ed.), *Culture, Politics, Race, and Diaspora: The Thought of Stuart Hall.* Kingston and Miami: Ian Randle Publishers and United Kingdom: Lawrence and Wishart, 2007, 249–68.

Hobbes, Thomas. *Leviathan.* London: J. M. Dent and New York: E. P. Dutton, 1957.

Hogeveen, Bryan. "After Sovereignty: Spectres of Colonialism." In Charles Barbour and

George Pavlich (eds.), *After Sovereignty: On the Question of Political Beginnings*. Abingdon and New York: Routledge, 2010, 115–29.

Huber Stephens, Evelyne, and John D. Stephens. *Democratic Socialism in Jamaica: The Political Movement and Social Transformation in Dependent Capitalism*. Basingstoke and London: Macmillan, 1986.

Huish, Robert, and John M. Kirk. "Cuban Medical Internationalism and the Development of the Latin American School of Medicine." *Latin American Perspectives* 34 (2007).

Hutton, Clinton, and Nathaniel Samuel Murrell. "Rastas' Psychology of Blackness, Resistance and Somebodiness." In Nathaniel Murrell, William Spencer, and Adrian McFarlane (eds.), *Chanting Down Babylon: The Rastafari Reader*. Kingston: Ian Randle, 1998, 36–54.

James, C. L. R. "The Black Jacobins." In Anna Grimshaw (ed.), *The C. L. R. James Reader*. Oxford (UK) and Cambridge (USA): Blackwell, 1993.

———. *The Black Jacobins: Toussaint L'Ouverture and the San Domingo Revolution*. New York: Vintage, 1963.

Joseph, Peniel E. *Waiting 'Til the Midnight Hour: A Narrative History of Black Power in America*. New York: Owl Books, 2006.

Joseph, Tennyson. *Decolonization in St. Lucia: Politics and Global Neoliberalism, 1945–2010*. Jackson: University Press of Mississippi, 2013.

Kamugisha, Aaron. *Caribbean Political Thought: The Colonial State to Caribbean Internationalisms*. Kingston and Miami: Ian Randle, 2013.

———. *Caribbean Political Thought: Theories of the Post-Colonial State*. Kingston and Miami: Ian Randle, 2013.

Kaufman, Michael. *Jamaica under Manley: Dilemmas of Socialism and Democracy*. London: Zed, 1985.

Kelley, Robin D. *Freedom Dreams: The Black Radical Imagination*. Boston: Beacon Press, 2002.

King, Martin Luther Jr. "I Have a Dream." In James Washington (ed.), *A Testament of Hope: The Essential Writings and Speeches of Martin Luther King Jr*. New York: Harper Collins, 1986, 217–20.

Klein, Naomi. "Privatization in Disguise." *Nation*, April 28, 2003, wwwthenation.com.

Krugman, Paul. "The Money Pit." *New York Times*, March 18, 2001.

LaGuerre, John. "The Indian Response to Black Power: A Continuing Dilemma." In Ryan and Stewart 1995, 273–308.

Lamming, George. "The Plantation Mongrel." In Richard Drayton and Andaiye (eds.), *Conversations: Essays, Addresses and Interviews 1953–1990*. London: Karia Press, 1992.

———. *The Pleasures of Exile*. London: Michael Joseph, 1960.

———. *Season of Adventure*. London: Allison and Busby, 1979.

Laslett, Peter (ed.). *John Locke: Two Treatises of Government*. Cambridge: Cambridge University Press, 1988.

Levi, Darrel. *Michael Manley: The Making of a Leader*. Kingston: Heinemann Caribbean, 1989.

Levitt, Kari. "Anti-model as Antidote." *Trinidad and Tobago Review* 24, no. 10 (October 2002).

———. Fifth Sir Arthur Lewis Memorial Lecture. St. Lucia: Eastern Caribbean Central Bank, November 22, 2000.

Levitt, Kari, and Michael Manley. "The Michael Manley/Kari Levitt Exchange." *Small Axe* 1 (1997).

Levy, Horace. "May 2010." Typescript, June 2011.

Levy, Horace, Barry Chevannes, et al. *They Cry Respect: Urban Violence and Poverty in Jamaica*. Mona: Centre for Population, Community and Social Change, University of the West Indies, 1996.

Lewis, Gordon. *Grenada: The Jewel Despoiled*. Baltimore and London: Johns Hopkins University Press, 1987.

Lewis, Linden. *Caribbean Sovereignty, Development, and Democracy in an Age of Globalization*. New York and London: Routledge, 2013.

Lewis, Patsy. "Beyond Bananas: Globalization, Size and Viability in the Windward Islands." Paper presented at the seminar Coming In from the Cold: Small States Responses to Globalization. Mona: Department of Government, UWI, January 1999.

———. "A Future for Windward Islands Bananas? Challenge and Prospect." *Journal of Commonwealth and Comparative Studies* 38, no. 2 (2000).

———. "Grenadian Reflections." *Stabroek News*, www.stabroeknews.com, September 14, 2009.

Lewis, Rupert. "Learning to Blow the Abeng: A Critical Look at Anti-Establishment Movements of the 1960s and 1970s." *Small Axe* 1 (March 1997): 5–17.

———. "Notes on the West Kingston crisis and Party Politics" Delivered at "States of Freedom, Freedom of States" symposium. UWI/Duke University, UWI Mona campus, June 16-18, 2010.

———. "Walter Rodney and the Cultural Politics of Rastafari and Rude Boy." Chapter 5 in Rodney 1998, 47–84.

———. *Walter Rodney's Intellectual and Political Thought*. Kingston: University of the West Indies Press and Detroit: Wayne State University Press, 1998.

Lewis, W. Arthur. "Jamaica's Economic Problems: A Series of Seven Articles." In Patrick Emmanuel (ed.), *Sir William Arthur Lewis: Collected Papers, 1941–1988, Vol. 2*. Cave Hill, Barbados: Institute of Social and Economic Research, 1994, 1438–70.

Lyday, Corbin, Margaret O'Donnell, and Trevor Munroe. *Corruption Assessment for Jamaica*. Washington: U.S. Agency for International Development, September 11, 2008.

Machiavelli, Nicolo. *The Prince*. Quoted in Ralph Miliband, *Socialism for a Sceptical Age*. London and New York: Verso, 1994, epigraph.

Mandle, Jay. "The Role of Migration in Caribbean Integration and Development." *Social and Economic Studies* 60, nos. 3–4 (September/December 2011): 3–20.

Manley, Michael. "Address to the 38th Annual Conference of the People's National Party, September 19, 1976." In Michael Manley, *Not for Sale*. San Francisco: Editorial Consultants, 1976.

———. *Jamaica: Struggle in the Periphery*. Oxford: Writers and Readers, 1982.

———. *The Poverty of Nations*. London: Pluto Press, 1991.

———. *Up the Down Escalator: Development and the International Economy: A Jamaican Case Study*. Washington: Howard University Press, 1987.

Manley, Norman Washington. "Mission Accomplished: The Wheel Has Come Full Circle." In Rex Nettleford (ed.), *Manley and the New Jamaica: Selected Speeches and Writings, 1938–1968*. Longman Caribbean, 1971, 368–84.

Manley, Rachel. *Drumblair: Memories of a Jamaican Childhood*. Kingston: Ian Randle, 1996.

———. *Slipstream: A Daughter Remembers*. Kingston: Ian Randle, 2000.

Marable, Manning. *African and Caribbean Politics: From Kwame Nkrumah to Maurice Bishop*. London: Verso, 1987.

Marley, Bob. "Concrete Jungle." The Wailers, *Catch a Fire*, Island Records.

Marley, Bob, and the Wailers. "Fire, Fire." Wail n Soul m, 45rpm, ca. 1969.

Mars, Perry. *Ideology and Change: The Transformation of the Caribbean Left*. Detroit: Wayne State University Press and Barbados, Jamaica, Trinidad and Tobago: University of the West Indies Press, 1998.

Marshall, Don. *Caribbean Political Economy at the Crossroads*. London and Basingstoke: Palgrave Macmillan, 1998.

Mbembe, Achille. "Fifty Years of African Decolonisation." *Chimurenga Online*, www.Chimurenga.co.za.

McVeigh, Shaun, and Sundhya Pahuja. "Rival Jurisdictions: The Promise and Loss of Sovereignty." In Barbour and Pavlich 2010, 97–114.

Meeks, Brian. *Caribbean Revolutions and Revolutionary Theory: An Assessment of Cuba, Nicaragua, and Grenada*. London and Basingstoke: Warwick University/Macmillan Caribbean, 1993.

———. "Cuba One." In Edward Brathwaite, *New Poets from Jamaica*. Kingston: Savacou, 1979, 58–59.

———. "The Development of the 1970 Revolution in Trinidad and Tobago." M.Sc. thesis, University of the West Indies, Mona, 1978.

———. *Envisioning Caribbean Futures: Jamaican Perspectives*. Kingston: University of the West Indies Press, 2007.

———. "Grenada, Once Again: Revisiting the 1983 Crisis and Collapse of the Grenadian

Revolution." In Rupert Lewis (ed.), *Caribbean Political Activism: Essays in Honour of Richard Hart*. Kingston and Miami: Ian Randle Caribbean Reasonings Series, 2012, 199–226.

———. *Narratives of Resistance: Jamaica, Trinidad, the Caribbean*. Kingston: University of the West Indies Press, 2000.

——— (ed.). "New Currents in Caribbean Thought." *Social and Economic Studies* 43, no. 3 (September 1994).

———. *Radical Caribbean: From Black Power to Abu Bakr*. Kingston: University of the West Indies Press, 1996.

———. "Reasoning with Caliban's Reason." *Small Axe* 11 (March, 2002).

———. "Reinventing the Jamaican Political System." *Souls* 3, no. 4 (Fall 2001, Special Issue, "Reinventing Jamaica: A Conversation about the Renewal of a Diasporic Society"): 9–21.

———. "Re-Reading the Black Jacobins: James, the Dialectic and the Revolutionary Conjuncture." *Social and Economic Studies* 43, no. 3 (September 1994): 75–103.

———. "Social Formation and People's Revolution: A Grenadian Study." Diss., University of the West Indies, Mona, Kingston, 1988.

Meiksins-Wood, Ellen. *Democracy Against Capitalism: Renewing Historical Materialism*. Cambridge: Cambridge University Press, 1995.

Millette, James. "Letter to Selwyn Ryan, re: Testimonial Conference in Honour of Lloyd Best." Oberlin College, Ohio, Sept 16, 2002.

Mills, Charles. "Marxism and Caribbean Development: A Contribution to Rethinking." In Judith Wedderburn (ed.), *Rethinking Development*. Mona: Consortium Graduate School of the Social Sciences, 1991.

———. *Radical Theory, Caribbean Reality: Race, Class, and Social Domination*. Kingston: University of the West Indies Press, 2010.

Morales Padrón, Francisco. *Spanish Jamaica*. Kingston: Ian Randle, 2003.

Mordecai, John. *The West Indies: The Federal Negotiations*. London: George Allen and Unwin, 1968.

Moses, Pablo. *Reggae Greats: Pablo Moses*. Mango Records, 162-539 790-2, 1984.

Munroe, Trevor. *Renewing Democracy into the Millennium: The Jamaican Experience in Perspective*. Kingston: University of the West Indies Press, 1999.

National Joint Action Committee. *Conventional Politics or Revolution?* Port of Spain: NJAC Publications, 1971.

Nelson, Cary, and Lawrence Grossberg (eds.). *Marxism and the Interpretation of Culture*. Urbana and Chicago: University of Illinois Press, 1988.

"The New Face of Capitalism: Slow Growth, Excess Capital and a Mountain of Debt." Editorial. *Monthly Review* 53, no. 11 (April 2002): 1–11.

Nurse, Keith. "Bringing Culture into Tourism: Festival Tourism and Reggae Sunsplash in Jamaica." *Social and Economic Studies* 51, no. 1 (March 2002): 127–43.

O'Brien Chang, Kevin, and Wayne Chen. *Reggae Routes*. Philadelphia: Temple University Press, 1998.

Oxaal, Ivor. *Race and Revolutionary Consciousness: An Existential Report on the 1970 Black Power Revolt in Trinidad*. Cambridge, MA, and London: Schenkman, 1971.

Pasley, Victoria. "Gender, Race, and Class in Urban Trinidad: Representations in the Construction and Maintenance of the Gender Order 1950–1980." Diss., University of Houston, May 1999.

Patterson, H. Orlando. *Emancipation, Independence, and the Way Forward*. Kingston: Ministry of Local Government, Jamaica, 2002.

Patterson, Maurice. *Big Sky, Little Bullet: A Docu-Novel*. Grenada: Maurice Patterson, 1992.

Pavlich, George. "On the Subject of Sovereigns." In Barbour and Pavlich 2010, 22–36.

People's Revolutionary Government. *To Construct from Morning: Making the People's Budget in Grenada*. St. George's: Fedon, 1982.

Planning Institute of Jamaica. *Economic and Social Survey: Jamaica, 1997*. Kingston: Planning Institute of Jamaica, 1998.

———. *Economic and Social Survey Jamaica, 2010*. Kingston: Planning Institute of Jamaica, 2010.

———. *A Growth Inducement Strategy for Jamaica in the Short and Medium Term*. Kingston: Planning Institute of Jamaica, 2011.

———. *1999 Survey of Living Conditions*. Kingston: Planning Institute of Jamaica, 2000.

Polanyi Levitt, Kari. *Jamaica: Lessons from the Manley Years*. Maroon Pamphlet No. 1. Morant Bay, Jamaica: Maroon, 1984.

Powell, Lawrence, and Balford Lewis. *Political Culture of Democracy in Jamaica, 2008: The Impact of Governance*. Washington: U.S. Agency for International Development, Latin American Public Opinion Project, March 2009.

Powell, William. *The Anarchist's Cookbook*. New York: L. Stuart, 1971.

"Principles and Objectives." Kingston: People's National Party, February 1979.

Pryor, Frederic. *Revolutionary Grenada: A Study in Political Economy*. New York: Praeger, 1986.

Puri, Shalini (ed.). *The Legacies of Caribbean Radical Politics*. London and New York: Routledge, 2011.

Reed, John. *I Saw the New World Born: An Anthology*. Moscow: Progress, 1976. Excerpted from *Ten Days That Shook the World*.

Regis, Louis. *The Political Calypso: True Opposition in Trinidad and Tobago, 1962–1987*. Barbados, Jamaica, Trinidad and Tobago: University of the West Indies Press, 1999, 86–90.

Robinson, Randal. "Forgiveness Day?" *Stabroek News*, www.stabroeknews.com, September 14, 2009.

Robotham, Don. "From Natty to Doggie." *Gleaner*, September 12, 2010.

Rohlehr, Gordon. *Calypso and Society in Pre-Independence Trinidad*. Port of Spain: Gordon Rohlehr, 1990, 57–68.

———. "Sounds and Pressure." In *My Strangled City and Other Essays*. Port of Spain: Longman Trinidad, 1992, 89.

Roopnarine, Rupert. "Resonances of Revolution: Grenada, Suriname, Guyana." Presented at the colloquium "Remembering the Future: The Legacies of Radical Politics in the Caribbean," Center for Latin American and Caribbean Studies, Pittsburgh University, April 3–4, 2009.

Rosenau, Pauline. *Post-Modernism and the Social Sciences: Insights, Inroads, and Intrusions*. Princeton: Princeton University Press, 1992.

Ryan, Selwyn. *Deadlock: Ethnicity and Electoral Competition in Trinidad and Tobago, 1995–2002*. St. Augustine: Institute of Social and Economic Studies, 2003.

———. *Democratic Governance in the Anglophone Caribbean: Threats to Sustainability*. St. Augustine: Institute of Social and Economic Research, 1997.

———. *Revolution and Reaction: Parties and Politics in Trinidad and Tobago 1970–1981*. St. Augustine: Institute of Social and Economic Research, 1989.

———. *Winner Takes All: The Westminster Experience in the Caribbean*. St. Augustine: Institute of Social and Economic Research and UWI, 1999.

Ryan, Selwyn, and Taimoon Stewart (eds.). *The Black Power Revolution 1970: A Retrospective*. St. Augustine: Institute of Social and Economic Research, 1995.

Said, Edward. *Representations of the Intellectual: The 1993 Reith Lectures*. London: Vintage, 1994.

Samuels, K. C. *Dudus, 1992–2010: His Rise, His Reign, His Demise*. Kingston: Pageturner, 2011.

Sandiford, Wayne. *On the Brink of Decline: Bananas in the Windward Islands*. St. George's: Fedon, 2000.

Schwartz, Mattathias. "A Massacre in Jamaica." *New Yorker*, December 12, 2011, 62–71.

Schwarz, Bill. *West Indian Intellectuals in Britain*. Manchester and New York: Manchester University Press, 2003.

Scott, David. "The Dialectic of Defeat: An Interview with Rupert Lewis." *Small Axe* 10 (September 2001): 85–177.

———. "The Permanence of Pluralism." In Paul Gilroy, Lawrence Grossberg, and Angela McRobbie (eds.), *Without Guarantees: In Honour of Stuart Hall*. London and New York: Verso, 2000, 282–301.

———. *Refashioning Futures: Criticism after Postcoloniality*. Princeton: Princeton University Press, 1999.

Seabury, Paul, and Walter A. McDougall (eds.). *The Grenada Papers: The Inside Story of the Grenadian Revolution and the Making of a Totalitarian State—As Told in Captured Documents*. San Francisco: Institute for Contemporary Studies, 1984.

Seaga, Edward. *My Life and Leadership Vol. 1: Clash of Ideologies.* Oxford: Macmillan, 2010.

Senior, Olive. *The Encyclopedia of Jamaican Heritage.* Red Hills, Jamaica: Twin Guinep, 2003.

———. *The Message Is Change: A Perspective on the 1972 General Elections.* Kingston: Kingston Publishers, 1972.

Shutt, Harry. *The Trouble with Capitalism: An Enquiry into the Causes of Global Economic Failure.* London and New York: Zed, 1998.

Sives, Amanda. *Elections, Violence, and the Democratic Process in Jamaica, 1944–2007.* Kingston and Miami: Ian Randle, 2010.

The Skatalites. *Foundation Ska.* Studio One, originally released 1964–65, rereleased 1997.

Stanley Niaah, Sonjah. *Dancehall: From Slave Ship to Ghetto.* Ottawa: University of Ottawa Press, 2010.

Starr, Amory. *Naming the Enemy: Anti-Corporate Social Movements Confront Globalization.* London: Zed, 2000.

Stone, Carl. *Class, State and Democracy in Jamaica.* New York: Praeger, 1986.

———. *Democracy and Clientelism in Jamaica.* New Brunswick, NJ, and London: Transaction, 1983.

———. *The Political Opinions of the Jamaican People (1976–1981).* Kingston: Blackett, 1982.

———. *Politics versus Economics: The 1989 Elections in Jamaica.* Kingston: Heinemann Caribbean, 1989.

———. "Report of a Committee Appointed to Advise the Jamaican Government on the Performance, Accountability and Responsibilities of Elected Parliamentarians." Typescript, Kingston, 1991.

———. "Survey of Public Opinion on the Jamaican Justice System." Unpublished report to U.S. Agency for International Development, Kingston, 1991.

Strange, Susan. *The Retreat of the State: The Diffusion of Power in the World Economy.* Cambridge: Cambridge University Press, 1996.

Suite, Winston. "The Arrogance of NJAC." in Ryan and Stewart 1995.

Sunshine, Cathy (ed.). *Grenada: The Peaceful Revolution.* Washington: Ecumenical Program for Interamerican Communication and Action, 1982.

Thelwell, Michael. *The Harder They Come.* New York: Grove Press, 1980.

Thomas, Deborah. *Modern Blackness: Nationalism, Globalization, and the Politics of Culture in Jamaica.* Durham and London: Duke University Press, 2004.

Thompson, E. P. *The Making of the English Working Class.* London: Penguin, 1980.

———. *The Poverty of Theory and Other Essays.* New York and London: Monthly Review Press, 1978.

Tucker, Robert. "The Theory of Charismatic Leadership." In Dankwart Rustow (ed.), *Philosophers and Kings: Studies in Leadership*. New York: George Braziller, 1970.

Ulysse, Gina. *Downtown Ladies: Informal Commercial Importers, A Haitian Anthropologist, and Self-Making in Jamaica*. Chicago: University of Chicago Press, 2007.

United Nations Development Program. *Human Development Report, 1998*. New York and Oxford: Oxford University Press, 1998.

———. *Human Development Report, 2000*. New York and Oxford: Oxford University Press, 2000.

Valenta, Jiri, and Herbert Ellison (eds.). *Soviet/Cuban Strategy in the Third World after Grenada: Toward Prevention of Future Grenadas*. Washington: Wilson Center, 1984.

Ventour, John "Chalky." *October 1983: The Missing Link*. Self-published, 1999.

Wade, Robert, and Frank Veneroso. "The Asian Crisis: The High Debt Model vs. the Wall Street-Treasury-IMF Complex." *New Left Review* 228 (March/April 1998).

Wallerstein, Immanuel. *The Decline of American Power*. New York and London: New Press, 2003.

Wallerstein, Immanuel, Terrence Hopkins, and Giovanni Arrighi. *Antisystemic Movements*. London: Verso, 1989.

Watson Hilbourne (ed.). *The Caribbean in the Global Political Economy*. Boulder and London: Lynne Rienner and Kingston: Ian Randle, 1994.

———. "Global Power Shift and the Techno-paradigm Shift: The End of Geography, World Market Blocs and the Caribbean." In Maribel Aponte Garcia and Carmen Gautier Mayoral (eds.), *Post-integration Development in the Caribbean*. Rio Piedras: Social Science Research Center, University of Puerto Rico, 1995.

———. "Themes in Liberalism, Modernity, Marxism, Postmodernism and Beyond: An Interpretation and Critique of 'Re-Reading the Black Jacobins.'" in Brian Meeks and Folke Lindahl (eds.), *New Caribbean Thought: A Reader*. Mona: University of the West Indies Press, 2001.

Weber, Max. *Max Weber: Economy and Society Vol. 2: An Outline of Interpretive Sociology*, Guenther Roth and Claus Wittich (eds.). London, Berkeley, and Los Angeles: University of California Press, 1978.

West Indian Commission. *Time for Action: The Report of the West Indian Commission*. Barbados: West Indian Commission, 1992.

White, Garth. "New World: Two Views." *New World Quarterly* 3, no. 4 (cropover 1967).

Wignall, Mark. "Failed State Status on the Horizon." *Jamaica Observer*, February 7, 2012.

Williams-Raynor, Petre. "Iron Fists Can't Curb Crime." *Sunday Gleaner*, June 19, 2011.

Workers Party of Jamaica. *Programme: Workers Party of Jamaica*. Kingston: Workers Party of Jamaica, 1978.

World Bank. *World Development Report 1999–2000: Entering the 21st Century*. New York: Oxford University Press, 2000.

Wright, Erik Olin, Andrew Levine, and Elliott Sober. *Reconstructing Marxism: Essays on Explanation and the Theory of History*. London and New York: Verso, 1992.

Wynter, Sylvia. "Beyond the Categories of the Master Conception: The Counter Doctrine of the Jamesian Poesis." In Paget Henry and Paul Buhle (eds.), *C. L. R. James's Caribbean*. London and Basingstoke: Macmillan Caribbean, 1992, 63–91.

Zakaria, Fareed. "Show Us the Money." *Newsweek*, March 26, 2001.

Zakheim, Dov. "The Grenada Operation and Superpower Relations: A Perspective from the Pentagon." In Jiri Valenta and Herbert J. Ellison (eds.), *Soviet/Cuban Strategy in the Third World After Grenada: Toward Prevention of Future Grenadas: A Conference Report*. Washington: Kennan Institute for Advanced Russian Studies and the Wilson Center, 1984.

CREDITS

Preface:
Excerpt from Martin Carter, "Looking at Your Hands," appears by kind permission of Red Thread Press.

Chapter 1:
Portions of the lyrics of "Third World," "Dis Place Nice," and "Every Brother Is Not a Brother" appear by kind permission of Anthony Emrold Phillip, also known as "Valentino."

Portions of the lyrics of "Blood Money," "We Should Be in Angola," "Give I Fe I Name," and "Grasshopper" appear by kind permission of Moses Publishing and Pableto Henry.

Chapter 3:
Excerpt from *The Poverty of Theory and other Essays* by E. P. Thompson appears by kind permission of the Monthly Review Press.

Chapter 4:
Excerpt from *Slipstream* appears by kind permission of Rachel Manley.

Quote from Michael Manley, "Address to the 38th Annual Conference of the People's National Party, September 19, 1976," appears by kind permission of Rachel Manley for the Estate of Michael Manley.

Chapter 6:
Portion of the lyrics from "Revolution" by Dennis Brown appear courtesy of the Dennis Brown Estate.

Chapter 7:
All quotes from Lloyd Best appear by kind permission of Carmel Best on behalf of his Estate.

Chapter 8:
Quotes from Claudius Henry and Fidel Castro appear by kind permission of the *Daily Gleaner*.

Chapter 12:
All excerpts from articles from the *Jamaica Observer* appear courtesy of Jamaica Observer Limited @ 2006.

Chapter 14:
Quote from Norman Washington Manley speech, "Mission Accomplished: The Wheel Has Come Full Circle," appear by kind permission of Rachel Manley on behalf of the Estate of Norman Manley.

www.ingramcontent.com/pod-product-compliance
Lightning Source LLC
Chambersburg PA
CBHW031124270326
41929CB00011B/1484